"This book is an exceptional
health-care debate. Martinuk br
health care and exposes it for what it is – an outdated, bloated, bureaucratic, government-controlled monopoly where patients rank well down the list of priorities and health-care workers are trapped in a regulatory maze over which they have no control. As such, it presents a compelling and irrefutable case for change. It's time for hospital executives across Canada, who are well aware of the serious shortcomings documented in this book, to speak up and stand up for change."

Tony Fell, Former Chairman, Board of Trustees, University Health Network; Former Deputy Chairman, Royal Bank.

"One of Canada's most enduring foundational myths is that we have the best health-care system in the world, that everyone gets timely, free health care, and that no one can buy his or her way to the front of the line. The reality, as aging boomers are discovering, is more prosaic. Susan Martinuk's new book is the sort of contrarian thinking we all should have been ingesting decades ago."

Neil Macdonald, Senior Correspondent for CBC News: The National; Award-winning journalist.

"Martinuk shares the experiences that far too many Canadian families have had when seeking health care and then provides the facts to explain why these tragic situations occurred. It left me to conclude that my own frustrated advocacy for our family health needs was just one small part of an ocean of angst that exists amongst Canadians who have been stymied in their attempts to get proper health care for loved ones. The book is written with compassion for patient needs, but the real takeaway is that Martinuk's research reveals radical changes are needed to stop the decline of patient care in Canada."

Lorna Dueck, former CEO; Consultant, Lorna Dueck Creative and Parkinson's Disease Advocate.

"Early in family practice, I discovered that much of the job involved putting suffering people onto waiting lists. Forty years later the waits are longer, and I look to our peer countries for a better way. Chapter after chapter, Martinuk's sharply indignant book sustains a justified condemnation of our authoritarian health-care monopoly and especially the delusional self-congratulation by which it self-perpetuates. Leaving the pretensions of the bureaucrats in tatters, Martinuk leaves us with some common sense to light our way."

Dr. Will Johnston, family physician.

"Canadians tend to accept wait times as if they are an inherent component of medical care, but they are not. Wait-times and waitlists are the symptoms of a challenged system, and they cannot be fixed in isolation of the governance, funding, and performance of the system as a whole. As with most circumstances, the protestations that focus on denial, blame, and polarization are distractions that keep positive change at bay. Martinuk's book indicates 'where there is smoke, there is fire' ... and solutions can only come from informed choices."

Dr. Simon Sutcliffe, President, Two Worlds Cancer Collaboration;
Past President and CEO of the BC Cancer Agency and Princess
Margaret Hospital/Ontario Cancer Institute.

"Martinuk's book is engaging, powerful, and should be required reading for all Canadians. We tend to be complacent about health care until our own quality of life is threatened; it is only then that we notice the systemic dysfunction that keeps patients from getting the care they need.

The present system makes it difficult for health-care professionals to provide the kind of care that heals, nourishes, and restores patients. There are no excuses, but perhaps it is just more evidence that this system doesn't work for anyone. This book is a timely catalyst for positive change and clearly shows why all parties (health-care workers, patients, and governments) must work together now to renew our vision of what Canadian health care should be: Caring, patient-centred, and accessible."

Elizabeth Sprinkle, RN.

For Simon,

PATIENTS AT RISK

Exposing Canada's Health-care Crisis

with heartfelt thanks
for your words and
support.

S McK
2022

PATIENTS AT RISK

Exposing Canada's Health-care Crisis

by

Susan D. Martinuk

FRONTIER CENTRE FOR PUBLIC POLICY

Patients at Risk: Exposing Canada's Health-care Crisis
by Susan D. Martinuk

ISBN 978-1-7776577-4-1 (print version)
ISBN 978-1-7776577-5-8 (electronic version)

Printed and bound in Canada.
1 2 3 4 5 6 7 8 9 10

Frontier Centre for Public Policy
203-2727 Portage Avenue, Winnipeg, Manitoba Canada R3J 0R2.
Email: admin@fcpp.org

Dedication

This book is dedicated to the millions of Canadians who have been denied timely medical care by our supposedly universal, equally accessible, and free health-care system.

Many of these people believed that Canada had the best health care in the world and faithfully supported it each year through their taxes, out-of-pocket payments, and charitable donations. They had no reason to doubt that it would be there to help them when they needed medical care. But when that time came, there was no healing to be found. Instead, they found themselves at the mercy of an archaic entity that is beholden more to ideology than providing care to patients; as a result, it can legally withhold medically necessary treatment for years and the only guarantee of care that it offers is access to a wait list.

Canadians deserve so much better and it is hoped that the patient stories and information presented in this book will become a tipping point for understanding the need to critically evaluate our health-care system, take stock of what is missing, and establish a framework that ensures patients and medical care take priority over a failed ideology that has no place in a modern, functional health-care system. Only then can we reimagine all that Canadian health care could—and should—be.

Acknowledgements

I would like to thank the Frontier Centre for Public Policy for their financial and administrative support. In particular, I am grateful to Gerard Lucyshyn, the Vice President for Research, for his suggestions, advice, and encouragement. An enormous debt of thanks is owed to Mrs. Theresa Odishaw for her kind assistance in conducting telephone interviews, researching topics, and preparing documents. Finally, I would also like to express my gratitude to the many friends, colleagues, members of the health-care profession, and unfortunate souls who (whether deliberately, mistakenly, or innocently and unknowingly) mentioned the words 'health-care system' to me over the past year. The ensuing conversations were always lively and, whether we agreed or not, your collective knowledge, insights, discerning comments, and ideas sharpened my perspective and enhanced my understanding of these complex issues and their impact on the lives of Canadians.

Table of Contents

PART V. WAITLISTS, THE COURTS, AND COMMON SENSE

PART VI. A NEW KIND OF HEALTH CARE

Author's Note

Please note that the comments and opinions expressed in this book are in no way intended to denigrate or disparage the excellent care provided by many of Canada's hard-working doctors, nurses, and health-care workers. The health-care problems discussed herein primarily place culpability on the 'system' and not those who diligently carry out their duties in spite of it.

In fact, our health-care personnel should be applauded for doing their best to faithfully deliver high quality medical care within a 'system' that has lost sight of its raison d'etre and now functions more to constrain medical care than provide it.

That said, some of the cases described herein involve errors (medical, administrative, or systemic) and situations where physicians, health-care workers, and/or clinical staff clearly failed their patients. In these circumstances, the names of those involved have been withheld and real names are provided only when identities have been already made public through media coverage.

It is worth noting that many doctors and patients did not want to publicly identify themselves in this book due to a fear of reprisals. Physicians are concerned that their criticisms of the medical system could harm their reputation with colleagues or patients; while some patients did not want to be identified out of concerns that publicizing their stories might have a negative impact on their medical care or their ability to access it.

Finally, readers should know that this book was written during the COVID-19 pandemic. It is clear that the pandemic will continue to exacerbate wait lists for hospital procedures and impact patient care in almost every way. But differences in the numbers and locations of COVID infections, variations in how provinces and hospitals have dealt with the virus, and the tremendous uncertainty about how long the pandemic will last have all made it difficult to consider the full impact of COVID-19 on patient care in Canada. For these reasons, please note that almost all data presented is from the pre-COVID era and, as such, likely represents the very small tip of an enormous, continuously expanding iceberg.

Introduction

Looking at Health Care through Patient Experience

There is a long-standing joke that tends to surface during discussions about problems inherent to the Canadian health-care system. The details and numbers may vary but, sadly, the point that underlies it remains true. Two patients enter two medical clinics on the same day with the very same complaint—they each struggle to walk and, based on their medical histories, it is likely that each one will need a hip replacement.

The first patient is named Jake. He asks to see his family doctor and discovers the earliest available appointment is in three weeks. So he waits, and when he is finally examined, the doctor refers him to an orthopedic specialist for treatment. In Canada, the wait time for this referral is 14.6 weeks.[1]

Months later, Jake finally sees the specialist. He is examined and then referred to a diagnostic clinic to undergo CT or MRI scans so the surgeon can obtain as much information as possible before deciding if hip replacement surgery is appropriate. If Jake lives in British Columbia and the year is 2019, he will likely have to wait at least another 12 weeks for an MRI scan. Once completed, a radiologist interprets the results and, about a week later, the orthopedic surgeon reads the radiology report and makes a final decision.

If Jake needs a hip replacement, the average wait for an orthopedic procedure will add another 24.5 weeks to his timeline for treatment. By the time he has surgery, Jake will have waited at least 55.1 weeks or 386 days.[2] That is, if he is lucky. As you will soon read, many people will wait two or more years for this procedure.

During that wait, Jake will have limped in pain and taken varying amounts of pain medication that may or may not have made a difference. He may or may not have been able to earn an income or even enjoy a positive

---

[1] Bacchus Barua and Mackenzie Moir. (2019). "Waiting Your Turn: Wait Times for Health Care in Canada," 2019 report, The Fraser Institute, https://www.fraserinstitute.org/studies/waiting-your-turn-wait-times-for-health-care-in-canada-2019.

[2] Ibid.

quality of life. There would be no tennis games, golf, or leisurely walks with a loved one.

After a long, painful wait of at least one year, he will undergo major surgery *and only then* will his badly inflamed and damaged hip joint begin the process of healing.

Patient 2 is also named Jake. He limps into a clinic where he is examined by a doctor and has X-rays taken that same day. Following a discussion, the decision is made to proceed with a hip replacement and Jake is booked for surgery the following week.

What is the difference between these two patients?

The first Jake is a Canadian. The second Jake is a German shepherd.

Welcome to Canada where we celebrate a health-care system that is governed by principles declaring it to be universal in scope, free of charge, and equal in terms of access and care. It sounds progressive, honourable, incredibly kind and, well, truly Canadian. But, as you will see throughout this book, it rarely lives up to these standards. In practical terms, these three principles (universal, free, and equal) have aligned to compromise patient access to medical care, to usurp the control that patients (and their doctors) should have over their care, and to make a mockery of "patient-first" health care.

Universal

This principle implies that there is comprehensive coverage of medical care for everyone. But simply declaring a health-care system to be universal does not make it so. Basic economics dictates that, realistically, such a system can only function if the intangible principle of universality is magically transformed into the day-to-day practice of rationing care and services.

In other words, universal care is rationed care. It is characterized by minimal numbers of doctors and specialists, a limited inventory of expensive diagnostic technology, and funding that covers only a limited number of procedures each year. Some procedures are not covered at all.

The only logical endpoint in the rationed-care game is denying care to patients and forcing them to wait their turn for treatment. As a result, Canada's waitlists for medical care are the longest in the developed world and are most often measured in terms of months and years. They now cover every aspect of care from getting a doctor's appointment to having surgery or even gaining access to a hospital bed. As patients languish on waitlists, they often suffer additional medical, financial, and personal consequences.

Free

There is no such thing as free health care and, frankly, there never has been. Via taxes, it costs the average Canadian a bare minimum of $7,000 per year and, to point out an obvious fact that is often ignored, that sum is paid whether they use the health-care system or not.

Equal Access and Care

This principle is as much a myth as the notion that Canadians cannot walk across the street without tripping over a beaver or a hockey stick. It is pure fiction, and as you will come to understand by reading this book, abject inequality exists in, pervades, and governs access to our socialist health-care system. As a result, one of George Orwell's most famous quotes may well provide the most honest description of the philosophy that undergirds Canadian health care: "All animals are equal, but some animals are more equal than others."[3]

A Patient's Perspective

The story of the two Jakes presents us with a vision of health care from the patient's perspective. Sadly, it reveals that (human) patients are essentially at the mercy of a health-care system in which treatment can be withheld for years and their only guarantee to health is access to a waitlist.

Patient care should be the single, most important component of any health-care system; yet, in Canada, it is almost never mentioned as a key goal during high-level discussions. Platitudes about patient care often appear in preambles to new initiatives or in metrics about patient outcomes, but beyond that, politicians and administrators tend to keep the focus on such traditional priorities as money, jurisdiction, organization, and transfer payments. Granted, numbers and statistics are integral components of any system and they must always be considered. But there is rarely any discussion as to how any of these issues affect the most important player in the health-care game—the patient.

What if we were to make patient care and experience our health-care system's primary goal? And what if we evaluated funding, personnel, numbers of procedures, and clinical organization in light of how best to serve those who need medical care?

---

[3] George Orwell, *Animal Farm,* (London: Secker and Warburg, 1945).

To do that, we first have to consider the concrete, day-to-day details of what happens to patients as they wait for referrals and scans, or linger for years on a waitlist for treatment. Such considerations include:

- What are the social consequences of leaving this patient untreated? How will it affect his/her ability to work and support a family?
- What can be done to ameliorate their pain and keep them comfortable while they wait?
- What are the mental/emotional consequences of a long wait for treatment?
- Will it diminish their overall health or quality of life?
- What are the medical consequences to the patient if this injury or illness remains untreated? Will there be further deterioration or disability?
- Will a longer wait result in greater costs to the health-care system?

Almost unbelievably, such questions are rarely considered before placing a patient on a waitlist. For that reason, reimagining health care from a patient's perspective might lead to better outcomes, financial benefits, and happier, healthier patients than continuing the same pattern of putting the money first, and then rationing numbers of patients, doctors, beds, procedures, and everything else to fit within the desired financial framework. After all, as the saying goes, doing the same thing over and over again while expecting a different result is the definition of insanity.

Patients are Gaining a Voice

Social media and the internet are changing the way we look at health care and hold it accountable. Increasing numbers of websites and hashtags are opening the vault to personal health-care experiences by providing a forum for patients (and health-care workers) to post stories, share frustrations, give updates, and submit ideas to bring about positive change.

Other websites allow patients to grade their physicians according to punctuality, knowledge, and helpfulness (among other things) in addition to describing their interactions. One person's experience may not provide an accurate assessment of a doctor's skills or attitude, but if 20 reviews make the same claims, they are likely to be a fairly good reflection of reality.

Individual contributions have now established a vast online reservoir of experience that patients and their families can access to get a glimpse of what to expect before heading to a hospital, undergoing a medical procedure, or meeting a new physician.

For that reason, telling the real-life stories of people and their experiences with Canadian health care has become a powerful means of communication and an effective tool for education, patient advocacy, and now, hopefully, change. Stories can provide us with a better understanding of what is happening in the system on a day-to-day basis and convey important information in a way that is more easily understood and recalled than that offered by graphs or statistics.

For example, most Canadians are unlikely to know the exact wait times for procedures such as open-heart surgery, but after reading this they will likely remember the story of Edward "Fox" Power, a 74-year-old Newfoundland cab driver and well-known local musician.[4]

In 2019, Edward was the subject of a *St. John's Telegram* news story on cardiac surgery waitlists because he had been forced to wait for weeks in a hospital room in order to undergo the triple bypass surgery that he needed to clear his clogged arteries. Doctors initially said that he would likely undergo the procedure within a week and felt that it was too risky for Power to go home to wait.

But as the days and weeks passed, Power became frustrated not only by the wait, but by the added expense that it was creating for the health-care system. As he sat in his hospital room (which he had begun to refer to as a "hotel"), he told the *Telegram*'s reporter that keeping people in the hospital while they wait for procedures is a clear example of how health-care costs escalate unnecessarily.

His thinking made common sense, yet the hospital had advised him that if he were to go home to wait for his surgery, he would lose his spot in the surgery queue and be reassigned to the bottom of the waitlist.

Power's story appeared in the *Telegram* on April 26, 2019. Just two weeks later, he was dead. He had passed away due to complications from heart surgery. What if Power had been operated on sooner? Would it have made a difference in his survival? Sadly, we will never know.

Similarly, we have all heard the dismal media reports documenting extensive waits in emergency departments, particularly in Ontario. An interim report on hallway medicine in that province documented the story of Sara, a

[4] Barb Sweet, "St. John's Man Says Wait for Cardiac Surgery is Too Long," *St. John's Telegram*, April 26, 2019.

94-year-old woman who endured humiliation, fear, and isolation as a result of the hallway medicine that is now a common feature of Canada's health-care system.[5]

On previous visits to the emergency department at her local hospital, Sara had been left unattended in busy, brightly lit hallways for eight to ten hours at a time, so on this particular trip, she knew that it would not be pleasant or easy to get care. Sure enough, after undergoing triage, she was placed on a stretcher in a nearby hallway that was already occupied by three other patients.

She felt frightened and vulnerable as she lay there and witnessed the staff deal with disturbances, police incidents, and lots of "yelling and cursing." The hallway was in a constant state of frenzied activity and noise. Her niece, Ida, was able to stay with her, but the only available chair was situated directly behind the head of the stretcher and out of Sara's sight, making it difficult for Sara to benefit from her reassuring presence.

Staff were far too busy to watch Sara, and Ida was the one who fetched her a blanket and took charge when her IV pole fell. At one point, Ida returned from getting a cup of tea to find Sara lying "completely exposed to everyone passing by" because her hospital gown and bed sheet had slipped off. Despite the high volume of hallway traffic, not one person had enough concern for Sara's dignity to take even ten seconds to cover and reassure her.

Ida says, "Sara was upset the whole time. It was awful to watch. She couldn't figure out what was going on, where she was, and whether she was in trouble because the police officer was there. She kept telling me she was scared and why couldn't she be in a room on her own? She asked, 'Can I turn the light out? Can I have a sleeping pill?'"

The worst part of this story is that this was just the first night. Sara spent 48 hours in that hallway before a hospital bed became available.

Can Stories Change Health Care?

Recounting these events from the patient's perspective is particularly powerful as it can open readers' minds to experience the very same frustration, anger, and loss of dignity that others have endured as they waited for medical treatment. These feelings create empathy, an emotion that allows readers to place themselves in that same situation and consider how they might feel if that had happened to them.

---

[5] The Premier's Council on Improving Health Care and Ending Hallway Medicine, "Hallway Health Care: A System Under Strain," First Interim Report, Province of Ontario, January 2019.

In other words, you may feel some sympathy for the patients in these stories but it is more likely that you will feel empathy—the same anger and frustration that you would have felt if Sara were your mother or Edward Power were your grandfather, uncle, or brother.

As Canadians read about the experiences of others and gain an understanding as to how our health-care system got to this place, hopefully we will all recognize the need to refocus health care on its initial, yet long-forgotten purpose—meeting patients' needs.

PART I

THE PATIENT EXPERIENCE

1

Debbie and Walid

Take a moment to imagine that your son has a serious medical condition that requires surgery and the pediatrician has just referred your child to a surgeon.

It is hard to see your child suffer, but as the doctor marks the referral "urgent," there is a feeling of moving forward. The problem will be fixed and healing will soon begin. You have every expectation that Canada's health-care system has the doctors, the skills, the resources, and the facilities needed to help him. You believe that things will soon be okay. But as the days and weeks pass, you notice that your son's condition is rapidly deteriorating.

The feeling of hope quickly slips away as you begin to realize that you have run head-on into an administrative bureaucracy where everyone wants their child to be the priority and the word "urgent" seems to have no relevance. You begin to make frequent and repeated calls to the surgeon's office, advising them of the change in your son's condition and asking for an immediate appointment. As the phone calls continue, the receptionist simply stops taking them.

Fourteen months later, your "urgent" referral finally gets to the top of the paper pile and you meet with the surgeon. He tells you that your son is in danger of developing severe and permanent damage to his internal organs. He needs surgery now, as further progression of the disease will make the surgery more complicated and greatly diminish the chances of a good outcome. As you try to process what he is saying, the doctor turns to you and in an accusatory tone asks: "Why didn't you bring him to me earlier?"

He callously places the blame on you, the one person who has been feverishly fighting to break through the wall of bureaucracy at his office to get an earlier appointment. Your eyes fill with tears at the cruel insinuation that you have somehow let your son down, but the doctor keeps talking and eventually says the words that sap your strength and almost break your heart: "Despite your son's urgent need for surgery, there is a two-year waitlist."

The tears fall freely now, and the words barely make sense. You try to comprehend what he is saying but your emotions are overwhelming your ability to think clearly. How can it be that your child needs "urgent" surgery, yet has to wait for two years?

For Debbie Waitkus of Kelowna, B.C., all of this was just the beginning of her journey to get urgent medical care for her son, Walid. Sadly, it would not end well. In the next year and a half, Walid would be left a paraplegic due to complications from a surgery that came far too late, and Debbie would be emotionally crushed by the very system which she, as a nurse, had long belonged to and supported. Her confidence in Canadian health care would be destroyed by her years-long struggle with an indifferent and obviously broken system that no longer serves the needs of those who need it the most.

What happened to Debbie and Walid has been the subject of many media reports and the names have not been changed.[6]

June 2009: The Diagnosis

At the age of eight, Walid was diagnosed with a high thoracic kyphosis, an abnormal curvature of the spine in his upper back that is defined by a curve of 50 degrees or more (a normal spine can bend from 20 to 45 degrees). It causes a deformed posture and, as it becomes more severe, it can cause permanent damage to the internal organs and spinal cord. At this point, Walid's curvature was measured at 53 degrees; surgery is recommended when the curvature measures 70 degrees or more.

Despite the diagnosis, Walid had a bright, infectious spirit and Debbie remained confident that Canada could provide the medical care he needed not just to survive, but to thrive, be physically active, and enjoy life.

Kyphosis progresses most rapidly during spurts of growth, such as puberty. Five years later, as Walid approached his 13th birthday, the curvature of his spine changed dramatically and that is when his Kelowna pediatrician sent an urgent request to the surgeon who specializes in pediatric spinal surgery at BC Children's Hospital in Vancouver.

As the days went by without any confirmation of an appointment, Debbie's anxiety grew. Walid's condition had deteriorated to the point where the curve in his spine caused him to assume an almost L-shaped posture and "his head entered the room before his body." She repeatedly called the surgeon's office to stress that rapid changes were taking place in Walid's spine, but it seemed as though a "fortress" of gatekeepers at the hospital prevented her from making any headway towards an immediate appointment.

---

[6] Ian Mulgrew, "Court Relives Waiting List Nightmare: Testimony Details Nightmare Her Son Endured as Spinal Treatment Delayed," *Vancouver Sun*, October 5, 2016; Pamela Fayerman, "Mother of Boy Paralyzed after Surgery Delays Throws Support Behind Private Clinic Owner's Lawsuit," *Vancouver Sun*, November 15, 2012; personal interviews and court documents.

After nine months, it was suggested that Walid return to his local pediatrician to obtain an updated assessment for the surgeon. This examination revealed that Walid's spinal curvature was now somewhere between 75 and 80 degrees, which meant that his condition had progressed beyond the point at which surgery is recommended. But even that was not sufficient to get an expedited appointment; it was another five months before Walid would have his first consultation at BC Children's Hospital.

August 3, 2010: The First Consult

As described earlier, the first consultation with the pediatric spine surgeon was emotional and filled with bad news. Beyond suggesting that Debbie was somehow at fault for not getting Walid the help he needed at an earlier date, the doctor said:

- The curvature of Walid's spine was 100 degrees;
- Walid needed surgery now, but the waitlist was two years long;
- The kyphosis was likely to progress "dramatically" as Walid waited, greatly increasing the probability of permanent damage to Walid's internal organs and spinal cord; and
- The increased curvature and Walid's young age substantially diminished the probability of a good surgical outcome.

None of it was good news, but the doctor assured them that he would monitor Walid closely and, if he felt the situation was becoming critical, he would make the surgery an urgent priority. In the meantime, Walid would get MRI and CT scans done and then return for another consult in five months.

Once more, Debbie felt a sense of relief in knowing that the surgeon would be watching Walid. But as the weeks passed and they heard nothing about dates for CT and MRI scans or a follow-up appointment, the anxiety returned. Debbie contacted his office only to discover that the doctor had not made any arrangements for Walid; no appointments had been made and no scans had been requested. As a result, Debbie's request for a follow-up appointment would have to go to the bottom of the waitlist. Again.

Debbie's mind turned to panic mode as she quickly considered the consequences of another 14 month wait. She called Walid's pediatrician to ask him to try to expedite the operation and then she hastily began looking for options. At this point, Debbie was willing to do anything to ensure that Walid had the surgery as quickly as possible, including relocating their family or remortgaging their home. But there was no relief to be found; there was nowhere else to go.

The surgeon informed the pediatrician that *the surgery could not be hastened and there were no alternatives for Debbie to investigate because Walid would receive the best care at BC Children's Hospital.* Besides, attempting to find care in another province would mean starting over at the bottom of the waitlist.

February 2011: The Second Consult

Knowing that their last encounter with the surgeon had been extremely emotional and, given her mounting frustrations since then, Debbie wisely asked a fellow nurse and friend to attend the February consultation with her and Walid.

The examination showed that Walid's spinal curvature was now at least 110 degrees and it was clear that surgery had to be done as soon as possible. *The surgeon promised that he would expedite the process and put Walid on an urgent-priority list.*

But nothing changed. Communication with the surgeon's office was non-existent and they heard only silence from the man who said he would take "urgent" action. There was no date for surgery and they had yet to hear anything about a date for the MRI and CT scans (which had supposedly been ordered six months earlier).

In April, Debbie asked the clinic if it would expedite matters if she were to pay to have private MRI and CT scans done. Once again, her efforts to take control over Walid's health-care matters were brushed off and she was told that the doctor preferred to have the diagnostic procedures done by BC Children's Hospital.

June 2011: Two Years Since Walid's Urgent Referral for Surgery

At this point, Debbie was under severe emotional stress and suffering from tremendous anxiety. She recalls making phone calls where she could barely speak because she was crying so hard. But the only information she gained was that Walid's name was not listed on the surgical roster for the 2011 summer months.

In other words, none of what the surgeon had promised materialized. There were no dates for diagnostic tests or surgery. There was no close monitoring of Walid's condition. There was no communication with the surgeon's office or the surgeon himself. That is when Debbie realized that she had let Walid down by trusting his care to Canada's public health-care system.

Debbie Takes Action

You can only push a mama bear so far before she will do anything to ensure her cub's safety. Knowing that every day without surgery compounded the risk factors and increased the chances of a negative surgical outcome for Walid, Debbie's emotions shifted from despair to the kind of anger that motivates and pushes people to do what seems impossible.

She initiated an advocacy and awareness campaign through a Facebook page called "No More Waiting for Walid." Through that outreach, she realized that this was not just her problem—a host of other families and individuals had also been left to suffer because of long waits for treatment. The Facebook page soon became a focal point for such patients and their families. Debbie contacted media groups, politicians, and advocacy groups. Walid's story was featured in various newspapers and on television.

In response, Shriners International, a non-profit group that assists children in need, contacted Debbie to say that Shriners Hospitals for Children in Spokane, Washington, would provide Walid with free health care and generous assistance with travel, accommodations, and food expenses.

The Final Straw

When Debbie called the surgeon to tell him of this new opportunity, he advised against going to the Shriners Hospital as he felt it did not possess the same kind of expertise that BC Children's Hospital offered.

Debbie was devastated by his words, but as there was still no surgery date for Walid and the potential of a positive outcome was dwindling with each day, she felt they had no other choice but to go to Spokane.

January 2012: Surgery in Spokane

In September 2011, Debbie and Walid travelled to Shriners Hospital in Spokane. Once there, she again realized that their problem was not so unique; the hospital was accustomed to treating frustrated Canadians whose children had lingered too long on waiting lists.

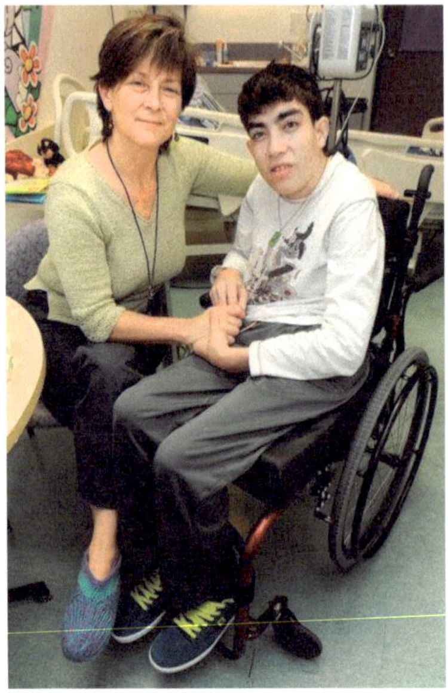

Debbie and Walid in 2012:
A picture of strength and determination.[7]

They also discovered that Walid's spinal curvature was now 127 degrees. As a result, he would have to undergo ten weeks of traction therapy before the surgery could take place. This would prepare his now-rigid spine for manipulation during surgery and prevent further curvature prior to surgery.

On January 9, 2012, 120 weeks after the urgent referral was sent to BC Children's Hospital, Walid underwent surgery in the United States. It was a gruelling ten-hour procedure that was classified as high risk. As Debbie had feared, there were complications during the surgery; Walid suffered a stroke and was paralyzed from the waist down. His life was forever altered.

Clinical recommendations call for a patient such as Walid to undergo surgery within 12 weeks of the diagnosis. By the time Walid had surgery, he had waited 120 weeks – 10 times longer than the clinical recommendations.

Over a period of two and a half years, the only treatment that Walid received at BC Children's Hospital was an X-ray and two half-hour consultations with the surgeon. There was no watchful monitoring of his condition. There was no communication. Appointments for diagnostic scans (MRI and CT) never materialized. Nor did a date for surgery.

---

[7] Photo is courtesy of the *Kelowna Daily Courier* and photographer Gary Nylander.

2

Ross and Don

Ross is a successful business owner; he is bright, polite, and accustomed to dealing with the public (including the occasional difficult customer). Two years ago, he (and his siblings) readily took on the challenge of helping their father, Don, access doctors and treatment for liver cancer. But, like Debbie in Chapter 1, they were shocked to find themselves stuck in a fragmented system laden with gaps and flaws that left them powerless and unable to access timely cancer care for their ailing father.[8]

Despite his well-honed people skills, it took just six months of attempting to navigate Toronto's health-care system to strip Ross of his confidence and bring him to the place where he felt utterly "disenfranchised and disempowered." When it was over, he said: "It felt like I had to resort to begging…just to get my father access to medical treatment."

Begging for care. Sadly, this too has become a reality in Canadian health-care.

Two Doctors Ignore Their Duty of Care

Don was retired, but active and physically fit. So, when he told his family physician (GP) that he was feeling unwell, the doctor ordered a series of blood tests. The results showed elevated levels of enzymes that could be related to a liver disease or perhaps even cancer. A CT scan was scheduled and, following a four-month wait, completed. When the clinic/doctor received the results, they were placed in the patient's file. There was no follow-up phone call and Don was never notified. Shortly thereafter, the doctor retired. As Don would later discover, the CT scan showed a 1.3-centimetre cancerous mass in his liver.

Prior to retiring, Don's doctor had made arrangements for another GP to take over his case files. As time went on and Don had still not heard the results of his CT exam, he booked an appointment with the doctor who had agreed to take over his care. In a very short visit, this doctor told Don that he

---

[8] Story from personal interviews; names have been changed to protect privacy.

was not able to take him on as a patient. He told Don to find another family doctor but he never bothered to give him the results of his CT scan.

Too Little, Too Late? Part I

More than 4.8 million Canadians (over 15 percent of the population) cannot find a family doctor.[9] Those of you who are members of this group know how difficult this can be. So it was somewhat of a miracle when Ross's sister was able to get Don an appointment with yet another GP within three months.

When the next GP perused his file, she asked Don where he was undergoing cancer treatments. This was how Don found out that he had cancer, nine months after the CT scan had revealed a mass in his liver.

The GP immediately referred him to a surgeon to see if the tumour could be resected, but a new CT scan showed that it was now too big for surgical removal. With that, the surgeon referred Don to an oncologist.

Waiting and Calling Part I

After several weeks of waiting, Don had not heard anything about an appointment and that is when Ross began making phone calls. But without knowing which oncologist would handle his father's case, it was difficult to speak to anyone in authority. Each time Ross called, they would tell him the same thing: "Someone will call you back later today or tomorrow." But no one ever returned his calls or, worse still, made an effort to help him.

A couple of months later, Don finally got an appointment with an oncologist, but before the doctor made any decisions, he wanted an "in-house CT scan." Knowing that Don was worried about more waiting, the doctor said he would "mark it urgent because I know you want this dealt with as soon as possible."

Waiting and Calling Part II

Once again, weeks passed without hearing about a date for the "urgent" scan and once again, Ross made multiple calls each day to the CT department to get a date for the scan. Eventually, a receptionist told Ross that they had the referral, but that it was not marked urgent, so it could be weeks or months before an appointment became available. He was told that if the doctor had

---

[9] Staff, "Despite More Doctors, Many Canadians Don't Have a Family Physician: Report," CTV News, September 26, 2019, https://www.ctvnews.ca/health/despite-more-doctors-many-canadians-don-t-have-a-family-physician-report-1.4611149.

made a mistake, then it was up to Ross or Don to get the doctor to fix the error.

Ross began calling the oncologist's office. The receptionist would tell Ross that the doctor would return his call later that day, but he never did. Ross kept calling. The receptionist became increasingly rude and then began to hang up as soon as she would hear his voice. With every phone call, Ross tried to be reasonable, saying, "I just wanted my father to be looked after. I was not rude…I wanted them to understand the urgency of the situation and that an error had been made."

Think about it. It was the kind of error that could have been fixed in a couple of minutes, yet the office staff would not listen to Ross long enough or care enough to take the time to fix the error that their office had made and which was now preventing a cancer patient from receiving care.

Too Little, Too Late? Part II

For the next month, Ross continued to make calls to the oncologist's office and to radiology. One day, his persistence was rewarded and a helpful receptionist in the CT department listened to his story and mentioned it to the head of the department who took action and called the oncologist. In less than a week, Ross's father had his CT scan.

As Ross and the family had feared, the scan showed that the cancer had grown significantly. It was horrible news, especially since they had tried so hard to get timely treatment for their dad. The doctor tried to put a positive spin on it by reassuring them that "we can fix this. Your dad is going to be okay."

Waiting and Calling Part III

The plan, of course, was for the oncologist to arrange the radiation treatments and then contact the family with a date. But the call never came. It took repeated phone calls from Ross and other family members to get a date for radiation treatment. Don's treatment was finally scheduled to start during the last month of December, almost 14 months after the first CT scan showed a cancerous mass and 18 months after Don first went to his GP to say he was not feeling well.

But one final CT scan just prior to beginning radiation treatment changed things again. The mass had now grown to more than ten centimetres and the oncologist quickly changed his prognosis. One month before, he had assured the family that all would be okay. Now he told them that he was not sure if radiation would be of any help to Don and that "it is time to pray for a cure."

Too Little, Too Late? Part III

The family was devastated. Ross says those words made for one of the most emotionally shattering moments in this experience. In 30 days, they had gone from "we can easily cure this" to "our only hope was prayer." Ross has no problem with praying or believing that prayer can help, but says, "I don't care what faith he comes from; I did not come to this cancer centre to ask for prayer. That is not the kind of help we want from an oncologist."

When Ross mentioned his disappointment at all that had transpired, the doctor immediately deflected any blame for what had happened, saying, "It's not my fault that there is a backlog in the wait for radiation and CT. My hands are tied." That is, he never mentioned, or took responsibility for, his error in neglecting to check the "urgent" box on the CT request form.

Because the mass had grown to almost eight-fold its original size, Don had to undergo a much higher dose of radiation than initially planned and it left him unable to do much other than eat small amounts and sleep. All quality of life was gone.

The radiation did buy the family some time but, one year later, the cancer has returned, leaving his family to wonder if Don would be cancer-free had it not taken so long to get treatment. As Ross says, "Surgery might have been able to eradicate it at the very beginning. Alternatively, a smaller tumour would have been treated by a lower dose of radiation, resulting in fewer side effects and a far better quality of life as he recovered."

At every step, beginning with his first visit to his GP, our health-care system failed Don and deprived him of the best opportunity to defeat his cancer. He, and every other Canadian, deserves so much better.

3

Laura

"Hello. I'm Laura Hillier. I'm in the ICU…with a bleeding mouth. I can't breathe. Soon, a tube will be stuck down my throat again. And for feeding as well. And I won't be able to talk. They said I may not wake up, but I really hope I do. But if I don't, I hope this never happens to anyone ever again. And that the government sees that there needs to be funding. Because people are dying when we can save them. We can save these people. Please help. Thank you."

Laura Hillier[10]

January 2021 marked five years since 18-year-old Laura Hillier died on a waitlist. She had an aggressive cancer and was waiting for a bone marrow transplant. But there were more than 30 patients ahead of her on the waitlist and, at that time, Hamilton's transplant program could perform just five transplants per month. While she waited, she and her family reached out to media groups to tell her story. They wanted the system to be fixed so no more teenagers, kids, mothers, and fathers would have to die because of rationed care.

Laura's courageous call for health-care change lives on through her story. A short video of her calling for change (with what she thought might be her last words) can be found on YouTube.[11]

For years, Laura fought the cancer that had invaded her young body. At 13, while her friends were enjoying the carefree existence of young teens, Laura was fighting for her life. Diagnosed with acute myeloid leukemia, she went through intensive chemotherapy treatments and endured brutal side effects that almost killed her. But she courageously took on each battle as it flared, including sepsis, a brain infection, and permanent damage to her

---

[10] Diana Zlomislic, "Plea from Dying Teen: 'Please Help,'" *Toronto Star*, April 26, 2016.

[11] *Toronto Star*, "Laura Hillier, 18, Records a Message Before Her Death," July 17, 2017, https://www.youtube.com/watch?v=8nYseLLPOQQ.

vision. It was awful, but she persevered through it all and won. The disease went into remission.

Four years later, in April 2015, the leukemia again attacked her body with a vengeance, producing a toxic rash, fever, throat pustules, mouth cancers, fatigue, bleeding gums, etc. As soon as the earliest symptoms emerged, Laura knew the cancer was back.

Her first trip to Juravinski Hospital in Hamilton accomplished nothing. In spite of her history of cancer and even though a spot test for infectious mononucleosis was negative, the ER doctors were convinced she had mono and sent her home. It was the same story the next day, as her family once again took her to the ER and the doctors once again remained unconvinced and unconcerned. There was no referral to an oncologist or for further tests.

Laura finally got a break when her parents called the children's oncologist at McMaster Hospital who had treated her years ago. The doctor agreed to see Laura (even though she was no longer considered a pediatric patient) and a subsequent bone marrow test confirmed their worst fears: The cancer was back. She underwent a round of chemotherapy and started to feel better.

In 1988, Laura's doctor was the first Canadian to perform a successful bone marrow transplant using unrelated donor cells from a central registry. The patient who receives the cells gets a boost as the new cells function to rebuild his/her immune system and that means that Laura had the perfect doctor to help her overcome her cancer. Yet, as time went on, he too would be powerless to work within the health-care system in time to save her.

Laura endured another round of chemotherapy and, once it was clear that she was in remission, the hospital found a donor that matched her and it finally seemed that all the pieces of the puzzle were falling into place. But one problem remained—the system that managed the transplant program for cancer patients was about to collapse under the load of waitlists. Consequently, instead of getting her transplant, "the teenager bore witness to one of the province's most devastating healthcare secrets and died trying to do something about it."[12]

The Waitlist Problem that was Killing People

For years, the doctors had warned Cancer Care Ontario (the name of the organization that coordinates cancer care and funding in that province) that there was "unprecedented demand" for the stem cell transplant procedure

---

[12] Diana Zlomislic, "Plea from Dying Teen: 'Please Help,'" *Toronto Star*, April 26, 2016.

and "inadequate resources." But nothing had been done. As a result, Laura's doctor told *Toronto Star* reporter Diana Zlomislic that "for the last few years, [he] has walked around with chronic rage."[13]

In May 2015, Laura's doctor and other transplant chiefs from across Ontario wrote a letter to Cancer Care Ontario "begging" for it to address the crisis of waitlists in the transplant program. The letter stated that the hospital program's capacity needed to be increased "by at least a third to perhaps as much as half" to address the backlogs on the waitlist and to provide "medically appropriate times to transplant." Without those additional resources, the only option was for doctors to put patients through what is termed, 'consolidation' chemotherapy, whereby patients are subjected to additional rounds of chemotherapy to keep cancer cells at bay while they wait for a transplant. In other words, the only plan or strategy to deal with the long waitlist for stem cell transplants was to subject patients to expensive, invasive, physiologically grueling, psychologically debilitating, and medically unnecessary treatment.

Laura's father, Greg, pressed hospital staff to admit that the consolidation treatment was medically unnecessary, and was quoted as saying, "You're rolling the dice with these patients. It's unconscionable." So, they began to look for options: SickKids Hospital in Toronto did transplants and did not have a waitlist. But Laura was now legally an adult and not eligible for treatment. Letters had to be written and Cancer Care Ontario's permission gained for Laura to go there.

By the time the approval came, it was August. SickKids then advised Laura that her donor would not be available for several weeks and encouraged her to undergo a mild chemotherapy as she waited. In September, SickKids called to say that the donor was "lost." No other explanation or information was given to Laura and her family. By November, tests at Juravinski Hospital showed that 80 percent of Laura's bone marrow cells were leukemic. Time, if there was any left, was running out.

Desperate to help Laura, her doctor found a hospital in California that was willing to do a stem cell transplant even though Laura was no longer in remission. But the very morning that she was to fly to California, she developed a brain bleed and went into cardiac arrest. She died shortly after.

In the end, Laura may have died from cancer … but it was the transplant waitlist that killed her.

---

[13] Ibid.

International standards of care call for cancer patients to have their transplant within two to three months of diagnosis. At that time, the wait at Princess Margaret Cancer Centre in Toronto was eight months.

4

Bill

There is a man in Kingston, Ontario, who lived for years with horrible pain and a condition that many would find socially embarrassing. Yet Canada's health-care system has offered him nothing but broken promises for treatment, eventually leading him to a point where he considered suicide or even taking a shotgun into a hospital and demanding care. (He did not and would not take such steps, but he admitted that these are the "stupid" ideas that fly around in your brain when your tolerance has reached its limit and your faith in the system has hit rock bottom.)

His name is Bill, and CBC reporters have followed his story.[14] In 2013, he was diagnosed with urethral stricture disease, which is scarring in or around the urethra that blocks the flow of urine out of the body. Years of attempts by surgeons to clear out his urethra only made the scar tissue worse. On more than a dozen occasions, he has had a catheter inserted into his bladder to relieve the discomfort, but it is a temporary solution and the infections continue.

As a result, Bill's life was a never-ending cycle of pain, infections, and discomfort. He could not work, walk, lift, or play with his grandchildren. He told reporters: "It's embarrassing when you go out because if you have too much urine in the bag and it starts sloshing, and you're wondering if everybody hears you or if they see the tube sticking out by your foot."

Surgery was the only answer, but Canada has only a few urologists with the required expertise to perform the operation, so a wait seemed inevitable. In the spring of 2016, he received the news that an Ottawa urologist would perform the procedure and that his surgery would be expedited. (As readers are likely beginning to understand, a promise to expedite surgery does not always end well.)

---

[14] Laurie Fagan, "Kingston Man Waits Years for Surgery to Relieve Painful Condition," CBC News, November 8, 2019; Neil Macdonald, "'Slosh, Slosh, Slosh': The Maddening, Twilight World of Medical Waiting Lists," CBC News, November 12, 2019.

The following sequence of events took place as Bill's surgery was supposedly 'expedited':

- In December 2016, Bill was told the surgery would happen before the fall of 2017.
- In October 2017, he received a call from a woman saying they had "misplaced" him on the list and would call back with a new surgery date. She never did.
- In April 2018, after complaining to the hospital's patient relations department, he received an apologetic call from the surgeon to assure him that the surgery would occur soon.
- In March 2019, he was told the surgery would take place on June 5.
- They told him that date was firm—until just 48 hours later when they called back to cancel the surgery because the required operating room was not available.
- In August 2019, he was given another date—November 4.
- Bill and his wife, Ann, drove to a hotel in Ottawa. At 7:00 a.m., a phone call came to say there had been an emergency and his surgery had been bumped again.

Bill had done his duty as a patient: He had made repeated calls to the office, asked about cancellations, and done his best to keep his name uppermost in their minds. But he says that the constant pain only made him made him feel "forgotten and trivialized." As time went on, his wife was increasingly worried about the state of his mental health.

So, it is hardly surprising that this call to his Ottawa hotel room—on the day of his promised surgery—led Bill to thoughts of rage, suicide, and utter despair. The agony, the infections, and the embarrassment had worn him down physically, mentally, and emotionally. He was done. The good news is that the media coverage of his story and a phone call from the reporter to the hospital administrators led to a surgery date within that week.

All of the above (endless delays and rescheduled surgery) was the result of one clerical designation: Bill's surgery had been declared "elective"—something that he wanted, not something that was medically necessary. That designation left him at the bottom of the list for priority procedures.

Uncontrolled pain. Constant infections. A urine bag around his leg. Unable to work. And in our health-care system where everybody gets treatment, *this is termed elective surgery*?

As CBC reporter Neil Macdonald describes, Bill's urologist had "repeatedly tried to clear [the scar tissue] out, inserting catheters and scopes and even a scope with miniature scissors into his penis, working up to his bladder. Each time, the scar tissue would just thicken." Does that sound to you like a fix that any man would undergo (repeatedly) if he did not have a desperate need?

Beyond the ridiculous classification as an "elective" surgery, why should people like Bill—or any other Canadian—be put in a position where they have to get media headlines just to obtain medical care?

5

Greg

Greg Price was a 31-year-old Calgary man; he was also an engineer and an avid baseball enthusiast who lived a great life and had a great life ahead of him. But all that changed when he put his trust in Canada's health-care system.[15]

He was first referred for a surgical consult when he noticed an unusual thickening on his testicle. But he heard nothing from the surgeon's office for three months. While he waited, unbearable pain forced him to attend a walk-in clinic, where he underwent more tests and an urgent CT was ordered. The scan, completed weeks later, detected a mass but the clinic never called him back with the results. When Greg called the clinic, he found out that the doctor had left the practice.

Multiple systemic and human errors resulted in the death of Greg Price.

[15] Susan Martinuk, "Use the Health-care System at Your Own Risk," *Calgary Herald*, January 10, 2014.

Greg went to see another physician who told him that he had testicular cancer and referred him to a urologist for surgery. So Greg waited again. He never received a phone call and, when he called the urologist's clinic, a recorded message told him that the doctor was away for an extended period of time.

Eventually, Greg was referred to another urologist and surgery was scheduled. Days before his operation, Greg sent an update to family and friends. Despite his difficulties in obtaining care, he sounded strong, gracious, and optimistic:

> "I am scheduled for primary surgery to remove one testicle at Rockyview General on Wednesday. It is planned for day surgery with the possibility of one overnight. Tissue samples will be taken and sent to the lab to determine the specific type of cancer cells and the pathology results will take about a week. This will give final confirmation of the diagnosis and guide the next treatment steps. The most likely treatment will be several rounds of chemotherapy, and/or further surgery.
>
> I am sure this is a little overwhelming and a shock to everyone, but I chose to not talk much about it until I knew for sure. Testicular cancer is one of the most treatable cancers with an extremely high cure rate. I am confident I can come out of this in several months stronger than ever."

The surgery went ahead as planned, but two days after his operation, complications developed and Greg was unable to reach his urologist. He went to the emergency ward only to be sent home and told that the cancer clinic would follow up. He died the next day.[16,17]

---

[16] Greg's family is using his tragic experience to advocate for change in health care. For more information visit www.healtharrows.ca.

[17] A film entitled, "Falling Through the Cracks: Greg's Story," uses Greg's experience as a tool to educate both patients and medical students. It can be viewed at https://gregswings.ca/fttc-gregsstory/.

6

What's Wrong with this Picture?

These experiences do not paint a pretty picture of health care, but they do reveal just how far our medical system has fallen from its primary purpose of providing care to the sick and injured. Even as we proclaim our pride in having a health-care system built on the principle of universal access, patient experience demonstrates the reality (and the irony) that health care has become inaccessible to those who need it most.

It is tempting to think that these just-described experiences are too extreme to reflect the typical interactions that take place between patients and their doctors. Admittedly, these stories often involve multiple human and systemic errors that conflate to override any chance of common sense coming to the rescue. But they are typical in that every one of us is likely to face at least one of these same human and/or systemic issues when we seek medical care that requires multiple visits to doctors, diagnostic tests, specialist care, and/or treatment. It is inevitable that some aspect(s) of care will be negatively affected by our fragmented system (of referrals and waits) and such unfortunate situations will become even more common as it is increasingly overwhelmed by an event such as the COVID-19 pandemic or our aging population.

What were the specific problems at the core of these stories? What insights can we gain from their experiences?

Every Step Forward is a Fight

There is a growing realization among Canadians that our health-care system is no longer there for us—the people who pay for it. Access to ongoing care often involves an exhausting battle against an inflexible and (sometimes) uncaring system to secure appointments for doctors, medical tests, diagnostic scans, and/or treatment. Continuity of care is often disrupted and there are months-long waits at every juncture of obtaining care, requiring repeated phone calls to push for appointments and dates for procedures, even when a referral has been sent. It can be exhausting and, as these stories demonstrate, fraught with emotion, anxiety, and frustration.

When your health is declining and your quality of life is diminishing daily, *there is nothing that so saps your strength as the feeling that you are not being heard by the only people who can help you.* People who are sick, particularly those with serious illnesses like cancer, should not have to devote their limited personal resources (time, strength, finances, and energy) to constantly press for the medical attention that they need just to get proper care.

> "You have to fight for everything. It is not enough that you pay for this free medical care…you have to wage constant war with everyone in the system that is taking your money. In case of emergency, BC healthcare is awesome. For maintenance health care, it's pure hell."[18]
>
> Roger S., B.C.

Ross said he was "not rude or disrespectful, but most times I had to beg just to be heard. It is a fight. Here I am, a grown man, a professional, and I have to beg to get medical care." He knew that he had to be persistent to get treatment for his father, but he was also increasingly fearful that his phone calls would be labelled as problematic and his father's care would suffer as a result. (Note that this is a common fear expressed by patients who share their stories).

Professionals say that Ross did the right thing. According to Jodi Glassford, head of Alberta Netcare's eReferral program, a provincial government program for clinicians that e-tracks referrals, the onus is on the patient to ensure their referral is moving forward. Glassford, who is also provincial director of access improvement for Alberta Health, says: "You've gotta follow up. You have to be that patient who's difficult, because who knows? You have no transparency into [the referral process so you don't know] am I on the list? Will I be seen?"[19]

Francesca Grosso, chairman of the board for an advocacy group called Patients Canada, echoes that advice. Commenting on the problems that COVID-19 has created for patients, she says: "...we don't have a system that

---

[18] Roger S, "Is Canadian Health Care as Bad as it Seems?", Quora, May 27, 2018, https://www.quora.com/Is-Canadian-health-care-as-bad-as-it-seems.

[19] Vanessa Milne, Joshua Tepper, and Maureen Taylor, "Anatomy of a Referral: Why Wait Times for Specialists are Still Too Long," www.healthydebate.ca, February 9, 2017.

really prioritizes patients in a way that flags…patients [who] require urgent follow up. It's sort of left up to the patient [to be] the squeaky wheel…"[20]

Referrals: Seemingly Ubiquitous, Yet Rarely in the Right Spot

The current referral process is disorganized, inefficient, and seemingly allows doctors on both ends of the referral (GPs and specialists) to deny having accountability for the patient's care and well-being. As a result, it is the patient who suffers from any administrative and bureaucratic mistakes.

Human errors happen all the time, but the current referral system seems doomed from the start. There are too many opportunities for mistakes:

- Sometimes referrals do not get sent. They are too often put in a paper pile and forgotten, mislaid, ignored, or simply lost;
- Or the doctor makes a note while talking to the patient and then promptly forgets to pass on the orders;
- Or perhaps a secretary gets distracted by a phone call and fails to make the necessary arrangements, despite the physician's instructions;
- Referral forms can be filled out incorrectly (as with Ross and Don);
- Referrals can be sent to a doctor in the wrong medical specialty (as shown in Dave's story below) or to the wrong doctor who has the same last name;
- Finally, even when referrals are sent, there is no guarantee that they will be responded to, or acted on. This results in situations like Greg faced as he waited for an appointment with a surgeon who was not even currently practicing.

A 2014 study from McMaster University in Hamilton showed that as many as 21 percent of requests for specialty consults failed to elicit any kind of response from the specialist's office.[21]

Three years later, these same researchers found that more than one-third (36.4 percent) of referrals had not been responded to by the end of the study's seven-week follow-up period.[22]

---

[20] Jennifer La Grassa, "After a Late-stage Cancer Diagnosis, Windsor Mom Says Her Son Fell Through the Cracks of COVID-19 Shutdowns," CBC News, December 3, 2020.

[21] I. Neimanis et al., "Committee on Utilization, Review and Education Common Referral Form," *Canadian Family Physician*, vol 60: 916, 2014.

In other words, more than one in three referrals never even makes it to the waitlist pile and is essentially moot. Obviously, this leaves a patient's care seriously compromised, as without any intervention (such as a phone call from the patient or a rare follow-up call from the referring doctor), the patient is left in limbo and in the dark. He/she could wait weeks or months without knowing that the call they are waiting for is not going to happen.

Researchers have also found it is not uncommon for doctors to refer patients to a doctor practicing in the right specialty but the wrong sub-specialty. As you can imagine, a misdirected referral can add many months to a patient's wait for treatment.

In February 2015, Dave ruptured a disc in his lower spine and was in excruciating pain.[23] He went to a family practice clinic at the University of British Columbia where he saw a doctor who was relatively new to Canada and did not have a good understanding of the English language.

The doctor gave him oxycodone for the pain and referred him to a specialist for further care. He survived on painkillers for three months while waiting for his orthopedic consult. But when the requisite wait was over and he finally saw the specialist, he was in for a shock—he had been referred to a foot surgeon, not a spinal surgeon!

Apparently, the medical system has no way to right that wrong by making a few phone calls. Instead, the onus was put back on Dave to return to a family physician, get another referral (to the right specialist), and then wait even longer for another appointment while still relying on oxycodone for pain control. He finally saw the correct specialist in October, nine months after his accident.

Even if the process runs smoothly and the right paperwork gets to the right doctor, it can still be declined because the specialist's caseload is already over capacity. For the patient, this situation is no different than when the referral never gets there. If a specialist fails to inform the referring doctor and/or patient that they are not accepting new patients, the referred patient is left sitting in the dark, thinking his/her healing pathway is moving forward when, in fact, it is at a standstill.[24]

Whether the paperwork flies between offices or sits in a pile, the only thing that a patient can be certain of is, in far too many cases, there is no one

---

[22] I. Neimanis et al., "Referral Processes and Wait Times in Primary Care," *Canadian Family Physician*, vol 63:619-624, 2017.

[23] Personal Interview.

[24] Vanessa Milne, Joshua Tepper, and Maureen Taylor, "Anatomy of a Referral: "Why Wait Times for Specialists are Still Too Long," www.healthydebate.ca, February 9, 2017.

overseeing the referral process to ensure that the patient's interests are protected.

The lesson in all of this? *Patients need to take responsibility for their own care and make phone calls to ensure a referral has been sent, received, and acted on.* The doctors' offices may not like it, but as long as you are polite and provide accurate information, you are right to do so. Of course, there are other, more innovative, and even pleasant ways to accomplish this.

Catherine is a health-care worker in a large hospital. Her father had been diagnosed with cancer and referred for a PET scan.[25] The appropriate referral was made and received by the diagnostic clinic, but the wait time for the scan was measured in months as, unfortunately, was her father's life expectancy.

She began dropping by the administrative desk every day, chatting with the scheduler, and often bringing her a Starbucks coffee. She was open about what she wanted—a PET scan for her dad. When an opening surfaced in the schedule, her father got the call. To show her gratitude, Catherine continued to periodically bring coffee and stop by for a chat.

They were Denied Access to Treatment

There is no guarantee of timely treatment or timely access to specialty care in Canadian health care. The Commonwealth Fund's 2016 International Survey found that Canadians had the worst access to specialist care of eleven wealthy, developed nations.[26] Almost one-third of Canadian patients (30 percent) waited longer than two months to access a specialist; in Germany, just three percent of patients waited that long. In many cases, delayed care is the same as no care, and this can be a harsh discovery for patients who have put their trust in Canadian health care and expect it to help them when needed.

In an anonymous Quora.com posting on the topic, "Is Canadian Health Care as Bad as it Seems?" one man described how his friend's 25-year-old son lost months of his life and suffered great agony as he waited for a urologist to fix a common problem with a relatively routine surgery.

> "It started with a sharp and unbearable pain in the side of his lower abdomen. When he was taken to the emergency department at Ottawa's Queensway Carleton Hospital, they told him he had a kidney stone. They also gave him painkillers, told him there were

---

[25] Personal Interview.

[26] 2016 Commonwealth Fund International Health Policy Survey of Adults, November 16, 2016.

no urologists available to see him, and that the nearest appointment was three months away. Then they sent him home.

The painkillers helped, at first. But then the pain became constant and debilitating. For the next number of weeks, my friend's young son could not work and remained in bed and in pain. On two occasions, the pain forced him back to the ER where an ultrasound showed he had a six-millimetre stone. But there was still no urologist available and the hospital staff said there was nothing they could do to expedite his appointment. They gave him more painkillers and sent him home.

He was in agonizing pain: He did not work, so he had no income. His parents were transferring money from India to help him survive. Three agony-filled months later, he finally saw a urologist. After examining him, the first thing the urologist said was: *"You should have come earlier."* Eventually the surgery was done and, despite some difficulties, this young man was finally on the road to recovery.

After this experience, my friend constantly wonders why he did not take his son to India as soon as the whole ordeal started. In India, his son would have been operated on and the problem solved within a day or two.

Like many Canadians, my friend's son waited for the first month - still under the illusion that the Canadian health-care system would come through. During the second month, they were certain they would receive a notice for a urologist appointment any day. By the third month, he was too ill to travel. Now there is no doubt in my friend's mind: If this were to happen again, he would immediately send his son to India."[27]

Professionalism: Missing in Action

Unprofessional Communication. These patient experiences are rife with unprofessional behaviour and a lack of communication by doctors and office staff with their patients. Both Ross and Debbie went beyond the norm to

---

[27] Anonymous, Quora.com, May 5, 2018, https://www.quora.com/Is-Canadian-health-care-as-bad-as-it-seems.

communicate in a way that was polite yet firm; in each case, something had obviously gone wrong with the paperwork and they were doing their best to get office workers or doctors to take a brief moment to understand the situation and then correct the problem.

Debbie is a long-time nurse and familiar with working in a hectic environment with busy doctors. Similarly, as a businessman, Ross knows that losing your patience is not the best way to resolve problems with customers. Yet, being polite got them nowhere. Their concerns went unheard; they encountered verbal abuse, silence, and a general lack of respect just because they were trying to get treatment for family members.

In addition, despite repeated promises of maintaining contact, doctors and their staff made virtually no attempt to maintain contact, to keep the patient updated, and/or to resolve systemic problems. Being subjected to such apathy and indifference only deepens the stress and anxiety that is already running rampant in the minds of seriously ill patients and their families.

Ross's story of the receptionist in the CT department who took time to listen to his problem and then took action to resolve it is very telling and shows that it can often take less time to resolve a recurring problem than to persist in playing the daily Whack-a-Mole game with phone calls from patients wanting answers. In this case, the receptionist spoke directly to her department head who then took a few minutes to call the referring oncologist. In less than a week, Ross's father, Don, was undergoing a CT scan. Compare the five to ten minutes that it took to fix the problem to the perpetual cycle of stress and frustration that was exacerbated over a period of weeks and months for the patient, his family, and those answering the phones at the CT desk.

Worse still are the actions of those receptionists who simply hung up on concerned patients. The College of Physicians and Surgeons of British Columbia has professional guidelines for its members to follow when making referrals and it should be noted that the preamble stresses the importance of maintaining communication with the patient and keeping the patient "at the centre of the referral-consultation process:"[28]

> "…physicians should be mindful that patient well-being is the single most important factor in ensuring an effective referral-

---

[28] College of Physicians and Surgeons of British Columbia, Professional Guideline Referral-Consultation. Last revised March 20, 2020. https://cpsbc.ca/files/pdf/PSG-Referral-Consultation-Process.pdf.

> consultation process. In all instances, patients and their families remain at the centre of the referral-consultation process, and physicians should show their willingness to work together courteously and respectfully to ensure patient care is not compromised. Keeping the patient informed throughout the referral process is of the utmost importance."[29]

In spite of this being a professional guideline, it has been reported that referring physicians continue to view it as optional. Based on the studies and examples shared herein, efforts to "ensure patient care" and keep the patient informed throughout the referral process do not seem to be a common reality for many patients.[30]

Cherry-picking. Another type of unprofessional behaviour, known as cherry-picking, describes a situation when family doctors refuse to take on patients who have chronic pain issues, mental illness, complex health problems, or are deemed to be "difficult." Any of these issues requires longer appointment times and can therefore have a negative impact on appointment schedules and physician incomes.[31]

Ross's father, Don, ran into this situation when the family doctor who had agreed to take on a retiring GP's patient load subsequently refused to provide care for Don. This practice is contrary to the Canadian Medical Association's Code of Ethics and Professionalism, yet it remains a relatively common occurrence.[32]

How common? An online survey of 1,181 Canadians found that 68 percent of readers had experienced it, while 23 percent knew of others who had. Remarkably, while these responders (91 percent) viewed cherry-picking as a significant health-care problem, those who had never experienced it (nine percent) did not consider it to be an important issue.[33]

---

[29] Ibid.

[30] Tola Overduin, "Continuity of Care Policy Exposes Fault Lines in the Medical Profession," *Canadian Medical Association News*, December 19, 2019.

[31] Vanessa Milne, Andreas Laupacis, and Mike Tierney, "Are Family Doctors Cherry Picking Patients?" www.healthydebate.ca, October 23, 2014, https://healthydebate.ca/2014/10/topic/family-doctors-cherry-picking-patients.

[32] Canadian Medical Association, "CMA Code of Ethics and Professionalism," https://policybase.cma.ca/documents/policypdf/PD19-03.pdf.

[33] Vanessa Milne, Andreas Laupacis, and Mike Tierney, "Are Family Doctors Cherry Picking Patients?", www.healthydebate.ca, October 23, 2014, https://healthydebate.ca/2014/10/topic/family-doctors-cherry-picking-patients.

Ignoring an Ethical Duty to Care. Debbie confronted a specialist who could not provide the timely care that Walid needed, yet was unwilling to discuss or seek out options for his care. Both the doctor and BC Children's Hospital had a professional and ethical duty to educate Debbie about options when it became obvious that they could not provide the surgery that Walid needed in a timely manner.

It is not enough for the doctor to merely dismiss the notion of referring to another doctor or clinic; in fact, it demonstrates an arrogance and a limited scope of thinking that fails to put the patient's well-being as the first priority. Considering the hospital could not even accommodate Walid for diagnostic scans over a two-and-a-half-year period, the doctor should have been honest about his chances of ever getting care at BC Children's Hospital and actively working to expedite his care at another facility.

That said, the number of options in the Canadian health-care system are limited. If you travel to another province for care, you go to the bottom of a waitlist. If you make a request to switch doctors, you go to the bottom of a waitlist. In some provinces, there is an option of attending a private clinic for surgery, but pursuing any of these options or bringing them up for discussion with the doctor can, in some cases, jeopardize future care.

Considering the seriousness of Walid's condition and Debbie's willingness to do anything (including remortgage her house), the surgeon should have had a strong focus on seeking other options and discussing this with Debbie in a helpful, cooperative manner.

Refusal to Take Responsibility. In his interview, Ross said that he wished that someone would have accepted responsibility for his father's care and taken action to get him the treatment he needed, like the receptionist in the CT department who took a moment out of her schedule to solve his problem. Instead, the oncologist told Ross "it's not my fault" that the CT and radiation departments had such a backlog and that his "hands were tied." Similarly, this same doctor refused to accept responsibility for his receptionist who had hung up on Ross and his siblings on multiple occasions as they attempted to get appointments for their father. When Ross mentioned her unprofessional behaviour, the doctor basically shrugged his shoulders and said there was nothing he could do about it. She had been there for 30 years and "that's just the way she is."

The first GP who took over Don's case from the retiring physician failed to act on his duty to care for Don, as did a subsequent physician who told Don that he had cancer and referred him to an oncologist, then washed her hands of any responsibility in helping him access that care when problems arose. She continued to provide general care to Don as he underwent investigations and treatment for his cancer, yet even as it was obvious that he was not getting proper access to specialists and scans, she refused to make any effort to rectify the issues and ensure that he could undergo cancer treatments in a timely fashion. Instead, the doctor said she could not interfere with the process—it was all up to the cancer clinic. (Apparently, she has never seen the motivational quote that says "the only real failure in life is not in failing to accomplish something, but in failing to try").

Greg's story is also a tragic example of what can happen when there is no one overseeing or taking responsibility for patient care during the referral process. This seriously disrupted his continuity of care, as on multiple occasions, doctors and/or staff did not follow up on test results, referrals, post-operative care, and/or communicating with the patient.

> "At times, I feel angry, powerless and just a nobody. The medical system needs a complete overhaul if people have to wait, wait and wait some more."[34]
>
> Kathleen

[34] Kathleen, "People Have to Wait, Wait, and Wait Some More," Charter Health, January 12, 2015, www.charterhealth.ca.

7

Where is Canada's Outrage?

In June 2019, CBC news reporter Neil Macdonald unexpectedly landed in a hospital for a painful hip injury and writes, "I found myself in the business end of the health-care system Canadians brag about so much: a big, crowded ward full of hurting people, some of them yelling profanely, and few staff in sight."[35]

After an overnight in the ER, he was moved to a room but still had no idea what was wrong with him. Nurses said he had to ask the doctor and kept pushing pain meds; technicians who took various scans repeated the seemingly standard response. According to Macdonald, the nurses were now his gatekeepers whose duty was to deal with his pain and not to divulge information about his medical problem. From this, he concludes, "nurses are better at guarding information than our security agencies."

This pattern continued for several days. They said the doctor would be by later. Or this evening. Or tomorrow. But he never answered his pages and he never came to see Neil, his patient. As a reporter, Neil had an inside track to finding people and he is not the type to shrink from ruffling a few feathers. He had previously called a 'missing-in-action' physician at his home late at night to get answers and, as he told his nurse now, he was quite willing to do it again. His blunt words finally inspired some action and the nursing staff made sure that his doctor was at his bedside the very next morning. After spending several days in the hospital, Neil finally met his doctor, heard a diagnosis, and received answers to his questions about his condition and his care. At 62 years of age, Macdonald has travelled the world and survived reporting from the midst of war zones; yet this one health-care experience led him to write that he now finds the prospect of another visit to a Canadian hospital to be "frightening."

---

[35] Neil Macdonald, "Canada's Health-Care System is Hopelessly Sclerotic. We Need to Wake Up," CBC News Commentary, June 12, 2019.

His suggestion for change? He says *it is time for Canadians to "stop bragging about our health-care system and start yelling about it* instead."

Waitlists are a Denial of Care

Waitlists have been prevalent in Canadian health care since the 1990s and have grown, almost unabated, since then. They eventually became a permanent fixture in health care and, more recently, have evolved to become the determining factor for when, or even if, health care is delivered to a patient. In other words, waitlists do not define Canadian health care so much as they officially define its denial of care, yet Canadians rarely show any sense of rage at the reality: Treatment that is provided three years after an injury is not a sign that we have a good health-care system.

It may be that growing up in a country with the always-present expectation and promise (however false it may be) of cradle-to-grave health care has lulled us into believing that this is how health care works and it is the best we can do. Or perhaps our expectations of service are relatively low because health care is a huge government-ordained monopoly and we rarely hold government institutions to the same standard as private sector services.

For years, the Canadian Institute for Health Information (CIHI), the Fraser Institute, and provincial governments have carefully tracked waitlists. Reports are published throughout the year but they rarely present any positive data and only serve to remind us that wait times for surgeries, specialists, diagnostic procedures, and medical treatment are getting longer.

If It Does Not Affect Me...

There is a saying that "perception is reality." That is, what you have seen and experienced impacts your thinking and, for good or bad, informs your opinion. In other words, most Canadians remain oblivious to the health-care chaos around them until it affects them. Those who have had limited experiences with health care, have had a regular family doctor for years, or have experienced excellent care in an isolated emergent situation are likely to believe that the system works well, even if long waits exist. As long as the lists are filled with the names of others, this group is not likely to be alarmed or mobilized by years-long waits for treatment.

For example, a February 2020 article in *The American Prospect* claimed to have the inside story on the Canadian health-care system.[36] It presented Medicare to our southern neighbours in terms of its noble ideals and idyllic

---

[36] Caitlin Kelly, "What Medicare for All Really Looks Like," *The American Prospect*, April 8, 2020.

principles, while brushing off realities like waitlists as mere inconveniences that Canadians are quite happy to put up with in exchange for free health care.

As proof of how well our system works, the article profiled a healthy, 28-year-old Ontario man named Dennis whose entire experience with health care involved a few visits to the emergency department for sports injuries. He has never had to pay for medical care and therefore continues to play recreational sports without "financial anxiety over potential injury." According to a young, strong, and healthy guy like Dennis, the Medicare system is great.

But another athletic young man named Corey had a very different experience and now claims that being forced to wait in pain for years without treatment "should not be considered ethical even in a supposedly free system."[37]

Corey injured his left hip during a hockey game and a physiotherapist later diagnosed it as a "cartilage issue." But not long after that injury, the same thing happened in his right hip as he bent over to pick up something off the floor, immediately transforming him from "a very athletic person to a guy who could barely walk a few blocks."

Doctors scheduled Corey for an MRI to properly diagnose the problem, but the earliest date for a scan was one and a half years after the injury occurred. So he paid to have MRI exams done at a private clinic and the scans revealed that he needed surgery on both hips. However, because of rationed care and the many constraints that exist in our health-care system, *he was told that he could only get treatment on one hip at a time*. Further, the first surgery had to successfully resolve the problem before they could operate on the other hip. In other words, he would be waiting for about three years for each hip. According to Corey, the limited access to treatment meant it was "basically a sentence to live in pain for six years."

It is simply not realistic for a young, active fellow like Corey to put his life on hold for that long. As a result, he paid to have the surgery done at a private clinic.

A Touch of Stockholm Syndrome?

It has been suggested that Canadians rarely get exercised about health-care issues because of what psychologists refer to as Stockholm syndrome.[38] The term stems from a 1973 bank robbery in Stockholm, Sweden, that turned into

---

[37] Adapted from Corey, "Not Ethical Even in a Supposedly Free System," Charter Health, October 24, 2016, www.charterhealth.ca.

[38] William D. Gairdner, *The Trouble with Canada … Still!: A Citizen Speaks Out*, (Toronto: Key Porter Books, 2010): 289–290.

a five-day standoff with the police. Almost inexplicably the hostages formed sympathetic bonds with their captors and even refused to testify against them.

This same phenomenon can also occur during situations of abuse or domestic violence, so the term has now become a rather general reference to any difficult situation where the victim feels powerless to bring about change and, as a means of protection, begins to create an irrational bond with the one who is persecuting them.

Is this an accurate picture of Canadians waiting three years for surgery? Or one year for an MRI scan? Are we really so grateful for "free" health care that we do not care when we get it or how much pain we have to endure before it can be treated?

Canadian author and intellectual Dr. William Gairdner muses that Stockholm syndrome might be one reason that millions of Canadians proudly consider Medicare a defining value of our nation, even when the system is incapable of providing timely care in all but emergent situations (and sometimes not even then) and when more than one million people are waiting for medical care. Far too many Canadians have been victimized by the very system that is supposed to care for them.

According to Gairdner, Canadians feel powerless to change the system because a lifetime of socialized health care ("a top-down bureaucratic control of government-rationed medicine") has led us to believe that we have very little control over our own medical care. [39] In other words, we are all trapped in a socialist jail and therefore grateful for the least bit of care we can get from a dysfunctional system that could just as easily deny us care. An example of this is comparing Canada Post with private couriers; you know the package will get there with Canada Post—you just do not know when. But it is often cheaper than a courier so we make allowances for the delays. Overall, Stockholm syndrome is just one intriguing theory. But is it correct? Who knows?

Casual conversations during the early months of the COVID-19 pandemic suggest there may be an element of truth to it. Some Canadians who were frustrated with various aspects of health care prior to the pandemic suddenly felt a sense of gratitude for a system that was free and open to anyone. In other words, the system may not be great, but at least we have one.

---

[39] Ibid., 285.

Too Sick and Too Tired to Protest

As American radio commentator Paul Harvey used to say, there is still "the rest of the story" and that stems from the shared experiences of the million-plus Canadians who are languishing on a waitlist for what their doctors have deemed to be "medically necessary" treatment.

This group includes those who are searching for an elusive diagnosis, suffering from mental illness, have chronic diseases that require ongoing care and treatment, need multiple diagnostic tests and visits to specialists, have long waits for procedures, or are lying in the hallway on a gurney because they cannot access a much-needed hospital bed.

If the healthiest Canadians tend to be unaware of our health-care crisis, it is incumbent upon the sick to advocate for change. But this is an unfair burden. The people in the stories herein are those most affected by rationed resources, yet least capable of carrying out an energized protest against the system that they need for their care. They simply do not possess the additional physical and mental resources that are required to take on governments, bureaucrats, and hospital administrators in the public square.

Consider the story of Suzanne Aucoin, a St. Catharines, ON, woman who was forced to spend the final months of her life battling bureaucracy instead of the cancer that was overwhelming her body.

She gained national attention when she fought for the government to cover her cancer treatments, including the cost of a new drug.[40] Five years after an intitial fight with colorectal cancer, a CT exam showed that the cancer had recurred and spread to her lungs and liver. She now had Stage IV cancer and her oncologist recommended that she take Erbitux, a new drug capable of shrinking tumours in advanced cancer patients but had yet to be approved for use or purchase in Ontario.

Aucoin applied to the provincial Ministry of Health for out-of-country funding to go to a hospital in the United States where she could receive the only drug that could help her. Her application was denied even though the ministry acknowledged that it had paid for other patients to receive Erbitux in similar circumstances. The media followed Aucoin's battle against the government and, at this point, she told them: "You can't wait with this cancer. You can't wait for people to make decisions about your health. You can't wait for forms to be filled out. You have to go where the drug is."

---

[40] Amy Ridenour and Ryan Balis, "Cancer Patient Takes on Canadian Health-care Bureaucracy in Desperate Fight to Live," *Shattered Lives: 100 Victims of Government Health Care*, (Washington, DC: The National Center for Public Policy Research, 2009).

She then took matters into her own hands and began weekly treatments (costing US$14,000 per month) across the border at a clinic in the state of New York. About six months later, Health Canada granted its approval to Erbitux but with very limited access. Under the new rules other Ontarians could access the drug, but Aucoin was still refused coverage.

Several months later, Aucoin was the first patient to be allowed Erbitux under a new Ontario Special Access Program for seriously ill patients, although she would still have to pay part of the costs (C$6,000 per month) for treatment at a Hamilton clinic. But this was not the positive news that one would expect as it gave the "system" more power to intrude in Aucoin's medical care:

- For some inexplicable reason, the Ontario health ministry agreed to fully cover Aucoin's treatment costs at a U.S. clinic, so she would no longer have to pay out of pocket.
- However, the very same provincial health-care ministry would not cover her treatments at the West Seneca, N.Y., clinic that Aucoin had previously attended. *Instead, it mandated that she attend a Buffalo, N.Y., cancer hospital that charged thousands of dollars more each month for treatments than the West Seneca clinic.*
- Then the ministry refused to reimburse her for the costs it had said it would cover!
- Aucoin was forced to appeal to the provincial ombudsman to be reimbursed $76,000 by the Ontario government. In his ruling, the ombudsman referred to health officials as "cruel" and condemned their "slavish adherence to rules at the expense of common sense."

In the end, Aucoin was devastated saying, "I am completely disgusted with our health-care system. I am very discouraged and frustrated by the lack of professionalism, the lack of consistency, and the lack of care for me as an individual patient. I should never have had to deal with this. It takes all my energy to fight cancer."

Within a year, Aucoin would pass away. But she had spent more than three years fighting a bureaucracy at the time that she most needed her strength to combat cancer and her time to be with family.

PART II

WAITING

8

A Nation that Waits

Over the past several years, Canada's wait times have reached two major milestones: We now have the longest wait times in the developed world and, beginning in 2017, our annual waitlists have exceeded the one million mark. Assuming that one person is waiting for each procedure, there were 1,062,286 people waiting for various treatments and procedures in 2019, a number that is roughly equivalent to three percent of our population.[41]

As you read this chapter, please keep in mind that the facts listed below (and in this entire book) are not meant to be a criticism of health-care workers or a comment on the quality of Canadian health care. But a particularly salient point about quality care in Canada is that it does not mean much if you cannot access it.

How Long do Canadians Wait?

The Fraser Institute has tracked wait times for over 25 years, evaluating the situation nationally, across the provinces, and in 12 medical specialties. Overall, the data provide ample evidence to demonstrate that Canadians do not have timely access to health care.

In its reports, total wait times are determined by adding together two consecutive time intervals: The time from a general practitioner's referral to the date of consultation with a specialist, plus the time from the specialist consultation until the patient receives treatment. (Note that waits are measured in weeks and presented as the median value, rather than an average. The median represents the "middle" value in the data set and is considered to be more representative of the real situation because it is less affected by unusually high or low numbers called outliers).

---

[41] Bacchus Barua and Mackenzie Moir. (2019). "Waiting Your Turn: Wait Times for Health Care in Canada," 2019 Report, The Fraser Institute, https:/www.fraserinstitute.org/studies/waiting-your-turn-wait-times-for-health-care-in-canada-2019.

In 2019, Canadians waited 20.9 weeks to be treated by a specialist (beginning with the date of referral from a family doctor). This is the second highest wait time recorded by the Fraser Institute since it began measuring wait times in 1993 (when this same interval was just 9.3 weeks).[42]

The Province of Ontario reported the shortest waits for treatment at 16.0 weeks, while Prince Edward Island had the longest at 49.3. In other words, Island residents will be waiting for almost an entire year to see a medical specialist. Not surprisingly, the longest waits across the country were for orthopedic surgery (39.1 weeks), while the shortest (4.4 weeks) were for medical oncology.

Year	Total Number of Procedures for which Canadians are Waiting	Interval 1 GP to Specialist *(weeks)*	Interval 2 Specialist to TX *(weeks)*	Total Wait from GP to TX *(weeks)*	Medical Oncology (shortest waits) *(weeks)*	Orthopedic Surgery (longest waits) *(weeks)*
1993		3.7	5.6	9.3		
2000	166,150	5.6	8.4	14	4.5	24.6
2005	782,936	8.3	9.4	17.7	5.6	40
2010	825,827	8.9	9.3	18.2	4.9	35.6
2015	894,449	8.5	9.8	18.3	4.5	35.7
2019	1,064,286	10.1	10.8	20.9	4.4	39.1

Table 1. Wait times for medical care from 1993 - 2019[43]

None of the above data is encouraging; according to the 2019 report's ultimate conclusion, "despite provincial strategies to reduce wait times and high levels of expenditure on health care, it is clear that patients in Canada are waiting too long to receive treatment."[44]

---

[42] Ibid.

[43] Based on annual reports from the Fraser Institute.

[44] Bacchus Barua and Mackenzie Moir. (2019). "Waiting Your Turn: Wait Times for Health Care in Canada," 2019 Report. The Fraser Institute, p.17. https://www.fraserinstitute.org/studies/waiting-your-turn-wait-times-for-health-care-in-canada-2019.

Where is the biggest holdup? The 2019 wait time from GP referral to a specialist was 10.1 weeks while the interval from specialist consultation to treatment was 10.8. (These waits are substantially longer than in 1993 when the same times were 3.7 and 5.6 weeks, respectively). A comparison of the intervals from 1993 to 2019 suggest that the wait from GP referral to the specialist appointment is now the source of the longest delay in the process.

Different Ways of Calculating Wait Times

There is one caveat to consider while looking at the medical wait times shown above: They will likely be very different from those found on government websites.

Governments tend to create their own methods of determining wait times and they have developed a very handy (and deceptive) way of minimizing "official" provincial waits. For example, some provinces only begin to measure wait times from the day that an operating room is booked or the hospital receives a request for a medical procedure. These calculations deliberately exclude the majority of the wait that the patient experiences, thereby making the numbers on provincial health websites appear much lower than they really are.

Using the provinces' magic formulas means that some patients may have waited several years before they are even added to a waitlist. For example, if this method was used to measure the wait time that Walid and his mother, Debbie, experienced, it would have miraculously concocted an official wait time of zero days, since his operation was never booked.

Another PR trick governments use to minimize the waitlist problem is to subtly shift the words used. Waitlists typically refer to patients waiting for treatment or procedures that a doctor has deemed "medically necessary." But politicians strive to confuse us all by claiming that patients are waiting for "elective" procedures. Words matter, and there is a huge difference in the public's perception of those waiting for "elective" procedures (like some types of plastic surgery) compared to "medically necessary" procedures (which can mean the difference between being able to walk or not, work or not, or care for a family or not). More importantly, it can even be the difference between life and death.

You can readily see 1) how problematic this can become for patients who have been waiting months and years, only to realize they are not yet even on an official waitlist, 2) that government waitlists greatly underestimate the size of the waitlist problem, and 3) that governments do what they can to minimize the problem when they report it to the public. The third factor is never indicative of a government that is keen on working towards a resolution.

Even as governments actively seek to minimize the waitlist problem, the reality is that some people can wait for years to get relief from their medical conditions:

> "The public health system has failed me on so many levels…by age 21, I developed debilitating upper limb pain. It took six years to receive a correct diagnosis, all while enduring job loss and financial ruin while attending to numerous appointments within the public health-care system. In between waiting for specialist appointments, I sought pain relief from private health-care treatments. They helped but were not financially sustainable. I was finally referred to a public surgeon who specializes in my condition...Two and a half years have passed and I am still waiting for a consult (not for surgery or treatment). I've been told I'm on the 'short list' and could be waiting up to 5 years in total. The 'long list' is up to 10 years. Since then, I have struggled with daily tasks, taking high doses of pain killers and mental health issues. Last year I attempted suicide and was hospitalized…my chronic pain was so unbearable, I tried to end my life to escape it."[45]

Benchmarks and Clinically Reasonable Wait Times

In 2005, Canada's federal, provincial, and territorial governments agreed to a set of common benchmarks for priority medical procedures which would set a time frame to treat 50 percent of the patients for that particular condition. Specialists are also routinely surveyed as to what they consider to be "clinically reasonable" waits for these same procedures and, not surprisingly, the time frames set by physicians are markedly shorter than those proposed by governments. Data for the past three decades show that the actual wait times typically exceed what is considered to be the clinically reasonable wait and, in 2019, waits for priority procedures exceeded the clinically reasonable times in 77 percent of cases.[46]

---

[45] Loki, "The Public Health Care System has Failed Me on So Many Levels," Charter Health, January 22, 2017, www.charterhealth.ca.

[46] Bacchus Barus and Mackenzie Moir. (2019). "Waiting Your Turn: Wait Times for Health Care in Canada," 2019 report, The Fraser Institute, p. 6. https://www.fraserinstitute.org/studies/waiting-your-turn-wait-times-for-health-care-in-canada-2019.

Different Perspectives on Wait Times

Governments may wish to dismiss the time that patients are required to wait for a consult with a specialist or for diagnostic tests, but if a patient is in pain or unable to work and support his/her family, this time period becomes particularly relevant to their wait-time experience and their quality of life.

Governments are not the only groups that have attempted to minimize the problems associated with long waits for health-care. Canadian Doctors for Medicare is an advocacy group that acts as a cheerleader for our health-care system and, over the years, its need to support what is obviously 'unsupportable' has made for rather outlandish claims about what constitutes timely medical care. In a 2012 speech, Dr. Robert Woollard provided an example of what he considers to be the excellent and timely care that one can expect in our country.

> "The public system has the nimbleness to provide speedy, quality care to those who truly need it. Just six or eight weeks ago, I had a patient come in who needed urgent attention to her knee. She was in severe pain. She was seen by a team within a week, and she was slated for surgery that will probably happen in the next two or three months."[47]

There are several points to consider in his comment:

- this doctor considers a five-month wait (at least) for surgery for a patient in "severe pain" to be an example of Canada's exceptional medical care.
- he uses the terms "nimble," "speedy," and "quality care" to describe the care that was given to a patient in "severe pain," who was seen "within a week," and is now waiting months for treatment to resolve that pain.
- how is the attitude of this doctor and the group that he represents enhancing patient care by proclaiming cases like this to be an example of success?

Compare his comments about Canada's "nimble" service to the two similar stories that follow.

---

[47] Brian Day, "Why the Medicare Madness Will Soon Come to an End," Canadian Healthcare Network, October 22, 2012, www.CanadianHealthcareNetwork.ca.

Diana from Vancouver, writes: "Six months ago, I began experiencing knee pain due to meniscal damage. My doctor referred me for an MRI, but when I called the clinic to book an appointment, I was told that it would take six weeks for someone to even return my call! Once I do get the MRI, it will be a six-to-eight month wait for a consult with a surgeon. After that, who knows how long until I can finally have surgery."[48]

Dianne, from Chilliwack, B.C. writes: "I've had five years of pain and lack of function. So far, I have waited: nine months for an MRI, three years for a consultation with a surgeon, and now, who knows how long for a surgery date."[49]

Linda is a mother who knows the frustration of watching a loved one as they wait years for medical care. Her active, healthy, mid-20s son began to suffer from fatigue, dizziness, and a general feeling of being unwell. He made repeated visits to his GP to ask for help but his doctor was reluctant to refer him to a specialist. It took two years for his doctor to determine that he was incapable of diagnosing and treating his condition, and only then did he refer him to specialists.[50] Once her son passed that hurdle, he faced waits of 18 months or more to see a GI specialist for a biopsy and a cardiologist. She writes that he is anxious to get on with his life, "but the Canadian medical system is too backed up and bogged down to help him."

Her son has been unable to work, attend school, or function since all of this started and she writes:

> "It should not take years and years and years for a young person to get a diagnosis. The more I connect with others online, the more I realize that [our] medical system is failing people and dysfunctional. If you want proof of this, just ask the Canadians who wait five to 10 years for a simple diagnosis."

So, are we really providing "excellent and timely care"? Is it nimble? Hardly. Speedy? Clearly not. Quality care? Does that matter? Even if it is quality care, does it matter if you cannot access it in a reasonable period of time?

---

[48] Diana, "I Can't Even Begin to Describe My Frustration," Charter Health, October 15, 2014, www.charterhealth.ca.

[49] Dianne, "Five Years of Pain and Lack of Function," Charter Health, November 1, 2018, www.charterhealth.ca.

[50] Linda, "My Son Has Been Suffering," Charter Health, July 14, 2020, www.charterhealth.ca.

9

Where the Wait Hurts the Most

"My husband became symptomatic in October of last year. He went to the doctor a couple of weeks later and he ordered a test. It was scheduled for March 19, almost five months after his visit to the doctor. He didn't make it to the test.

He landed in the emergency department on March 1 and was admitted. Two days later, he was diagnosed with Stage 3 adenocarcinoma esophageal. That was soon changed to stage 4 metastatic cancer. He chose to have radiation and chemotherapy in the hopes of slowing down the progression but died of a spontaneous GI bleed just three days after his last treatment.

The doctors tell me that the tumour was large and most likely had grown into the artery and burst it. It is also possible that the radiation shrunk the tumor and in doing so it unplugged from the artery and opened the dam. Either way, he died.

If he had gotten the test within days or weeks of it being ordered rather than months, the cancer may not have had an opportunity to grow so large and he may still be here with me and our teenagers. I will never know, and he will never see his children finish growing up or meet his future grandchildren."[51]

Julie, Nanaimo, B.C.

Waits are long for most procedures and for access to most specialists. However, there are several areas of particular concern:

---

[51] Julie, "My Husband Passed Away," Charter Health, August 19, 2014, www.charterhealth.ca.

Diagnostic Procedures

People tend to minimize the value of time spent waiting for diagnostic procedures, making the assumption that if it was truly urgent, then patients would have immediate, or at least reasonable, access. But that is not always the case. As the table below shows, wait times for diagnostic technologies have not improved over the years, in spite of a growing inventory of diagnostic equipment. As a result, Canadians waited a median of 4.8 weeks for a CT scan, 9.3 weeks for an MRI, and 3.4 weeks for an ultrasound examination. That translates into at least one month, and maybe even two, just to get a scan that will become the starting point for a pathway to healing. (Also note that these times vary considerably based on your location in Canada).

Year	CT	MRI	Ultrasound
2000	5	12	2.5
2005	5.5	12.3	3.4
2010	4.2	9.8	4.5
2015	4	10.4	4
2019	4.8	9.3	3.4

Table 2.
Median wait times for diagnostic procedures
(measured in weeks)[52]

Without a diagnosis, doctors and patients cannot move forward and that places patients in a vulnerable position where they have no power to take control of their own healing. From the perspective of a patient named Sherry, this unending wait for tests borders on the inhumane. Sherry writes: "the emotional and physical strain on patients waiting for tests is cruel."[53]

Delayed diagnostic tests can impact or compromise patient care to such an extent that any treatment becomes, as they say, non-curative. As shown with Don in Chapter 2, delayed imaging precludes the early detection of serious diseases such as cancer, postpones the onset of treatment and greatly diminishes the chances of a successful outcome.

---

[52] Based on annual wait time reports from the Fraser Institute.
[53] Sherry, "I am Appalled …" Charter Health, July 17, 2014, www.charterhealth.ca.

Rebecca writes: "My mother waited eight weeks to fail a stress test and then be told that she required a triple bypass 'yesterday.' My father waited six months to be seen by an ENT specialist and be diagnosed with an ultimately fatal form of head and neck cancer."[54]

An early diagnosis is not only helpful in life-threatening situations. As described below, it can also pay dividends in terms of getting highly specific treatment that restores a patient's health much more quickly and limits the drain on health-care resources.

Compare the following two stories: Fredrik was a healthy, active executive who spent his weekends on the slopes at Whistler, B.C. One day, all was going well until he hit a rock that was hidden under the powdery snow. He heard a "pop" in his knee and immediately assumed that his ski season was over.[55] He managed to get down the mountain on his own and then headed over to the Whistler Medical Clinic for an examination. An X-ray showed there were no breaks, but he would need an MRI to determine the full extent of the damage done to his muscles and ligaments. The doctors at the clinic had no idea as to when an MRI appointment might first be available; however, Fredrik was well aware of the horror stories about long waits for diagnostic scans and surgery, so he quickly decided that he would pay to have the scan done at a private diagnostic clinic.

Two days later, an MRI showed damage to three ligaments and extremely bad bruising on the inside of his knee. He took his results to a private orthopedic specialist who, to Fredrik's surprise, said surgery was not necessary at this point. Instead, he was told to undergo a very specific regime of physiotherapy. Three or four months later, he was back on the slopes.

Looking back, the key to Fredrik's rapid recovery was not the doctor or his advice to hold off on surgery. It was the rapid MRI scan that allowed both the doctor and the physiotherapist to understand the specifics of his injury right away—and then develop a highly specialized therapy program to guide his recovery.

In our current system, many people in this same situation see a doctor and a physiotherapist months before they are able to undergo an MRI examination to accurately diagnose the problem. As a result, they may be put through a more general type of therapy which may or may not be what is best for that particular condition. As shown below, sometimes not knowing the specifics of the injury can cause more harm than good.

---

[54] Rebecca, "My Mother Waited 8 Weeks to Fail a Stress Test," Charter Health, May 19, 2015, www.charterhealth.ca.

[55] Personal interview.

Compare Jill's experience to Fredrik's: Jill tore the meniscus in her left knee at the age of sixteen. (The meniscus is a piece of cartilage that acts as a cushion in the knee joint and it is often damaged during sporting activities that put pressure on the knee or where the knee is subject to quick rotations, such as in basketball or hockey). In Jill's case, the surgeon removed the entire meniscus, allowing her to once again enjoy a healthy and active life. But that is not the end of the story.

At the age of 49, Jill experienced a sudden and severe swelling in that same knee. She underwent therapy, but writes, "I foolishly waited four months for an MRI only to find out that the exercises that were prescribed to me were understandably incorrect for my problem." As a result, she says, "half my knee is that of an elderly person, bone on bone, no cartilage left. It is excruciatingly painful. My surgery is scheduled for 14 months from now. I cannot and will not wait that long."[56]

It is likely that prompt access to a scan may have resulted in an exercise regime that would have provided Jill with a better outcome.

Cancer Treatment

The only good news about Canada's waitlists is that the wait times to begin cancer treatments are the lowest of any medical specialty. Even so, cancer patients across Canada are still waiting longer than one month to begin treatment. The time from referral by a GP to treatment was determined to be a median of 4.4 weeks for medical oncology (chemotherapy) and 4.5 weeks for radiation oncology.[57]

The importance of an early diagnosis for beating cancer is the core message that has been repeatedly drilled into Canadians' minds through every cancer awareness campaign for every cancer that exists. An enormous investment of money has gone into these media campaigns and the warnings are clear: Be vigilant in watching for symptoms. Take part in screening programs.

But these messages seem to be lost on governments, health-care planners, and administrators as timely access to specialists, diagnostic technology, surgery, and treatment remains difficult, as Frank, who lives in Toronto, experienced:

---

[56] Jill, "As a Small Business Owner, the *Canada Health Act* is Making My Life Worse," Charter Health, n.d., www.charterhealth.ca.

[57] Bacchus Barua and Mackenzie Moir. (2019). "Waiting Your Turn: Wait Times for Health Care in Canada," 2019 Report, The Fraser Institute, p.5. https://www.fraserinstitute.org/studies/waiting-your-turn-wait-times-for-health-care-in-canada-2019.

> "November 2019. I have a history of skin carcinoma. I found a suspicious patch on my skin and visited my family doctor two months ago. He said he would refer me to a dermatologist. After a month of nothing happening, I returned to my family doctor and he said he would refer me to another dermatologist. It has been more than two months and I still do not have an appointment date.
>
> December 2019 Update. I just got the appointment with the dermatologist. April 11, 2020. Wait time seven months…and with a previous history of carcinoma."[58]

Compare Frank's comment with that of a U.S. surgeon: "I'm in the US and blessed with good insurance, but coincidently I had minor surgery today to remove a carcinoma from my arm. I was chatting with my surgeon and learned that she trained in Toronto. She made the comment that cancer tumors in Canada tend to be bigger than what she sees in the U.S. When I asked why, she said because it takes Canadians so much longer to get surgery scheduled unless they go outside the system. I was surprised."[59]

This off-the-cuff remark by Bill's American surgeon appears to be supported by Canadian doctors who similarly associate larger tumours with wait times. This has long been an issue, but the COVID-19 pandemic seems to have made the media more curious about the situation and doctors more willing to speak out.

For example, Dr. Antoine Eskander, a surgical oncologist at Sunnybrook Health Sciences Centre in Toronto, estimates that there has been a 20 to 50 percent drop in cancer surgeries because of the pandemic and, as a result, patients are coming in "with larger tumors" and presenting at a stage where they "absolutely need an emergency procedure."[60]

One factor that is often lost in considering surgery waits for cancer is additional surgeries. What happens if a second surgery is necessary? Do

---

[58] Frank, "Is Canadian Healthcare as Bad as it Seems?" Quora, November, 2019, www.quora.com/Is-Canadian-health-care-as-bad-as-it-seems.

[59] Bill Clemmons, "Is Canadian Healthcare as Bad as it Seems?" Quora, May 23, 2018. ww.quora.com/Is-Canadian-health-care-as-bad-as-it-seems.

[60] Ben Cousins, "'Collateral Damage': Doctors Worry Patients Diagnosed with More Advanced Cancers because of Delays," CTV News, August 13, 2020, https://www.ctvnews.ca/health/coronavirus/collateral-damage-doctors-worry-patients-diagnosed-with-more-advanced-cancers-because-of-delays-1.5063815.

patients have to go back to the bottom of the waitlist? In short, no. But in some cases, those who are fortunate enough to get a timely first surgery may find that scheduling the second or even third operation remains complicated:

> "My friend underwent surgery for breast cancer but subsequent pathology showed that the margins were not clear. In other words, cancer cells remained. While the first surgery involved a reasonable wait, the surgery that she now needs to clean up the rest of the cancer does not. So far, she has waited three months for that surgery.
>
> I am a nurse and it's criminal. Every day we hear...of prolonged wait times, deteriorating health and mental well being. Canadians deserve better. We all deserve choice and the ability to manage our own health."[61]
>
> Nancy, Vancouver, B.C.

Mental Health

Every January, Bell Canada supports extensive media awareness campaigns across Canada to promote discussions about mental health issues and, hopefully, reduce the stigma that is associated with such conversations. The commercials come out, famous people share their struggles with depression, and we are all instructed to encourage those nearest to us (friends, family members, or co-workers) who are suffering, to seek treatment.

It is a great campaign, but it is also the source of considerable frustration for those who decide to take a leap of faith, talk to a doctor, and obtain appropriate professional help. It does not take long for them to discover the reality that such help is not readily available. Unless they are willing to go to an emergency department and be evaluated within the context of having a mental health emergency, chances are high that their efforts to obtain care will go unrewarded for months or even years.

Because of a small sample size and other complicating factors, the Fraser Institute calculates psychiatric wait times separately from those of other specialties. According to its 2019 report, "Waiting Your Turn," the median wait from a GP referral to receiving psychiatric treatment was 24.4 weeks

[61] Nancy, "We Must have Choices to be Proactive," Charter Health, April 16, 2016, www.charterhealth.ca.

across Canada.[62] However, wait times varied significantly depending on location. The shortest waits were in Saskatchewan (12.8 weeks), while the longest (and truly outrageous waits for those in mental distress) were in the Maritimes (Nova Scotia, 53.6; Newfoundland and Labrador, 50.5; and New Brunswick, 47.9 weeks).

As with other specialties, there is a substantial difference between the actual wait and the wait times that psychiatrists believe to be clinically reasonable. For psychiatric care in Canada, the actual wait exceeded the reasonable clinical wait in 94 percent of cases, and not just by a small amount; actual waits were 209 percent greater than what the medical profession has deemed to be reasonable.[63]

Parksville and Qualicum Beach are two idyllic retirement communities located on the eastern coast of Vancouver Island. They are widely known for fabulous beaches, trails, and easy access to lakes. You cannot help but enjoy the surrounding nature and the senior citizens who live there tend to be healthy and physically active. It sounds idyllic for retirement and that was the plan for Susan and Gary when they moved to Parksville from Ontario.

But their plans changed when Gary, 68, suddenly became quiet and forgetful, and his fun-loving nature disappeared. He became progressively worse until he slipped into a catatonic state. At that point, Susan rushed him to Nanaimo Regional Hospital where he was treated for severe depression and anxiety.

After six weeks, Gary left the hospital with the understanding that he would continue to receive psychiatric care on an outpatient basis. But more than six months later, Gary still had not received any professional help. Susan says Gary is not stable, often in bed, and simply cannot function. He is sad and needs someone to help with his medications. Although Susan took their story to the local newspaper in an effort to get help, the B.C. government responded with a rather apathetic statement acknowledging that there is a shortage of psychiatric specialists and it is working to address the issue.[64]

---

[62] Bacchus Barua and Mackenzie Moir. (2019). "Waiting Your Turn: Wait Times for Health Care in Canada," 2019 Report, The Fraser Institute, p. 60. https://www.fraserinstitute.org/studies/waiting-your-turn-wait-times-for-health-care-in-canada-2019.

[63] Ibid., 65.

[64] Karly Blats, "Parksville Couple Urges Province to Address Shortage of Psychiatrists," *Vancouver Island Free Daily*, July 3, 2019, https://www.vancouverislandfreedaily.com/news/parksville-couple-urges-province-to-address-shortage-of-psychiatrists/.

Surgery

As with most provinces, the surgical waits in British Columbia were particularly serious even before the COVID-19 crisis. In 2019, the BC Anesthesiologists' Society released a discussion paper called "Far Too Long, Far Too Many" and sent a letter to all MLAs encouraging the government to take steps to curb the growing waitlists. The report presented evidence to show that wait times in B.C. were at the highest point ever and previous efforts to manage the problem had accomplished little.[65]

For example, in the past 20 years, B.C.'s surgical waitlists have increased at a rate that is approximately three times the growth rate of the province's population during that same time. By September 2019, 91,000 people were waiting for surgical procedures that had been deemed medically necessary by their doctors; almost one-half of them had been on the list longer than benchmarks set by the B.C. government. Waits for surgery can prove critical, no matter how long:

> "I was naive to believe our health care system would take care of her. I didn't know that our healthcare system was this broken. My late mother fractured her hip on May 9, 2014 and was taken by ambulance to Chinook Regional Hospital where her condition wasn't considered life threatening. She spent close to two hours in the hallway outside of the ER and when she finally got into the ER she wasn't seen by a doctor until three hours later.[66]
>
> My mother waited almost 51 hours for surgery following her fateful fall. She developed a large clot between her heart and lungs during surgery and never recovered. She died on May 20, 2014, her birthday.
>
> I wonder how many other patients have died similar to my Mom as they too waited for surgery? Who will be the watchdog to ensure future patients get timely surgery to save their lives?

---

[65] BC Anesthesiologists' Society, "Far Too Long, Far Too Many," Report, January 2019, https://bcanesthesiologists.ca/wp-content/uploads/2019/01/BCAS-Far-too-Long-Far-Too-Many-Discussion-Paper.pdf.

[66] Sharon (Davies) Fogtmann, "I was Naïve to Believe our Health-care System Would Take Care of Her," Charter Health, May 20, 2015, www.charterhealth.ca.

My late mother had a keen mind, lived on her own and loved life. She deserved a chance at life but died needlessly waiting for surgery. Our daughter's dog broke its femur on a Sunday a few weeks after my mother died. Their dog was operated on within three hours of the accident and is alive and well today unlike my late mother.

How strange it is that our pets receive immediate medical attention while someone like my mother dies waiting for medical attention!

Nothing about the past losses I have experienced prepared me for the loss of my mother. A mother, after all, is your entry into the world. She is the shell in which you divide and become a life. Waking up in a world without her is like waking up in a world without sky: Unimaginable.

Not only did the hospital let her down, but I did too as I was naive to believe our health care system would take care of her. I will live with that guilt the rest of my life!"

Sharon (Davies) Fogtmann, Lethbridge, AB

By June of 2020, it was obvious that already lengthy surgical wait times across Canada would be further impacted by measures taken to stem the COVID-19 pandemic. A research team at McMaster University used models to estimate that more than 28 million surgical procedures were cancelled (world-wide) during an initial 12-week shutdown of operating rooms during COVID-19, including an 82 percent reduction in orthopedic surgeries.[67] Since then, the numbers of surgeries each hospital allows have varied based on the number of COVID-19 cases.

But even as health systems have reopened surgical facilities, there has yet to be a return to 100 percent of pre-pandemic surgical activity. At best, the authors optimistically believe that some systems might be able to return to 90 percent pre-pandemic capacity in 12 months.

With that as the best-case scenario, there would be a 3.4-times increase in orthopedic surgical wait times. For example, a pre-COVID-19 wait time of

[67] H. Johal and M. Bhandari, "A Surgical Deep-Freeze: Backlogs, Burden and New Beginnings," *OE Insights*, article no. 7, June 1, 2020.

six months would become an approximate 21 month wait. The worst-case scenario (if capacity should drop to less than 90 percent due to further outbreaks) would produce a seven-fold increase in wait times, whereby a six-month pre-pandemic wait would become a 42 month (or 3.5 years) wait.

Children

It has long been frustrating that the management of priority wait times has focused primarily on adults. But long waits can have a far more critical impact on children and, in many cases, their physical and emotional development is even more at risk during extended waits, as they are in a stage of rapid growth and development.

It is interesting to note that just as Debbie and Walid were struggling to access treatment, a pediatric surgeon at the Hospital for Sick Children in Toronto was conducting and publishing research on wait-time targets for pediatric surgery[68] and for adolescents with the same problem as Walid.[69] A study of 88 adolescents who waited longer than six months for surgery to correct a curvature of the spine showed that almost 15 percent required additional surgery compared to just 1.6 percent of those who had surgery within six months. In addition, patients who waited longer than six months (like Walid) had greater progression of the curvature, longer surgeries, longer stays in the hospital, and the degree of surgical correction was less than those who had surgery within six months. As a result, the authors recommended that the access target for surgery be three months rather than the six months others suggested.

In February 2020, Children's Mental Health Ontario (CMHO) released a report called "Kids Can't Wait"[70] which showed that 28,000 children and youth were waiting for mental health services in Ontario. This number is double that of 2017 (12,000 children and youth) and even more shocking was the finding that wait times could be as long as two and a half years for some community mental health and treatment programs. In polls conducted as part of the report, Ontarians shared their concerns that children and youth should

---

[68] J. G. Wright, et al. "Development of Wait Time Access Targets," *Canadian Journal of Surgery* 54(2), 2011:107–110.

[69] H. Ahn, et al. "Empirically Derived Maximal Acceptable Wait Time for Surgery to Treat Adolescent Idiopathic Scoliosis," *Canadian Medical Association Journal* 183 (9), 2011: E565–E570.

[70] Children's Mental Health Ontario, "Kids Can't Wait," Report, 2020, https://cmho.org/wp-content/uploads/CMHO-Report-WaitTimes-2020.pdf.

not have to wait at all for mental health care and, if they do, the maximal wait should be no more than two days.[71]

Another segment of the young patient population that is rarely considered in discussion is pediatric dentistry.

In September of 2019, dentists determined that Luke, a seven-year-old boy, would have to have his four molars capped. Because of his young age and his anxiety levels, it was also decided that the procedure should be done in a hospital and under general anesthesia. He was supposedly put on a list, and despite repeated calls from his mother, there was no date for surgery.[72] He was finally given a surgical date of July 17, 2020, ten months after a surgical date had been requested.

On June 26, in preparation for his surgery, Luke had X-rays taken and the doctors discovered that two of his molars had deteriorated so much that they could no longer be capped and had to be pulled. He will likely now require braces and more extensive dental work.

COVID-19: One More Challenge to Wait Times

For many Canadians, the COVID-19 lockdown has been a challenge in terms of overcoming the most minor inconveniences of life: No shopping. No eating out. The gym is closed. Travel is limited. But we are slowly becoming more aware of a subset of our population that has had to sacrifice much more than that as they have been unable to access the medical care that they need. In some cases, they have had to pay the ultimate price, which is death.

Most non-emergent surgeries were cancelled at the start of the pandemic (March 11, 2020) in the expectation that hospitals would be overrun by COVID-19 patients. The surge associated with the first wave of illness had a rather selective impact on hospitals across the country. In many cities, there were reports of empty surgical units and bored staff.

Licia Corbella, a long-time columnist with the *Calgary Herald*, has followed the case of Jerry Dunham, a 46-year-old father and husband who died from heart failure after a routine procedure to install a pacemaker/defibrillator was postponed because of the COVID-19 lockdown.[73] Apparently, it had been labelled as a "non-essential" surgery and

---

[71] Ipsos, "28,000 Children and Youth on Wait Lists for Mental Health Services In Ontario, with Wait Times Up to 2.5 Years," https://www.ipsos.com/en-ca/news-polls/28000-Children-And-Youth-On-Wait-Lists-For-Mental-Health-Services-In-Ontario.

[72] Personal interview.

[73] Licia Corbella, "When it Comes to Health, the Price of Caution May Be Higher than We Think," *Calgary Herald*, August 14, 2020.

was therefore cancelled to clear hospitals of unnecessary patients and keep beds open for what was expected to be a massive influx of those with COVID-19.

That influx never happened at the Medicine Hat hospital where Dunham was taken. Nurses there assured the family that they did not need to be concerned about catching the virus while there because "the hospital's almost empty."

Dunham was a talented musician who played with various bands and, just two months before his June 7, 2020, death, he wrote the following on his Facebook page: "I was basically told that the government is willing to risk my life to save my life. Let me say again, my government told me they're willing to let me die, which, according to them, is for my own safety."

It proved to be prophetic as he suffered a cardiac arrest on May 30 and, deprived of oxygen to his brain, died eight days later surrounded by his family in a Medicine Hat hospital.[74]

The very next day, a spokesperson for Alberta Health Services responded to Corbella's questions by writing: "All urgent, emergency and cancer surgeries have been available throughout the pandemic. Albertans who need urgent surgery will get it. AHS has indicated that they are not aware of any deaths due to cancellations of scheduled surgeries."

Unfortunately, Canada's existing issues in developing, maintaining, and consolidating electronic health records make it difficult to fully document the harm that patients have suffered from reduced access to diagnostic or treatment procedures.[75] As a result, there are no official statistics or data to assist our governments in making plans to ensure that health care is not compromised again during future waves of coronavirus.

> "Heart surgery [is] apparently considered non-essential … but it's pretty goddam essential to me. Now I'm told [it] could be [another] year or two?
>
> So … what? I'm just supposed to kiss my ass goodbye?
> I'm starting to freak out here. Wondering what I should do?"
>
> Jerry Dunham, Facebook

[74] Licia Corbella, "Alberta Man Died from the Lockdown, not COVID-19," *Calgary Herald*, June 30, 2020.
[75] David Zitner, "The 'Price of Caution' during a Pandemic," MLI Commentary, August 13, 2020.

The best information we have comes from the news stories and research studies documenting lives that have been taken and/or put at greater risk because of panicked measures put in place for the pandemic that officials had long told us was coming yet failed to properly plan for.

For example, there have also been multiple reports of cancer patients becoming what one man aptly terms "collateral damage" as a result of cancelled surgeries, cancer treatments, and diagnostic procedures.

CTV news featured Dr. Bill Gardner, a cancer patient and epidemiology professor at the University of Ottawa, in a story on cancer patients and the problem of accessing proper care during the coronavirus pandemic.[76]

In March 2020, Gardner had a sore throat and some trouble swallowing but could not access an appointment because of delays caused by the pandemic. Four months later, as he began to cough up blood, he was able to undergo diagnostic tests and was subsequently diagnosed with Stage II oropharyngeal cancer. He is now undergoing radiation treatment that will have to be more intensive and more toxic because the cancer is bigger than it would have been had a diagnosis been made four months earlier. He is realistic about his situation and does not place the blame on anyone, saying, "I am—to some degree—collateral damage. It doesn't mean it's anybody's fault, but that's a good way to describe my situation."

Gardner is documenting his progress in a personal blog[77] and he hopes that his story will lead to better care for cancer patients in the future, stating, "It's time to think through the policies…that have reduced access to primary care, that have reduced access to diagnosis and screening (and) that have made it more difficult for people to get out-patient care."[78]

Beyond surgeries, COVID-19 has also had a serious impact on the screening programs for cancer and waits for diagnostic procedures. As

---

[76] Ben Cousins, "'Collateral Damage': Doctors Worry Patients Diagnosed with More Advanced Cancers Because of Delays," CTV News, August 13, 2020, https://www.ctvnews.ca/health/coronavirus/collateral-damage-doctors-worry-patients-diagnosed-with-more-advanced-cancers-because-of-delays-1.5063815.

[77] Bill Gardner, "The Incidental Economist," Blog, July 8, 2020. https://theincidentaleconomist.com/wordpress/i-have-serious-news-a-cancer-patient-in-the-covid-19-epidemic/.

[78] Ben Cousins, "'Collateral Damage': Doctors Worry Patients Diagnosed with More Advanced Cancers Because of Delays," CTV News, August 13, 2020, https://www.ctvnews.ca/health/coronavirus/collateral-damage-doctors-worry-patients-diagnosed-with-more-advanced-cancer-because-of-delays-1.5063815.

mentioned above, Canada does not yet have the data to determine how much of a decline has taken place in terms of cancer diagnoses.[79]

> "Is it time to rethink our policies? Absolutely. We cannot morally or ethically continue to deny medical care to those who need it as this pandemic continues or as similar scenarios occur in the future."
>
> Dr. Bill Gardner

A cancer diagnosis for Dr. Bill Gardner, an epidemiologist at the University of Ottawa, was delayed by four months because of COVID-19 shutdowns that cancelled surgeries, cancer treatments, and diagnostic procedures.[80]

But in the United States, one study has already reported that there may be as many as 33,890 additional deaths in the next year due to delays in cancer diagnosis. The *Journal of the American Medical Association* has already reported a 46 percent decline in the weekly diagnosis of cancers in that

[79] David Zitner, "The 'Price of Caution' During a Pandemic," MLI Commentary, August 13, 2020.
[80] Photo Credit: Photo used with permission from Dr. Bill Gardner.

country.[81] The lead author of that study, Dr. Harvey W. Kaufman, can easily see where this trend is heading and says, "The delay in diagnosis will likely lead to presentation at more advanced stages and poorer clinical outcomes."[82]

In Canada, statistics from the Canadian Cancer Society show that an average of 617 Canadians are diagnosed with cancer each day.[83] If 40 to 50 percent of those were unable to access their doctors or undergo diagnostic tests for any length of time (as suggested in the data from the United States), it can be assumed that the "collateral damage" (the term Gardner uses) to those with cancer will be high.

> "COVID isn't going anywhere, anytime soon, and neither is cancer. We need to find a way to work within the confines of a pandemic to provide the best possible care for our patients."[84]
>
> Dr. Antoine Eskander

CBC's national radio show, *As it Happens,* interviewed Dr. Jonathan Irish about the impact of the pandemic on cancer patients. He noted that screening programs were down "over 80 percent," the number of diagnostic scans were down, and "as a head and neck cancer surgeon, in my unit, we've done ten laryngectomies. (This is) an operation done for the most advanced voice box cancers, or larynx cancers. And we've done more in the last two months than we usually do in a full year."

He added: "We're hearing from our colleagues that patients are presenting increasingly with more advanced cancers…this has implications, meaning more advanced surgery, longer surgeries, longer stays in hospitals

---

81 H. W. Kaufman, et al., "Changes in the Number of US Patients with Newly Identified Cancer Before and During the Coronavirus Disease (COVID-19) Pandemic," *JAMA Network Open*, 3(8): e2017267, 2020. doi:10.1001/jamanetworkopen.2020.17267.

82 Ben Cousins, "'Collateral Damage': Doctors Worry Patients Diagnosed with More Advanced Cancers Because of Delays," CTV News, August 13, 2020, https://www.ctvnews.ca/health/coronavirus/collateral-damage-doctors-worry-patients-diagnosed-with-more-advanced-cancers-because-of-delays-1.5063815.

83 Ibid.

84 Ibid.

and, of course, implications for all sorts of post-operative care, including radiation and chemotherapy."[85]

[85] Jonathan Irish, "As it Happens," CBC, Transcript, October 27, 2020. https://www.cbc.ca/radio/asithappens/as-it-happens-tuesday-edition-1.5778707/backlog-in-screenings-causes-influx-of-patients-with-advanced-cancers-says-ontario-doctor-1.5778751.

10

Waiting has Consequences

> "39 cancer patients died while still on wait-list for Halifax gastroenterologist: study."
>
> The Chronicle Herald, April 23, 2019.

The headline from the *Chronicle Herald* in Halifax was hard to miss and, for many, hard to accept. But the underlying point was unmistakable: Nova Scotia needs more GI specialists and if they do not get them, the consequences for patients are dire.

According to the study, "The demand for GI services at our academic centre has exceeded available resources and only urgent referrals are being seen within recommended time frames."[86]

The Canadian Association of Gastroenterology recommends that patients with symptoms of colorectal cancer have an endoscopic examination within two months. Yet the study reported that 90 percent of Haligonians wait:

- 329 days (almost one full year) for an endoscopic procedure;
- 268 days for a GI consult for laparoscopic surgery;
- 492 days for laparoscopic surgery;
- 163 days for a GI tract surgery consult; and
- 195 days for the GI tract surgery.

Those waits do not come without serious consequences, including:

Mortality

The 39 deaths occurred between March 2015 and September 2017. If that is the situation for a two-year period of GI cancers (only) in Nova Scotia, can you imagine the numbers of deaths that have occurred from waiting for

---

[86] Staff, "39 Cancer Patients Died While Still on Wait-list for Halifax Gastroenterologist: Study," *Chronicle Herald*, April 23, 2019, https://www.thechronicleherald.ca/news/local/39-cancer-patients-died-while-still-on-wait-list-for-halifax-gastroenterologist-study-304737/.

treatment for all cancers and every disease across Canada during that same time period?

Researchers at the Fraser Institute asked that same question and then developed a mathematical model to provide the answers. Based on the calculations, there is a relationship between delayed access to medical services and mortality and it is estimated that increased wait times for medically necessary care in Canada may have resulted in an additional 44,273 deaths (between 25,456 and 63,090) among females from 1993 to 2009.[87]

Bacchus Barua, one of the report's authors, rightly notes that "large as this number is, it doesn't even begin to quantify the possibility of increased disability and poorer quality of life as a result of protracted wait times."[88]

Waitlists accounted for an additional 44,273 deaths among females from 1993 to 2009.

Why were deaths so high among females only? The report offered several explanations including a societal trend toward increased female deaths (likely due to greater numbers of women taking on more active roles outside of the home, high-stress jobs, commuting, and greater participation in higher risk activities like smoking and drinking). Second, women tend to fall more and falls account for increased mortality in the elderly. Finally, and perhaps most significantly, the disparity may suggest that women find it more difficult to obtain health care in a timely fashion, may not act quickly to seek health care, or they may not be taken as seriously as men when reporting symptoms to doctors.

The researchers concluded that the estimated increase in female mortality rate was "likely unnecessary" and lay the blame solely on protracted waiting lists that are unique to Canada's health-care system. They write that the deaths are "the result of a health-policy regime that imposes longer wait times on Canadians that are not found in the universal-access health care systems of other developed nations."

In most situations, a discovery that 45,000 (and perhaps as many as 63,000) Canadian women had died unnecessarily would produce a mass outcry for political action. Women across the country would be marching in protest and calling for a national inquiry. But that has not happened; the

---

[87] Bacchus Barua, et al. (2014). "The Effect of Wait Times on Mortality in Canada," The Fraser Institute.

[88] Bacchus Barua, "While Politicians Dither, Patients Die," *Alaska Highway News*, n.d., https://www.fraserinstitute.org/article/while-politicians-dither-patients-die.

enormity of the deaths associated with waitlists remains hidden in a maze of statistics and apparently, the consequences are only visible to the friends and families of those who waited and died.

In December 2020, SecondStreet.org released a policy brief on death and waitlists. They filed freedom-of-information requests to get data from hospitals and health ministries across Canada. Fewer than half of the facilities in the country responded, but they managed to get "partial data from eight provinces" as evidence of 1,480 patients who died while waiting for surgery in 2018-2019. The deaths resulted from waits as short as one month and as long as eight years.[89]

Unbearable Pain and Suffering

Paula's story below is a damning indictment of our medical system; it reveals a woman so devastated by pain and despair as she waits for hip replacement surgery that she is considering suicide or "the option of taking a fall to break your hip" just to move up the list for hip replacement surgery. That she knows two others who have deliberately done so provides further evidence of how utterly dysfunctional our health-care system has become.[90]

Her thoughts very clearly reveal the desperation associated with chronic, unrelenting pain. It can produce the perfect storm of physiological and psychological conditions that create suicidal thoughts; finding out that it may be years before their pain can be treated adds more fuel to the fire. Paula's story should serve as a warning to Canadians: The system needs to change.

> "This is how desperate I feel…Here's a dirty little secret about how awful it is [to wait for surgery] and it forces some people to take extreme measures. It can cause depression, some people begin to have thoughts of suicide to escape it, even when they have lives they cherish.
>
> Chronic intractable pain changes you and the prospect of trying to endure it for years on a waitlist for surgery (hip replacement) can drive people to all kinds of thoughts. You don't want to end your life, but you're desperate to stop the pain and you begin to consider other options.

---

[89] Colin Craig, "Died on a Waiting List," Policy Brief, SecondStreet.org. December 2020.

[90] Paula, "This is How Desperate I Feel," Charter Health, March 11, 2014. www.charterhealth.ca.

> [That includes] the option of taking a fall to break your hip to speed up the process.
>
> I know two people who've done this and while it's probably not something that most people could bring themselves to do (who knows how many have) you wouldn't exactly be open about it. Yet this is how desperate I feel. I am considering this."
>
> Paula, Victoria, B.C.

> "I have severe scoliosis and am on a waiting list for a spinal fusion.
>
> Every day, I suffer from back spasms, immense pain and difficulties breathing, but because I am not an "emergency," I am pushed to the bottom half of the list.
>
> I have been on this surgical waitlist for almost two years in September. It has been three years since I was referred to a neurosurgeon.
>
> I have put my life on hold for the past three years for nothing. If it continues this slowly, I will be lucky if I get a surgery date before 2022. How is this acceptable?"[91]
>
> Gloria, Winnipeg, MB

Permanent Disability

One of the most perverse rules that governs waitlists is an apparent triage system whereby doctors arbitrarily determine whether or not you are in enough pain to earn a priority place on the list or, in some cases, to even get on the list. But some people face the prospects of permanent disability if they wait too long to have the problem fixed. That can happen through waitlists or if the examining physician somehow determines that the patient's injury is not serious enough. Either way, it puts the patient into a pattern of "wait and see" (like Walid in Chapter 1) which can often lead to unintended consequences.

---

[91] Gloria, "On a Waiting List for Spinal Fusion," Charter Health, July 31, 2018, www.charterhealth.ca.

Mark entered into this surreal situation when he experienced numbness in his fingertips that eventually travelled up his arm into his neck. His family doctor diagnosed a pinched nerve and referred Mark to a neurologist. During his wait to see a specialist, Mark's physical condition deteriorated even more. He could not use his arm and felt as though he was barely hanging on in the midst of the pain. He learned that he could prevent the numbness from running up his fingers and into his neck if he kept his head at an awkward downward angle. In the evenings, he would take three NSAID anti-inflammatory pills along with two or three beers or glasses of wine just so he could fall asleep. This went on for eight months.

Mark eventually saw two neurosurgeons and they both gave him the same opinion: His suffering and his inability to work were not enough to get him on a high-priority list for surgery. Realistically, Mark was looking at a minimum wait of three years. Mark could not believe what he had heard, saying that the words seemed like a bad and cruel joke. But then the surgeon continued in absolute seriousness: "The good news is that you can move up the priority surgery list if you lose all function in your arm. The bad news is if you lose all function in your arm, it cannot be recovered."

Those were the words that pushed Mark to open his wallet and pursue surgery at a private clinic. It took just two weeks to make the decision, fly across the country for a surgical assessment, and then undergo surgery the next day. Just three days after his operation, Mark went for a short, pain-free hike before flying home and heading back to work the next day.[92]

Financial Losses

Patients bear a direct financial cost as they wait for rationed health-care services and it is not inconsequential. For 2019, the cost of waiting per patient is estimated to be about $1,963 and that is if only normal working hours are considered to be lost. If all hours of the week (with the exception of eight hours of sleep per night) were considered to be lost to productivity, then the economic loss would be as much as $5,972 per person.[93]

With over one million Canadians waiting for treatment in 2019, the total value of lost wages and productivity is about $2.1 billion. Note that these costs are borne by the patient alone and do not include the impact on family members and their ability to earn an income. As wait times vary from province to province, so does the cost of waiting for care. In 2019, Manitoba

[92] Personal interview.

[93] The Fraser Institute, "Medical Wait Times Cost Canadian Patients More than $2 Billion in Lost Wages before COVID-19," News Release, May 7, 2020.

residents paid the steepest price for waiting at $3,011, while those living in Quebec paid the least ($1,381).

In Chapter 9, you met Jill, a 49-year-old financial planner, whose delayed MRI scan meant that she spent four months doing the wrong physio/exercises while attempting to rehabilitate her left knee. She was left "completely disabled," unable to walk because of her original knee injury and now, the overuse of her good knee, as she awaits knee replacement surgery.[94]

This unfortunate series of events occurred at the same time that her financial business tripled and she was poised to expand her operations, hire more staff, and make an even greater contribution to the local and provincial economies as a small-business owner. Instead, she is in limbo while waiting for surgery. Jill writes:

> "I cannot risk losing what I have worked so hard to build because of a political agenda that will not allow me to obtain the help that I need in a timely fashion. The solution to my problem is very simple—replace the knee.
>
> What is wrong with me being treated outside the system if it permits me to continue to be a valuable member of society?
>
> Or is it better to let me risk losing my business, not hire extra people and/or become addicted to narcotics and antidepressants?
>
> Why would it be so terrible if the province paid for what they normally pay for and I cover the rest myself?
>
> How did it come to be that Workers Comp is able to opt out of the Canada Health Act to better serve Canada's workers and yet small business owners and the rest of Canadians are subject to torture by the very people they elect?
>
> My surgery is scheduled for 14 months from now. I cannot and will not wait that long ..."

Note that she questions the hypocrisy in Canadian health care—that the *Canada Health Act* does not treat workers—or Canadians—equally. It allows

---

[94] Jill, "As a Small Business Owner, the Canada Health Act is Making My Life Worse," Charter Health, n.d., www.charterhealth.ca.

some (e.g., Workers Compensation Board and anyone with federal health insurance) to opt out of Canada's health care and have their private surgeries paid for, while small business owners and the rest of Canadians have to wait years for surgery and are, essentially, subjected to "torture by the very people they elect."

A Diminished Quality of Life

The most urgent cases are defined solely by medical need, as arbitrarily assessed by the doctor. But urgency can be defined in various ways depending on a person's living situation. There are a whole range of factors and events which one must face each day that ultimately affect one's health, well-being, family, and livelihood while waiting.

Derek Bolen suffered a spinal cord injury in June 2020. Six months later, he is still lying on the floor of his home in the only position that offers any comfort for the pain. It took him eight weeks to get a referral for spinal surgery, but the BC Ministry of Health has told him it could take months or even years before he hears from the surgeon.[95]

Apparently, even a spinal cord injury is not sufficient to get you priority (or even emergency) surgery in the midst of the COVID-19 pandemic and the years-long waitlists that were present even before that. What kind of damage can such a wait inflict on someone like Derek? The losses are already overwhelming and it has only been six months. He was healthy and successfully employed, but is now unable to work. He has had to temporarily give up custody of his son. He has no mobility and, for obvious reasons, suffers from depression. He is the founder of an organization that promotes an alcohol-free lifestyle, yet he has been put on opioids to try to control the pain.

Derek has it all—pain, suffering, financial losses, personal losses, immobility, and his quality of life is—well, you can imagine. His friends raised $15,000 for him to have private surgery, only to find out that the BC Supreme Court's September 2020 ruling on private health care (covered in Section V) now prohibits him from paying for private medical care. He has a spinal cord injury and cannot access medical treatment.

This is the medical system that we are so intent on keeping?

---

[95] Darcy Gerow, "The Tragic Human Face of Canada's Government Healthcare Monopoly," *Western Standard*, October 1, 2020.

11

Why are We Waiting?

Public health-care systems will always have waitlist problems and that will remain true as long as there are an unlimited number of patients trying to access a system with finite resources. In other words, waitlist issues will not change substantially until the health-care system is somehow reimagined.

As has been observed over the past 25 years, simply adding more resources (i.e., money) to the system may offer a temporary reprieve, but it does not result in consistent or sustained improvements. Indeed, the national wait time as recorded by the Fraser Institute is now almost twice as long as it was in 1993.

All of these issues raise the question of "Why?" Why are we waiting for so long?[96]

A Shortage of Doctors and Specialists[97]

This point cannot be made more clear: We need more doctors; both family physicians and specialists.

General Practitioners. One indication that we need more doctors and specialists comes from studies that have evaluated our ability to access them; frankly, the results show that our national condition is critical. Data from the Canadian Institute for Health Information (CIHI) show that almost five million Canadians (about 15 percent of the population over age 12) do not have a family doctor.[98]

---

[96] Bacchus Barua, "Canada is Failing to Deliver Healthcare Services in a Timely Manner. Here's Why," *National Post*, December 22, 2015.

[97] A full discussion of numbers of doctors and access to them can be found in Chapters 13 and 14.

[98] Staff, "Despite More Doctors Many Canadians Don't Have a Family Physician: Report," CTV News, September 26, 2019, https://www.ctvnews.ca/health/despite-more-doctors-many-canadians-don-t-have-a-family-physician-report-1.4611149.

In January 2021, Lynne Karch told the media that the doctor shortage had made her literally "afraid for my life." She had recently moved from Calgary to Penticton, B.C., to care for her aging mother and enjoy the beauty and quality of life that many find in the Okanagan. But she was "flabbergasted" when she discovered that finding a local doctor meant putting your name on a centralized waitlist alongside 5,000 other names. Who knows when she will get access to a primary caregiver?

Karch has a serious heart condition and says, "Six years ago, I died. I had a massive cardiac arrest, and no symptoms, no pain." So her fears of not surviving without a doctor to keep a constant eye on her condition are very real.[99]

She holds the government responsible for "a lack of leadership and urgency," and says: "Go out and find doctors, bring them from other countries. Do what you need to do to advocate for these people!"

Like waitlists, the doctor shortage seems to have crept up on Canadian patients and health-care planners. We have more doctors than ever, but we also have far more people than ever before. In addition, most of those people are getting old and developing chronic conditions that need physician oversight and management.

One has to wonder if we are headed back to a dreaded time in the 2000s, when doctors and even health-care districts made headlines by holding lotteries to randomly determine who gets medical care. Appalling as that might be, some doctors who felt overwhelmed began to use lotteries to just as randomly cull patients from their practices:

> "A new family practice in Newfoundland held a lottery last month (July 2008) to pick its caseload from among thousands of applicants. An Edmonton doctor selected names randomly earlier this year to pare 500 people from his heavy caseload. And in Ontario, regulators have heard reports of a number of other physicians also using draws to choose, or remove, patients."[100]

---

[99] Shelby Thom, "'I'm Afraid For My Life': Okanagan Woman Renews Call to Solve Doctor Shortage," Global News, January 7, 2021.

[100] Tom Blackwell, "Ont. Doctor Uses Lotteries to Pare Down Patient List," *National Post*, August 5, 2008.

Specialists. International comparisons by the Commonwealth Fund ranked Canada dead last in terms of timely access to specialist care.[101]

Perhaps the worst situation that can develop for both doctors and patients (and one that is most indicative of a system that is incapable of treating patients in a timely manner) is when the timeline for a specialist to see a new patient has become so ridiculously long that the specialist is no longer able to accept patients.

In November 2017, Dr. Joy Hataley of Kingston, ON, went to social media to sound the alarm about wait times.[102] She had referred a patient to a neurologist in that city, only to receive a return form letter stating: "Our current wait time for a new patient referral is approx. 4.5 years. As such, we are unable to book new appointments at this time. We will hold your referral and mail an appointment slip to your patient when one is available."

In an interview with CTV News, Hataley said that while she did not consider this to be the norm, the fact that it even occurred is "shocking" and "an alarm bell." In further comments, she stated that the referral situation was now "irrelevant" to her patient's well-being and a sure sign that the system "has hit a wall."

This situation is not unique to Ontario or to any one province. Nor is it only a recent phenomenon.

Several years ago, Fred, of Airdrie, AB posted a copy of the letter that he received from the Spine Triage and Assessment Clinic at the University of Calgary/Alberta Health Services.[103] After paying for his own MRI to get a diagnosis, he was referred to the clinic for treatment. That is when his family doctor received a letter similar to the one mentioned above, stating: "We regret to inform you we cannot accommodate your patient for consultation. Due to increasing numbers of referrals, a substantial waitlist, increasing wait times coupled with insufficient resources, the Division of Neurosurgery has unfortunately had to stop accepting referrals for spine related problems. We currently have 1,803 referrals on the waitlist…"

---

[101] The Commonwealth Fund's International Health Policy Centre, System Stats. https://www.commonwealthfund.org/international-health-policy-center/system-stats/wait-for-specialist-appointment.

[102] Rachael D'Amore, "'I Actually Thought I Misread it:' Doctor 'Stunned' over Years-long Wait for Specialist Appointment," CTV News: Toronto, November 3, 2017, https://toronto.ctvnews.ca/i-actually-thought-i-misread-it-doctor-stunned-over-years-long-wait-for-specialist-appointment-1.3662822.

[103] Fred, "I Find this Ridiculous at Best!" Charter Health, May 26, 2015, www.charterhealth.ca.

Fred's comments on his situation? "I am paying—but don't get service…I wonder when they are going to start giving us a reduction in our personal tax base to offset the lack of available care."

It is interesting that the above letter did offer other suggestions to the patient and, frankly, Canadian patients would benefit if we all acted on the second point:

1. If urgent care is needed, go to an ER; and
2. If you are upset by the inability to access care, write your MLA.

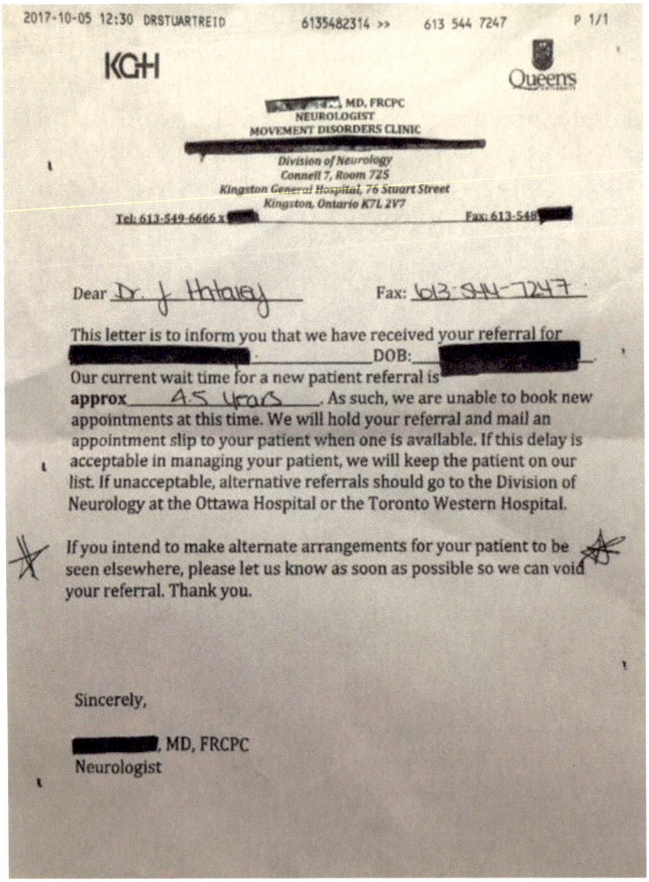

2017-10-05 12:30 DRSTUARTREID 6135482314 >> 613 544 7247 P 1/1

KGH

Queens

[redacted] MD, FRCPC
NEUROLOGIST
MOVEMENT DISORDERS CLINIC
[redacted]
Division of Neurology
Connell 7, Room 725
Kingston General Hospital, 76 Stuart Street
Kingston, Ontario K7L 2V7
Tel: 613-549-6666 x[redacted] Fax: 613-548[redacted]

Dear Dr. J Hataley Fax: 613-544-7247

This letter is to inform you that we have received your referral for [redacted] DOB: [redacted]. Our current wait time for a new patient referral is **approx** 4.5 years. As such, we are unable to book new appointments at this time. We will hold your referral and mail an appointment slip to your patient when one is available. If this delay is acceptable in managing your patient, we will keep the patient on our list. If unacceptable, alternative referrals should go to the Division of Neurology at the Ottawa Hospital or the Toronto Western Hospital.

If you intend to make alternate arrangements for your patient to be seen elsewhere, please let us know as soon as possible so we can void your referral. Thank you.

Sincerely,

[redacted], MD, FRCPC
Neurologist

Reply to Patient Referral Letter.

But letter-writing campaigns are not likely to provide an immediate response to medical needs, especially in Ontario where, as Hataley suggested, there is a marked shortage of neurologists.

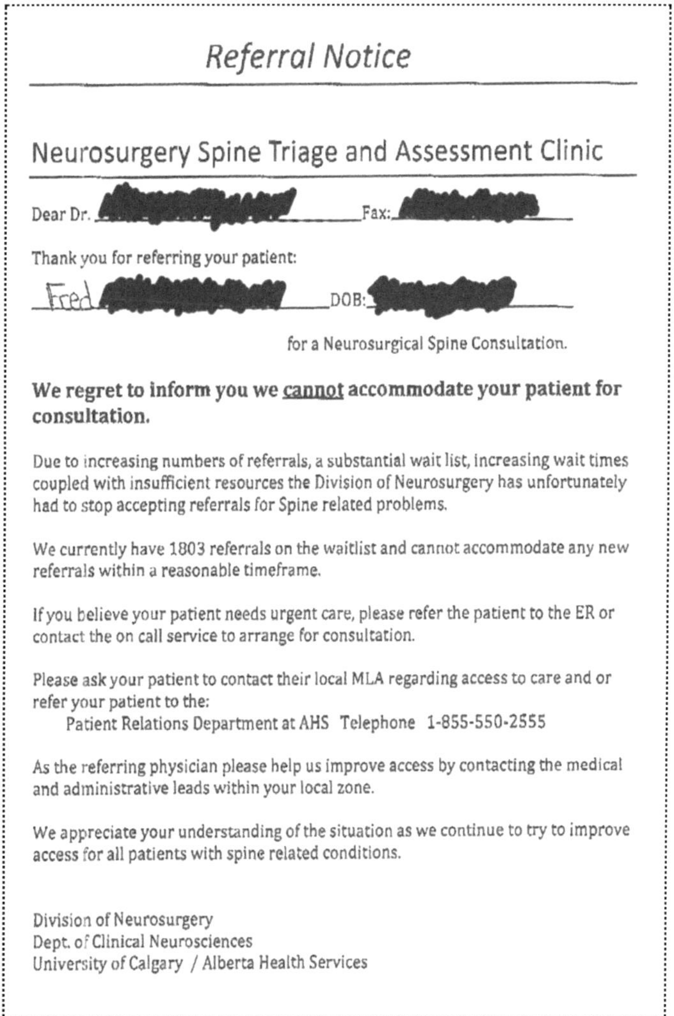

Referral Notice

Neurosurgery Spine Triage and Assessment Clinic

Dear Dr. [redacted] Fax: [redacted]

Thank you for referring your patient:

Fred [redacted] DOB: [redacted]

for a Neurosurgical Spine Consultation.

We regret to inform you we cannot accommodate your patient for consultation.

Due to increasing numbers of referrals, a substantial wait list, increasing wait times coupled with insufficient resources the Division of Neurosurgery has unfortunately had to stop accepting referrals for Spine related problems.

We currently have 1803 referrals on the waitlist and cannot accommodate any new referrals within a reasonable timeframe.

If you believe your patient needs urgent care, please refer the patient to the ER or contact the on call service to arrange for consultation.

Please ask your patient to contact their local MLA regarding access to care and or refer your patient to the:
Patient Relations Department at AHS Telephone 1-855-550-2555

As the referring physician please help us improve access by contacting the medical and administrative leads within your local zone.

We appreciate your understanding of the situation as we continue to try to improve access for all patients with spine related conditions.

Division of Neurosurgery
Dept. of Clinical Neurosciences
University of Calgary / Alberta Health Services

Referral Notice.

A former CEO in Toronto unexpectedly came to that realization when her husband was diagnosed with Parkinson's disease. The diagnosis came as a shock to them both, as did the discovery that, due to rationed care, Ontario's Parkinson's patients are limited to just two ten-minute visits per year with a neurologist. A devastating, emotional, and life-altering diagnosis that raises dozens of questions about medical care and it all has to happen within two ten-minute visits per year!

She resolved some of these issues by becoming an activist and online investigator. She listens to podcasts, attends support groups, and does all she can to learn about and understand this disease.[104]

There is Nowhere Else to Go

Our health-care system is essentially maxed out in terms of the numbers of people it can serve, even as our population continues to grow and age. Health care already consumes about 40 percent of our tax dollars, so without major changes to the system itself there is very little opportunity for expansion. In addition, as you have seen in many of the patient profiles herein, few options exist for patients who need care. When the system is overwhelmed, patients have three options: Wait, find and pay for private care somewhere in Canada, or travel to another country to pay for medical care there.

Christina Paruag is a 25-year-old Ontario woman who has endometriosis and she lived with this painful condition for five years while waiting for proper specialist care. She met with various specialists who either declared the case to be too mild to be concerned about, too complicated for their care, or offered her surgery at some point two years or more down the road.

While she waited for treatment, her symptoms progressed until she could no longer get out of bed, shower, or cook without assistance. About once every three months, she was forced to go to the emergency department to get help in controlling her symptoms. A host of other medical issues developed until her entire body seemed consumed by illness.

Since no one in Canada seemed able to help her, she turned to the internet and then travelled to the United Kingdom for surgery. It was there that they discovered that, while she waited for care, her endometriosis had spread substantially and it now affected her ovaries, ureter, kidneys, bowels, and even her diaphragm.[105]

---

[104] Personal interview.

[105] Brooklyn Neustaeter, "Ontario Woman Gets Endometriosis Surgery in the UK after Canadian Doctors Dismissed Her Symptoms for Years," CTV News, November 25, 2020.

Bottlenecks

The most frustrating and common waits are for patients with complicated diagnoses or chronic issues that require ongoing management of care with multiple specialists and a variety of diagnostic procedures.[106] As discussed earlier, these patients enter into a fragmented sequence of referrals and care that offers plenty of opportunities for delays (i.e., bottlenecks) and errors at each juncture.

For example, a patient sees a family physician for pain in the abdomen. He is then sent for blood tests and diagnostic imaging. In Canada, waits for imaging can be weeks or even months. The results are sent to the doctor, and the patient goes back for a review. The doctor suspects cancer and the patient is then referred to an oncologist where, very often, the same tests are repeated for confirmation. After all that, a diagnosis is confirmed and a treatment program is established. Even then, the patient still has to wait his turn to get the treatment.

This is referred to as a gatekeeper system whereby patients must first see a GP (the gatekeeper) to get a referral to a specialist. It serves to limit the number of patients who attend specialists and, consequently, limit the higher health-care costs associated with specialist fees. In order to garner these savings, however, the system sacrifices a tremendous amount of efficiency.

In some cases, this sequence of events can take months and, as shown by Ross's story in Chapter 2, that time period can make a crucial difference between dealing with an early-stage, treatable cancer and a late-stage cancer that has metastasized and is not likely to be controlled by a treatment program.

Finally, our referral system also contributes to a lack of continuity in care. As Ross's story shows, the patient is often left in limbo (between doctors) with nowhere to turn for advice and no doctor to advocate for/or take responsibility for their care.

Rationed Services

Hospitals are funded through global budgets that are pre-determined at the beginning of each year. This incentivizes hospitals to treat fewer patients in order to stay within their budgets and they do this by rationing care—restricting access to specialists, limiting numbers of physicians, and closing hospital beds and wards during summers.[107]

---

[106] Bacchus Barua, "Canada is Failing to Deliver Healthcare Services in a Timely Manner. Here's Why," *National Post*, December 22, 2015.
[107] Ibid.

Canadian health care is based on principles of equality and universality, but the real principle that drives our day-to-day health care is rationing—limiting the availability of medical care and resources. It is hard to imagine that we would be so supportive of our health-care system if we knew the key to its success was rationed care instead of universal care.

Terminology

A system with finite resources has to find some way to limit access and provincial health-care systems do that by having a limited list of what they call medically necessary treatments and procedures that they will fund. These procedures have been rather arbitrarily chosen and therefore coverage of some medical procedures differs among the provinces.

Abuse of the System

There are no cost-sharing disincentives for those who choose to visit the emergency department or see a doctor, or seek surgical treatment for medical issues that can only be classified as trivial. As a result, abuse, stupidity, and ignorance are inevitable and the taxpayer is stuck paying the bill.

According to an online post by Jess (who claims to have worked at Health Canada): "I should have a frequent flier card and I need to stop taking the ATVs up such dangerous mountains, as on occasion I can be quite accident prone. (I've had at least five 2.5 to 3 hour Medevac flights, completely covered. A flight for just me, my escort and a medic.) I love my health care system. This is my view from my many visits to hospitals/clinics in and around British Columbia."[108]

[108] Jess Turner, posting in "Is Canadian Health Care as Bad as it Seems?" Quora, www.quora.com/Is-Canadian-health-care-as-bad-as-it-seems.

PART III

SYMBOLISM, MYTH, AND REALITY

12

Symbolism

Our universal-access, single-payer health-care system has long been a cherished part of Canada's history and identity. On a national level, the flag that boldly bears a single maple leaf may invoke the highest level of patriotism, the beaver will bring everyone a smile, and hockey will always draw the biggest crowds. But when we consider long-standing contributions to bettering our society or even humanity itself, Canadians tend to claim universal health care (aka Medicare) as the most positive reflection of our values and one of our most prized touchstones.

One of the most commonly quoted polls in public discussions on health care showed that an astounding 94 percent of Canadians believed that universal health care was an important source of Canadian pride.[109] In many cases, a poll declaring virtually unanimous support would seem to be some sort of statistical anomaly. Yet, over the decades, multiple polls and surveys continue to reveal that an almost unquestioned loyalty exists between Canadians and their health care.

In 2019, the numbers of Canadians associating health care with national pride dropped to 73 percent.[110] The percentage may be dropping, but it is still a strong indication of support when three out of four Canadians agree on anything, particularly when it involves a long-held policy that is subject to the shifting whims of various governments and their budgets. In fact, it is difficult to recall any other policy that has such a strong and enduring track record of public approval.

---

[109] Canadian Press, "Poll: Canadians are Most Proud of Universal Medicare," CTV News, November 25, 2012, https://www.ctvnews.ca/canada/poll-canadians-are-most-proud-of-universal-medicare-1.1052929.

[110] Jack Jedwab, "Sources of Personal or Collective Pride in Canada," Association for Canadian Studies, June 28–July 1, 2019, https://acs-aec.ca/wp-content/uploads/2019/06/ACS-Sources-of-personal-or-collective-pride-in-Canada-EN.pdf.

Support for Symbolism is NOT Support for Health Care

It should be noted that many publicly quoted surveys are deceptive in that they involve an assessment of Canadians' *feelings* about universal health care as a symbol of our identity and our national pride. Consequently, they are not a legitimate measure of support for our health-care system or for how well that system is accomplishing its purpose of providing medical care.

Linking health care to our intrinsic sense of patriotism is an illusory PR trick that has long been used by governments, unions, and strong supporters of our present-day Medicare system (as it is) in an effort to keep substantive changes at bay. After all, if statistics (even those taken out of context) show that Canadians love their health-care system, why would we change it?

As an example of how deceptive statistics give way to misleading rhetoric, one Health Council of Canada report on health-care performance began with the claim that 85 percent of Canadians believed that "eliminating public health care" would produce a "fundamental change to the nature of Canada." Those surveyed also indicated that changing public health care would have a greater negative impact on our country than abandoning English and French as our two official languages, eliminating peacekeeping, or cutting ties with the monarchy.[111]

There is no data or information offered to provide any support for these statements, yet this high-profile report is somehow able to suggest that Canada as we know it would cease to exist without Medicare. This is what results from the careless use of polling data and baseless rhetoric; it eventually becomes the opening argument for a government report!

Of all the government-commissioned reports, studies, and analyses into our health-care system, the 2002 Romanow report deserves special mention for its rather shameless attempt to tug on our patriotic heartstrings instead of giving realistic options for bettering health care.

Its title, "Building on Values: The Future of Health Care in Canada" may seem innocuous to some, but the overt connection between values and health care was widely criticized as an unseemly attempt to create an emotional link between Canadian symbolism and support for health care. The report's

---

[111] Stuart N. Soroka, "A Report to the Health Council of Canada: Canadian Perceptions of the Health Care System," February 2007, https://healthcouncilcanada.ca/files/2.06-Public_Perceptions_English_Final_Feb-07.pdf.

comments and suggestions focussed on health care as an expression of our "values," while failing to provide substantive details, such as costs.

That prompted Norman Spector, a former ambassador and well-known political pundit, to warn Canadians to "Be vigilant, and hold on to your wallet when your leaders go on about 'values' but refuse to talk about value for your money."[112] His comment was true then, and it remains true today.

Others felt that voicing any disagreement with the report put them at risk of "being accused of betraying cherished Canadian values" or, more tacitly, the values that Roy Romanow had seemingly determined to be those of all Canadians.[113] Their concerns make clear the reality that health care is so closely entwined with our national pride that our views of it are most often distorted by a sense of history, patriotism, and familiarity. Unfortunately, all of these perspectives make for a rather crowded view of health care and do not leave much room for concepts like reality to influence the vision.

Beyond Symbolism: What Makes Canadian Health Care so Great?

There is ready evidence to demonstrate the confusion that is created in the minds of Canadians when symbolism and reality are forced to meet. A 2009 Nanos Research poll may be dated, but its numbers are still used to attest to Canadians' unanimous support for universal health care. It reported that nine out of ten Canadians "supported" universal health care as a policy and four out of five went so far as to give it their "unqualified support."[114]

At this point, the poll seemed to be heading in the same direction as most, Canadians' support for a generalized and undefined notion of health care. But then, in a rather unusual move, pollsters began to troll for specifics; they gave Canadians a list of concrete, real-life components of our health-care system and asked them to choose one that they believed to be its "key strength."[115]

The results were both startling and informative. The largest group (61.4 percent) cited the ideals that undergird health care as its key strength; that is,

---

[112] Norman Spector, "Federal Screw-Ups a Legacy of Power," *Edmonton Journal*, December 20, 2002.

[113] Richard C. Fraser, "The Exploitation of Canadian Values: Building on Values, The Romanow Report," *Health Ethics Today*, vol. 13:1, 2003.

[114] Nik Nanos, "Canadians Overwhelmingly Support Universal Health Care; Think Obama is on Right Track in United States," *Policy Options*, November 1, 2009, https://policyoptions.irpp.org/magazines/health-care/canadians-overwhelmingly-support-universal-health-care-think-obama-is-on-right-track-in-united-states.

[115] Ibid.

we have a system that is *free, public, and accessible to everyone*, and this founding principle remains its strongest attribute.

Surprisingly, no real-life attribute or component of health care even came close to having as much support as this intangible principle. Frankly, Canadians seemed hard-pressed to come up with any tangible strengths that are critical to sustaining the health-care system to which they offer their "unqualified support." As further evidence of this, the second most popular choice (20.7 percent) for a key strength of our health-care system was *unsure/no answer*.

From there, support for anything associated with health care dipped into the low, single digits, further revealing Canadians' bewilderment at naming a positive aspect of their beloved health-care system. The third highest selection (at 4.5 percent) was a *general positive attitude* (which can hardly be considered unique to Canadian heath care), while 4.3 percent claimed its greatest strength was, literally, nothing.

Just 4.0 percent remembered that the people who are charged with the daily care of patients might play a critical role in health care and gave their support to personnel: Doctors and nurses. The endorsement is minimal, but it speaks volumes that this slice of reality still ranked a notch lower than *nothing*.

Does this seem like a health-care system that should have the "unqualified support" of anyone?

It is astounding to comprehend that support for anything relating to the realities of health care (such as quality of care, emergency services, home care, modern technology, etc.) was utterly insignificant (their percentages of support were almost negligible) when compared to support for the philosophical ideal of universal care.

This is the sad reality of universal health care in Canada. We believe that it is a sacred icon that defines our nation and cannot be touched, yet we are apparently at a loss for words when asked what makes it so great.

Canadian health care will surely collapse if we continue to travel blindly down this road. Now is the time to shift our health-care conversation from public opinion about symbolism to public thought about health care.

13

Myth

It speaks volumes when our federal health minister stands before Canada's doctors and admits that our health-care system is one of the worst in the developed world. Yet, in a 2016 address to the Canadian Medical Association, Dr. Jane Philpott blatantly stated, "It's a myth that Canada has the best health-care system in the world."

Former federal health minister Dr. Jane Philpott tells Canada's doctors "it's a myth" that Canada has the best health care in the world.[116]

The discouraging admission continued as she said, "We spend more per capita on health care than many other countries. What's worse is that, while we do this, we get poorer outcomes for our patients…the Commonwealth

---

[116] Remarks from the Honourable Jane Philpott, Minister of Health, to the Canadian Medical Association Annual General Meeting, August 23, 2016. https://www.canada.ca/en/health-canada/news/2016/08/remarks-from-the-honourable-jane-philpott-minister-of-health-to-the-canadian-medical-association-annual-general-meeting.html.

Fund ranked us second from the last in a study that compared Canada to places like Australia, the UK, France, and Germany. The OECD also ranks us poorly on a number of specific areas that will be critical to our future health as a nation."[117]

So much for a rousing and encouraging keynote speech. Which way to the bar?

But kudos to Philpott for being one of the first politicians to be honest in telling Canadians that it is false to claim or even suggest that we have the best health-care system in the world. Every significant study and report makes it clear that we do not have the best access. Or the most hospital beds. Or an adequate inventory of diagnostic technology. Or timely medical care.

Instead, we have a health-care system that is built on, and controlled by, a flawed and outdated principle that dictates health care should be free, accessible to all, and equal. When this ideal meets the reality of day-to-day medical services, the notion of government providing free, open-ended care to every citizen for almost all of their medical problems quickly becomes unmanageable, unattainable, and, most of all, unsustainable. Consequently, health care is neither free nor accessible and, frankly, it is anything but equal.

How Free is Health Care?

> "Anybody who thinks healthcare is free needs to do some research. Keep in mind, the government has no money except what they take from us."[118]
>
> Barney Biggs

Canadian Health Care is Anything but Free. All costs are paid for by our tax dollars and that means every Canadian is paying for the system even if they have not used it that year or for years before that. In 2019, our so-called free health-care costs were expected to amount to $264 billion, an amount that equals $7,068 for every Canadian.[119]

In addition, not all health care is funded by the government. Provincial governments are selective in terms of what procedures or treatments they will pay for, so Medicare coverage can vary significantly from province to province. In addition, many provinces have/have had/or once again will have

[117] Ibid.

[118] Barney Biggs, "Is Canadian Healthcare as Bad as it Seems?" Quora, May 13, 2018, www.quora.com/is-Canadian-health-care-as-bad-as-it-seems.

[119] Effective Public Healthcare Panacea Project, "How Much does Canada Spend on Health Care?", 2018, https://ephpp.ca/healthcare-funding-policy-in-canada/.

a monthly medical services fee (an amount that is typically scaled to income) charged to families and individuals as a means of supplementing health-care costs. In such cases, health care is not only not free, but people are essentially forced to pay twice, once through taxes and then again as a monthly fee—whether they use the system or not.

The diagram below shows the breakdown of Canada's 2018 health-care costs. Government payments covered 64.2 percent of all health expenditures while 4.8 percent was covered by other public sources.[120] Canadians paid 15.4 percent of all health-care costs out of their own pockets and private insurance covered another 12.4 percent via policies offered to employees of large companies.

If we assume that the out-of-pocket percentage (15.4) stayed the same in 2019 when total expenditures were $264 billion, then Canadians directly paid over $40.7 billion out of pocket for their own health care in addition to about $170 billion in taxes. Again, that is paid whether they use the system or not, and whether or not they can obtain medical care when they need it. Even worse is that the one million-plus Canadians waiting for medical treatment must still pay for the health care that they cannot access.

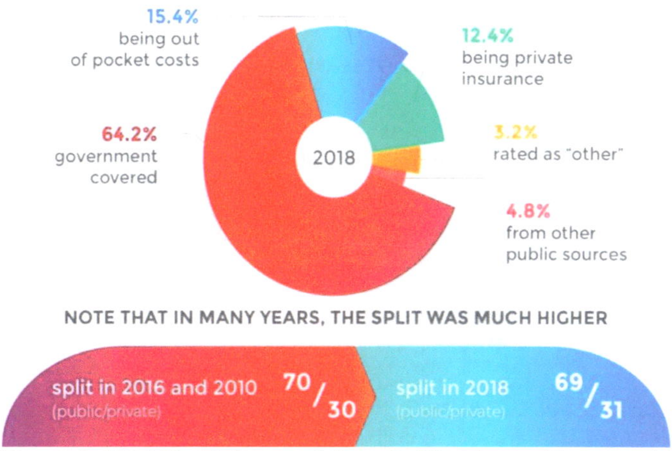

Figure 1. 2018 Breakdown of Canada Healthcare Expenses[121]

Paying for care that they cannot access is a growing frustration with Canadians like Pierre. He is in his mid-fifties, lives in Vancouver, and enjoys

[120] Ibid.

[121] Canadian Institute for Health Information, "Health Spending," 2018, https://www.cihi.ca/en/health-spending.

running to keep in shape. But one day, after a run, he began to experience pain in his left knee. He saw his family doctor and had X-rays taken but they only provided enough information to indicate that he needed an MRI.[122] The wait for that MRI scan? Three to 18 months.

Left with little choice, Pierre paid for a private MRI to get a quick diagnosis; he had a torn meniscus that required surgery. For Pierre, that meant the real wait—for surgery—was just beginning. As time passed, his back began to give him problems because of his limp and, eventually, he could no longer do his job because it required walking, lifting, and bending.

It was not long before Pierre concluded that he would need "private surgery to fix this quickly before it causes more issues." Perhaps more maddening than Pierre's story is the truth that underlies his final comments: "I am paying—but there is no service. Why is MSP receiving my monthly payments for medical and they are not providing me with the service that I need? I am paying for services that MSP cannot provide to me and that is a breach of contract."[123]

How Accessible is Health Care?

Medicare's principles dictate that health care must be accessible to all Canadians and this myth of accessibility continues, even though there is a plethora of evidence to show that it is not: Waitlists to access essential care, minimal access to technology, limited numbers of health-care personnel, and a bloated, outdated bureaucracy are both the causes and the symptoms of a system that can no longer respond to the needs of patients in a timely manner.

Waitlists. Canada has the longest waitlists in the developed world. Each year, since 2017, more than one million Canadians have had to wait for medically necessary treatment and at the end of 2019, there were an estimated 1,062,286 people waiting to be treated for illnesses and/or injuries.[124]

---

[122] Pierre, "I am Middle 50s, Work Full Time and Fit. One Day after a Run," Charter Health, October 24, 2015, www.charterhealth.ca.

[123] MSP was the provincial agency that collects monthly Medicare payments in B.C. The NDP government eliminated it on January 1, 2020 and replaced it with an employer health tax which shifts the burden to employers and, naturally, has led to an outcry from B.C. businesses.

[124] Bacchus Barua and Mackenzie Moir. (2019). "Waiting Your Turn: Wait Times for Health Care in Canada," 2019 Report, The Fraser Institute, https://www.fraserinstitute.org/studies/waiting-your-turn-wait-times-for-health-care-in-Canada-2019.

Canadians also have the longest wait times to access care by a specialist. According to the Fraser Institute, most people waited 20.9 weeks to access specialist care in 2019. That figure varies significantly depending on location and the procedure(s) required, but outside of an emergency department, there are never guarantees of care. For example, if you live in a Maritime province, chances are high that you will be waiting for at least one year to see any medical specialist. The median waits (from time of referral from a family doctor to treatment by a specialist) for residents of Prince Edward Island, New Brunswick, and Nova Scotia were 49.3, 39.7, and 33.3 weeks, respectively. That same wait period is substantially less for residents of more populated provinces like Ontario and Quebec, where waits were 16.0 and 16.3 weeks, respectively.

When evaluating wait times by the type of medical procedure, it is not surprising that the longest waits are for orthopedic surgeries (39.1 weeks or about ten months) and the shortest for oncology (4.4 weeks for medical oncology, i.e., chemotherapy, and 4.5 weeks for radiation oncology).[125]

Oncology waits seem entirely reasonable when compared to those for orthopedic surgeries, as there is almost a ten-fold differential. But in a health-care system that is supposedly guided by the principle of accessibility, no one should have to wait for care. Health care cannot be termed accessible when people who know they have cancer are forced to wait a month for treatment and healthy individuals like Pierre are sidelined for months or even years (unable to walk, work, or participate in the activities of daily living) because they cannot access routine surgery.

Not Enough Doctors. In Canada, the family doctor serves as a gatekeeper to screen and diagnose patients; he/she will then either treat them or refer them to a specialist. That means your first step to getting care in Canada is having a family doctor and, for a growing number of people, that has become an almost impossible task. According to 2019 CIHI data, 4.8 million Canadians (approximately 15 percent) reported that they could not access a family physician to guide their care.[126] The percentages varied across provinces, but 25.6 percent of Quebecers, 18.7 percent of Saskatchewanians and 18 percent of Albertans could not find a regular family physician. It is not unusual to hear of people making 20 or 50 telephone calls in an attempt to find an MD who is accepting patients.

---

125 Ibid.

126 Staff, "Despite More Doctors Many Canadians Don't Have a Family Physician: Report," CTV News, September 26, 2019, https://www.ctvnews.ca/health/despite-more-doctors-many-canadians-don-t-have-a-family-physician-report-1.4611149.

Without a family doctor, it becomes even more difficult for people to get specialized care or, frankly, even routine care; studies have shown that those who do not have a regular family doctor are less likely to get a flu shot or follow cancer screening guidelines.[127] The stories of Don in Chapter 2 and Greg in Chapter 5 highlight the pitfalls in care that can occur when there is no family doctor to manage a patient's care in a fragmented patient referral system.

The 2016 Commonwealth Fund report that looked at accessibility to physicians by adults in 11 wealthy OECD countries confirmed that Canadians continue to report longer wait times for doctors, specialists, and emergency department visits than their peers in other countries.[128] In fact, our waits to see a specialist were the worst of all 11 countries surveyed, meaning that we ranked dead last in terms of access to specialist care. Our reputation did not fare any better when the report evaluated accessibility to family doctors. Only 43 percent of Canadians were able to get a same- or next-day appointment at their regular place of care when they needed medical attention. Once again, this finding put Canada in last place when compared to other countries.[129]

Gatekeepers. In the Canadian health-care system, the GP is expected to play the gatekeeper role in terms of limiting the number of patients who are passed on to the higher priced specialists. As a result, your family doctor's attitude and skill can impact how long you must wait to see a specialist or even if you can see one.

Some GPs will put off making a referral because they do not believe the problem is serious enough to warrant a specialist consult. Ironically, it may function to save the system some money, but it can leave the patient frustrated, in limbo, and in pain. It can also leave some otherwise healthy patients waiting for their condition to deteriorate sufficiently so they can be referred for specialist care.

Cheryl is a 55-year-old woman in Nanaimo, B.C., who suffered from gallbladder pain for more than a year and a half. That meant regular struggles with nausea and horrific pain, as well as being forced to endure more than a dozen full-blown attacks that can occur at any time. Her only recourse was to go to the hospital for morphine and Gravol to control the pain. As a result, she said her quality of life was "very poor."

---

[127] Ibid.

[128] Canadian Institute for Health Information, "How Canada Compares: Results from the Commonwealth Fund's 2016 International Health Policy Survey of Adults in 11 Countries—Accessible Report," 2017.

[129] Ibid.

She was referred to a surgeon but had to wait five months for the consult and then even longer for the inevitable surgery. When a gallbladder attack forced her to the emergency department, she asked the doctors if her consultation with the specialist could be expedited. The doctors responded to her request by saying that "the surgeon wouldn't even consider seeing me because I was not ill enough."

Cheryl and her husband then determined that quality of life was worth more than money and they paid for private surgery that very quickly resolved the problem.[130] (Imagine the full costs to our medical system as Cheryl was forced to wait, get additional medical care, and make multiple visits to the ER.)

In another case, the initiative of the patient and his family resulted in a life-saving diagnosis when they were confronted with a GP who was unwilling to consider further investigations.

When Ron began to exhibit some strange behaviours, his own GP diagnosed him as having "transient global amnesia" and determined that there was no need to send him to a neurologist. His wife, Wendy, was unconvinced that the problem had been dealt with and, knowing they could not access a neurologist in the public system without their GP's help, made arrangements for Ron to see a neurologist at a private clinic.[131]

The neurologist suspected a stroke and immediately sent Ron for a CT scan. The diagnosis was confirmed and within four weeks Ron was undergoing major vascular surgery to resolve the problem. Wendy writes: "I cannot express our relief at being able to bypass the 'gatekeeper' GP system who, in this case, utterly failed us. My only option was to use the alternative private health system, available to Canadians for a price. If it were not for the private consultant, Ron would probably still be at risk and possibly have had another stroke."

It is the same story for Cade, an 18-year-old athlete from Fort St. John, B.C., albeit with non-life-threatening consequences. Cade developed a sore shoulder after a bench-press accident in the gym. His GP sent him to a physiotherapist, but the treatments only made it worse. After four weeks, his shoulder was "still very sore" even though the doctor continued to reassure Cade, saying, "Just rest; you will be fine."

Most people (athletes in particular) know their bodies well enough to detect when something is not right. Two months after the accident, Cade was

---

[130] Cheryl, "Very Serious Problem with the Health Care System," Charter Health, January 20, 2017, www.charterhealth.ca.

[131] Wendy, "My Alternative was to use the Alternative Private Health System," Charter Health, January 6, 2017, www.charterhealth.ca.

"fed up with these doctors not doing anything." He called a private MRI clinic and got a scan that very same day. Within two days, his results were back. Cade had a "full thickness tear in my infraspinatus," meaning that he had tears in multiple tendons in his shoulder.[132] There was no indication as to when Cade finally saw a specialist, but at least he had evidence to show his family doctor that rest alone was not going to be enough to regain the function in his shoulder.

How Equal is Our Health Care?

> "We already have a two-tier system—one for the rich and the government … and one for the rest of us."[133]
>
> Candice

One of the biggest myths about Medicare is that of equality. This principle is at the very foundation of our health-care system and so, for years, it has created the perception (or myth) that all Canadians are treated equally. That is why the very idea of two-tier health care is so repulsive to us. We truly believe that Canadian health care is the great equalizer of the rich and poor. When we need medical care, we all get the same treatment. No one can buy their way to faster or better care. But, as you will soon see, health care does not treat rich and poor the same, Canadians do not share equal access to treatment, and money can buy faster care.

A host of inequalities exist and even though we are careful to not say the words out loud, Medicare itself has created an unofficial two-tier health-care system for Canadians based on the factors described below.

> "If we are all supposed to be so equal, then why do workers' compensation cases, public employees and even jail inmates have priority over us suffering average Canadians, even if we want to pay for the extra insurance?"[134]
>
> Vivian

---

[132] Cade, "My Name is Cade and I am 18 Years Old," Charter Health, April 14, 2018, www.charterhealth.ca.
[133] Candice, "I Started Having Intermittent Lower Back Pain," Charter Health, April 15, 2015, www.charterhealth.ca.
[134] Vivian, Charter Health, n.d., www.charterhealth.ca.

Wealth. Canadians are adamant about not allowing private clinics because we do not want wealthy people to get better or faster access to medical care. But guess what? They already do. It is rarely spoken about, but there is always a way for wealth to speed up the process. Some specialists offer patients the option of paying a fee (e.g., $300 to $500) to jump the queue and access the next available appointment.

Justin from Abbotsford, B.C., discovered this when seeking a diagnosis of a rare condition that had completely disabled him. As he sought answers, his doctor put him on waitlists for various specialists, but each list was more than one year long. Justin writes, "I had to pay in order to see the specialists sooner and, even then, they were unable to help."[135]

An even more interesting take on this practice of buying an appointment comes from a woman who responded to a *Globe and Mail* story on wait times by sharing her own experience:

> "You can pass a doctor in Montreal or Toronto a few grand and you will get in much quicker. My friend's mother received a hip replacement within three months after she gave the specialist two grand in cash. Voilà! Another friend's father bought their neighbour (an orthopedic surgeon) a plasma TV. Knee surgery within two months. My dad gave his surgeon a very expensive golf club; he had his eye surgery completed in time for golf season. Unacceptable, but it exists."[136]
>
> Victoria43

Wealthy Canadians also have (and have always had) the option of flying to the United States or some other country to take part in a growing trend called medical tourism. "Flight of the Sick," a policy brief by a Calgary-based think tank called Secondstreet.org reports that 217,500 Canadians left the country for health care in 2017. If those travelling with the patients are included in the count, the total rises to 369,700 people.[137]

---

[135] Justin, "After Coming Down with a Rare Condition that Completely Disabled Me," Charter Health, February 16, 2016, www.charterhealth.ca.

[136] Victoria43, Online comment, www.theglobeandmail.com/opinion/article-bc-where-access-to-a-wait-list-is-considered-access-to-healthcare, May 8, 2018.

[137] Jane Stevenson, "More Canadians Leaving Country for Health Care: Report," *Toronto Sun*, March 12, 2019, https://torontosun.com/news/national/canadians-continue-to-leave-the-country-for-health-care-says-new-report.

Our politicians seem to forget that these patients take their money with them when they head to other countries for medical care. Statistics Canada estimates that Canadians spent $690 million on health care abroad in 2017. (The federal agency did not distinguish between patients seeking medically necessary procedures and those leaving Canada for cosmetic surgery.) That translates into $1.9 million per day that Canadians spent in another country just to receive timely medical care.[138] Many say the expense is worth it.

William needed a shoulder replacement due to advanced arthritis and other damage. He waited nine months for a diagnostic MRI and now has to wait another six months to see a specialist. After that, it will likely be an even longer wait for surgery. Overall, it will likely be three or more years before he can get help. No wonder he closes off his story with the comment, "considering going to Puerto Vallarta for surgery…Max cost to me US$16,500."[139]

In another little twist of the knife to Canadians lingering on waitlists, visitors to our fair country are welcome to bring their cash and pay up front for medical services at a doctor's office, a clinic, or a hospital. In return, they get care right away. There is no waiting list for tourists with credit cards; waitlists are a purely Canadian phenomenon and, apparently, are only for Canadians.

People who 'Know' People. You can pretty much bet that Canadians with influence in the health-care system and politicians of all stripes and at all levels are not waiting months or years for care. Author William Gairdner relates a rather blunt quote from Pierre Lemieux, a Quebec economist and fellow with the Montreal Economic Institute: "In Québec, you can be relatively sure not to wait six hours with your sick child in an emergency room if you know how to talk to the hospital director, or if one of your old classmates is a doctor, or if your children attend the same private school as your pediatrician's children, or if you deal with a medical clinic in the business district."[140]

Those opposing private care tend to raise public fears by painting a picture of doctors who work in both the public and private systems, charge huge fees for treatments, and shuffle patients from the public system into their private service as a means of eliciting higher payments. In other words,

---

[138] Ibid.

[139] William, "An MRI has Determined that I Need a Shoulder Replacement," Charter Health, April 16, 2018, www.charterhealth.ca.

[140] William D. Gairdner, *The Trouble with Canada ... Still!: A Citizen Speaks Out*, (Toronto: Key Porter Books, 2010): 308.

they believe that the doctors will scam the system if they are allowed to work in both public and private care.

To those who worry about doctors manipulating the multiple health-care systems in some sort of "get rich quick" scheme, relax. Anybody (doctors, administrators, and others) who wants to manipulate any system for self-gain will do it; a quick search on Google indicates there are a number of physicians who have committed fraud in the public system. If a doctor lacks moral and ethical character, it will not make any difference if they are in the private or public system, or both.

Federal Government Health Insurance. Some perks take place under the table, but others occur right in front of us. Few Canadians are aware of the perks associated with having federal government health insurance, but they should be because it firmly entrenches a two-tier health-care system. Those benefiting from this insurance include members of the RCMP, members of Parliament, federal civil servants, judges, and even inmates incarcerated at federal prisons. Yes, *even prisoners have better access to health care than most Canadians.* Each of these groups can use their federal insurance (paid for by taxpayers) to jump the queue in the public system, gain quick access to private surgery and treatment centres, and obtain private medical care paid for by our tax dollars.

The irony of being a politician who has vowed to protect our Medicare system is rich. The very people who ration the services and make the rules that force Canadians onto waitlists are the same ones who use our tax money to buy private health-care services and immediate care for themselves.

Workers who are covered by insurance from the Workers Compensation Board (WCB) also share in these special privileges. Apparently, governments have determined that these injured workers must get back to their jobs as soon as possible to keep the economy going and, consequently, they are given priority access to medical care. Of course, injured workers who are not covered by WCB are placed on the same waitlists as other Canadians, waiting months or longer for medical care.

> "It has taken me three years to get surgery on my nasal passages. Two years on a waiting list just to get on the waiting list for my surgery. The doctor was only allowed four surgeries a month! What a crock our system is. Even prison inmates are ahead of you

and me. WCB patients, sports teams, CEOs with private plans to go out of the country get better service."[141]

Steven, Richmond B.C.

Professional Athletes. When is the last time you heard of a professional hockey player in Canada getting injured in a game and then put onto a nine-month waitlist to get a diagnostic MRI? It never happens. They undergo scans within hours. Professional athletes, Olympians, and sporting franchises are all privy to the same special access privileges as those with federal insurance. While the rest of us wait months for a diagnostic MRI or surgery, professional athletes pay to get immediate access and care to diagnostic technology, medical procedures, surgery, rehab facilities, and even vaccinations.

Remember the swine flu scare of 2009? Public controversy ensued when the Calgary Flames received fast-tracked H1N1 flu shots in a private clinic while the rest of Albertans had to stand in long lineups at public clinics. In fact, it was not just the players; as was later reported, special access was given to players and 150 of their closest associates and family members. The public was outraged and the fiasco eventually cost one provincial health-care bureaucrat his career.

The same scenario played out in Toronto where the Raptors and Maple Leafs both got flu shots before priority patients. In contrast to the above (or maybe because of it), then-Ontario health minister Deb Matthews offered a sharp rebuke, saying, "I don't care who you are, how rich you are, how famous you are. If you're not in the priority group, get out of line and let the people who are in priority groups get their vaccination."[142]

Firing bureaucrats and stern warnings make for good headlines in the papers, but they do not change the reality that has long been part of the system. Professional basketball, football, hockey, soccer, and baseball players do not wait months for health care and if they ever did, professional sporting franchises would be heading south very quickly.

All of this raises the question of "when is it my turn?" That is what 88-year-old Ron asks as he waits for back surgery.

Ron is a former PE teacher, basketball player, and coach. Throughout his life he has exercised regularly, watched his weight, and done all he could to maintain a healthy, active, and enjoyable life. In his late seventies, he began

---

[141] Steven, "It Has Taken Three Years to Get Surgery," Charter Health, February 5, 2020, www.charterhealth.ca.

[142] Lee Greenberg, "Health Minister Angry as Pro Athletes Jump H1N1 Queue," *Ottawa Citizen*, November 5, 2009, https://ottawacitizen.com/news/health-minister-angry-as-pro-athletes-jump-h1n1-queue.

to experience increasing pain down his leg and foot, and was ultimately diagnosed with a deteriorated L4/5 disc.[143]

He cannot take major pain medications as they make him agitated and confused, so he now uses nerve blockers. They also have side effects such as mild tremors and numb, unsteady legs. As a result, he can only walk a few feet because of pain and fear of falling. He needs to have someone or a railing nearby to steady him as he walks and says, "I now find myself unable to do anything active which is impacting on my heart and respiratory health, as well as my ability to do all the things which I have enjoyed all my life."

He adds, "At 80, without the ability to exercise, I can only see my general health declining while I await my turn." Ron says he noticed that "ICBC, WCB, and pro athletes have immediate access to care. Perhaps their lives have more value to society than those of us who worked for 40 years, paid taxes, and expected nothing in return. Now when we are in need of care, we are treated like second-class citizens who may or may not receive care in time for us to receive any benefit from it."

The Urban/Rural Divide. There is a well-documented urban/rural divide in the medical care that is available to Canadians. The vast majority of physicians (92 percent) work in urban centres, meaning that only eight percent work in rural areas, even though Canada's population is scattered over a massive expanse of land.[144] In addition, high-tech diagnostic machines such as PET, CT, and MRI scanners and most specialists are located only in the largest centres and that means the patient, no matter how sick, must make a trip that may have a negative impact on their health and wallet.

Depending on distances, those from rural areas can end up having to pay considerable sums of money (hotel, travel, meals) and these expenses can be multiplied many times if they have to repeat the trip, stay for any amount of time, or even travel to other centres.

---

143 Ron, "I Began Experiencing Increasing Pain Down My Leg and Foot," Charter Health, April 12, 2016, www.charterhealth.ca.

144 Canadian Institute for Health Information. Physicians in Canada, 2018. Ottawa, ON: CIHI; 2019, secure.cihi.ca/free_products/physicians-in-canada-2018.pdf.

> "I've been wondering why the public and the news media who report on medical issues seem to be almost totally unaware of how many WCB patients jump the queue and are treated at private facilities?"[145]
>
> Dr. Raymond Grant

Indigenous Groups. Access to most health care by Indigenous people living in remote locations is extremely limited and has even been termed third-world care. There are myriad problems in getting proper health care to remote communities; however, further discussion of this important issue falls beyond the parameters of this book and is surely worthy of its own book.

Age. It is impossible to say just how much influence age has in determining priority placement on a waitlist. Referrals are determined by priority and may be rather arbitrarily assigned by the doctor who may or may not consider age as a factor. But the general, unofficial consensus is that older people often wait longer. Many of the online stories are from older, retired people who simply want to enjoy their remaining years. In general, they are frustrated that they have paid into the system for years and now that they need medical assistance, it is not available. When you are in your late seventies or eighties, waiting a year or two for medical treatment can make a huge difference between having a good quality of life and just surviving.

Juliet, of North Vancouver, B.C., waited months for hip replacement surgery only to have it cancelled by the hospital when it was forced to shut down a number of operating rooms to accommodate summer holidays for doctors and nurses. As a result, she had to wait even longer. She writes, "so now I have to wait again, not knowing when my surgery will be scheduled. This means I cannot make plans to do anything else. I already am in pain and who knows when it will be done. I am 77 and do not wish to spend the rest of my days in unnecessary pain. The system is terrible and causes people much pain which they do not need to go through."[146]

Similarly, Dominique, who lives in Surrey, B.C., injured himself during a fall and paid privately to have an MRI scan and X-rays done immediately. He had hoped to expedite the process, but in the end, his added effort did nothing to hasten an appointment with a specialist, and he has been on the

---

[145] Dr. Raymond Grant, "Politicians and Worker's Compensation Board Patients Jump Queue," Charter Health, n.d., www.charterhealth.ca.

[146] Juliet, "The System is Terrible and Causes People Much Pain," Charter Health, June 19, 2017, www.charterhealth.ca.

waitlist to see an orthopedic surgeon for almost a year. But he is soon turning 80 and time is precious. He writes, "A year ago I still was able to walk three or 4 miles daily, go to the gym/pool, and I HAD A LIFE." He adds, "the system must believe that I will croak before anything is done for my condition" and that we have "an absolutely disgusting healthcare system now compared to 20 years ago."[147]

All of the above should set off alarm bells in our heads and prompt those Canadians who still think we have the best health care in the world to ask themselves, "What exactly are we so proud of?"

> "I am 70 years old, but I still have places to go, things to do and people to meet. I need a knee replacement; my knees are getting worse and thus my life is more limited.
>
> I have seen two surgeons, but each one has determined that a referral was unnecessary. Then it is back to my doctor to get another referral to see another surgeon. There will be more waiting once the surgeon agrees to the operation and then there is the recovery time. This is wasting my life."[148]
>
> Myrna, Calgary, AB

[147] Dominique, "Absolutely Disgusting Health Care System," Charter Health, January 21, 2019, www.charterhealth.ca.

[148] Myrna, "I Still Have Places to Go, Things to Do and People to Meet," Charter Health, May 19, 2014, www.charterhealth.ca.

14

Reality

> "Just because something is universal doesn't mean you have access to it. Calling something universal doesn't override the laws of economic scarcity."
>
> Dave, September 15, 2018, Twitter

Numerous surveys compare our health-care system to those of other developed or wealthy nations. In general, the numbers and rankings remain similar from study to study (meaning they are likely accurate) and show our health-care system to be one of the worst in the world.

No health-care system is perfect, but evidence from other countries that offer some form of universal health care indicates they either do not have the same waitlist and access problems that we have or that they are minimal when compared to ours. Frankly, international comparisons rarely offer any reassuring or hopeful news to Canadians.

Access to Physicians

The number of physicians in Canada has grown steadily since 1997 and, according to the Canadian Institute for Health Information (CIHI), Canada was home to 89,911 physicians (or 2.41 per one thousand Canadians) in 2018 and that number is almost evenly split between family medicine physicians (1.22 per thousand) and specialists (1.19 per thousand).[149]

Over the past year, CIHI has tried to focus media attention on the statistics showing that we have more doctors per capita than ever before and the flow of doctors into the system is outpacing population growth: Between 2014 and 2018, the growth rate of the physician population was more than twice that of the regular population.[150]

---

[149] Canadian Institute for Health Information, Physicians in Canada, 2018. Ottawa, ON: CIHI; 2019, secure.cihi.ca/free_products/physicians-in-canada-2018.pdf.

[150] Ibid.

That particular talking point may work well for PR purposes, but as you will see in the patient stories, these statistics present a very limited picture of reality: Five million Canadians cannot find a family doctor to manage their care, almost 40% of our doctors will be over the age of 55 and closing in on retirement within three to five years,[151] and while the number of physicians may currently be increasing, it still remains well below that of other developed nations.

In 2019, the *Telegram*, the largest daily newspaper in Newfoundland and Labrador, did an in-depth, multiple-issue feature on the desperate need for doctors in Atlantic Canada.[152] It described dire conditions in which doctors are unable to recruit others to take over their caseloads when they move or retire, leaving patients on their own to find another care provider.

Based on provincial government statistics, the *Telegram* estimated 175,000 people in the Atlantic Provinces do not have a family doctor, and then calculated that the four provinces would have to attract 146 new doctors who were willing to see 1,200 patients each just to clear the waitlist.

The *Telegram* profiled 62-year-old Everest Howse who lives in a small village just outside Corner Brook. In 2016, for the first time in his life, he found himself without a family doctor to watch over his health (which includes a history of two aneurysms, heart surgery, and a back injury). Howse contacted about 20 family doctors in the area, visited clinics, and made dozens of calls. But no doctor would take him on.

In an ultimate act of desperation that proves the squeaky wheel gets the grease, he made a large cardboard sign "displaying his displeasure" (according to the *Telegram*'s polite wording) and began a one-man protest outside of the Corner Brook hospital. That public demonstration finally got the attention of the local health authority and he was eventually placed with a doctor.

That "I'm mad as hell and not going to take it anymore" kind of activism may have worked for Everest, but not every story ends that well. Ralph Coughlin of Prince Edward Island has been waiting for a kidney transplant since early 2018. But he may miss out on the opportunity for a new lease on life because he does not have a family doctor.[153] The transplant team in Halifax quite reasonably requires recipients to have a family doctor to provide ongoing care and follow-up after the procedure. Coughlin went to seven clinics on the Island with no luck in finding a doctor.

---

[151] Steven Globerman et al. (2018). "The Supply of Physicians in Canada: Projections and Assessment," The Fraser Institute.

[152] Glen Whiffen and Nancy King, "Atlantic Canada Needs More Doctors: Where are They?" *Telegram*, November 15, 2019.

[153] Ibid.

> "Medicare, a pillar of pride for most Canadians, doesn't feel universal for those struggling, sometimes waiting years, to access a family doctor."[154]
>
> Rebecca Renkas,
> University of Toronto

The clinics he visited advised him to put his name on a provincial patient registry, which he did, only to find out that it has a two- to three-year wait.

The irony in the above stories is that Statistics Canada's 2017 data show that Newfoundland and Labrador, Nova Scotia, and New Brunswick all had a lower proportion of residents (aged twelve and older) without a primary health-care provider than the national average of 15.3 percent, ostensibly suggesting that Maritimers have better access to family practitioners than Canadians in other provinces. Similarly, these same statistics indicated that Ontario patients had better access to physicians than the national average -- even though 1.45 million Ontarios do not have a doctor! As evidenced herein, statistics may tell the larger story of what is happening in a population but they can be meaningless to individuals looking for a family doctor and outright misleading when used to assess real health-care needs in a province. After all, a January 2020 headline in Peterborough's local paper read, "8,000 People Now Without a Family Doctor in Peterborough."[155]

Statistics aside, the situation in Atlantic Canada reflects what is happening in every province across the country -- there are not enough doctors to adequately serve Canadians.[156]

Overall, Quebec appears to be in the worst shape for numbers of doctors as 25.6 percent of its population (twelve or older) were without a

---

[154] Rebecca Renkas, "Female Doctors Better for Health Care, but Experience Gender Pay Gap, Discrimination and Depression: U of T Expert," *U of T News*, October 30, 2019, https://www.utoronto.ca/news/female-doctors-hey-gap-discrimination-and-depression-u-t.

[155] Joelle Kovach, "8,000 People Now Without a Family Doctor in Peterborough," *Peterborough Examiner*, January 14, 2020.

[156] Statistics Canada, "Primary Health Care Providers, 2017," February 21, 2019, https://www150.statcan.gc.ca/n1/pub/82-625-x/2019001/article/00001-eng.htm.

regular physician in 2018.[157] In B.C., Saskatchewan, and Alberta, that same number is more than 18 percent.[158]

The confusion between statistics and reality also comes into play with Canada's claim that Canadians living in urban areas are more likely to be without a regular health-care provider (15.9 percent) than those in rural regions (12.6 percent).[159] This poses somewhat of a dilemma for Canada's medical planners as the CIHI data place the urban/rural divide for physicians at 92 percent urban and eight percent rural.[160]

It is true that not all individuals without a family doctor need or even want one. But, as we have witnessed first-hand during the COVID-19 pandemic, personal health can change in an instant and for that reason alone, we should all have access to one. Anyone with a chronic disease or with serious health problems must have a family doctor to oversee their care. In addition, studies show that those with regular family doctors are more likely to get vaccinations and undergo cancer screening procedures, both of which are important to maintaining health.

Nancy, who lives in Vancouver, received a diagnosis of type II diabetes at the University of British Columbia's Urgent Care Centre three years ago and has been unable to find a family doctor ever since. The Care Centre gave her a list of general practitioners who were taking new patients, but when she contacted them, all but two declined because their practices were full. The two who did respond positively turned out to be unsuitable for the situation.[161] She has had enough and says she is now ready to pay for her care "even though money is extorted from me by the government for my medical care. The care is not available and I have no choice. This is a dangerous and disgraceful situation."

How Does Canada Compare to Other Countries?

According to data compiled by the Commonwealth Fund's International Health Comparisons survey (2017), Canada ranked 13th of 17 countries when looking at the number of physicians per one thousand population. It credited

---

157 Staff, "Despite More Doctors Many Canadians Don't Have a Family Physician: Report," CTV News, September 26, 2019.

158 Ibid.

159 Statistics Canada, Primary Health Care Providers, 2017," February 21, 2019, http://www150.statcan.gc.ca/n1/pub/82-625-x/2019001/article/00001-eng.htm.

160 Canadian Institute for Health Information, Physicians in Canada, 2018, Ottawa, ON: CIHI, 2019.

161 Nancy, "A Dangerous and Disgraceful Situation," Charter Health, February 22, 2014, www.charterhealth.ca.

Canada with 2.7 physicians per thousand, still far below other OECD countries such as Norway (4.7) and five other European nations that each registered higher than 4.0 doctors per thousand.[162]

Unfortunately, this study is not a statistical anomaly and multiple reports have produced similar findings over the past number of years. In 2019, the Fraser Institute showed that Canada had 2.8 physicians per thousand population, but that still put us far below the OECD average of 3.6.[163] As a result, when compared to other OECD countries, Canada ranked 26th out of 28 countries in terms of numbers of physicians. Other data ranks Canada's supply of doctors as 26 out of 35 high-income countries[164] and 29th out of 33.[165]

Another measure of access to family doctors comes from determining the percentage of patients who are able to get same-day or next-day appointments when sick.[166] Only 43 percent of Canadians were able to see a doctor in this time frame, but that was well below the Netherlands where 77 percent were able to access care within 48 hours. Canada tied for last place in this category.

Specialists

> "Specialist care is good…but you need a referral from a doctor; and if you don't have a doctor, you can't get the referral."[167]
>
> Kirsty

Numbers of Specialists. The Fraser Institute has tracked the total numbers of physicians (both general practitioners and medical specialists) over the

---

[162] The Commonwealth Fund, "Number of Practicing Physicians per 1,000 Population," 2017, https://www.commonwealthfund.org/international-health-policy-center/system-stat/practicing physicians.

[163] Bacchus Barua and Mackenzie Moir. (2019). "Comparing Performance of Universal Health Care Countries," 2019. The Fraser Institute.

[164] OECD Data. Doctors per 1,000 Inhabitants. https://data.oecd.org/healthres/doctors.htm.

[165] Steven Globerman et al. (2018). "The Supply of Physicians in Canada: Projections and Assessment," The Fraser Institute.

[166] The Commonwealth Fund, "International Health Care System Profiles: Selected Health and System Statistics," 2017. https://www.commonwealthfund.org/international-health-policy-center/system-stats.

[167] Kirsty, "Is Canadian Health Care as Bad as it Seems?" Quora, May 16, 2018, www.quora.com/Is-Canadian-health-care-as-bad-as-it-seems.

years. It estimates that from 2015 to 2030, the number of physicians per one thousand Canadians will increase from 2.74 to 2.97 if immigration numbers are included and to 2.84 if we relied on Canadian-trained doctors only. Either way, Canada's numbers for 2030 will still fall far short of the current average for OECD nations (3.4) and *this suggests that for the next decade at least, Canadian patients will have even greater restrictions in accessing a family physician or getting a speedy referral to a specialist.*[168]

According to the Fraser Institute report, "there is sufficient evidence to support the assertion that Canadian policymakers should be concerned about a relative scarcity of physicians as described in this report." When health policy reports call on policy-makers to be concerned, Canadian patients should join with them in sounding the alarm.

Access to Specialists. Three immediate issues affect access to specialist care in Canada. One, as Kirsty notes above, is that you need to be seen by a family doctor to get a referral. Two, the family doctor serves as a gatekeeper to the specialist which means that the doctor has to agree that the problem is something that he/she cannot fix and therefore requires specialist care. Three, specialists must be accepting new patients. In Canada, all three of these situations can be problematic for the patient.

Beyond these variables, access to specialists is most often determined by factors such as time from referral to a consultation appointment or time from referral to treatment. According to the latest statistics from the Commonwealth Fund, Canada is last in each category.[169]

It is appalling to know that, compared to others, our system is one of the worst in the world, but it is even worse to know that we spend more money on our health-care system than almost every other country.

---

[168] Steven Globerman et al. (2018). "The Supply of Physicians in Canada: Projections and Assessment," The Fraser Institute.

[169] The Commonwealth Fund, "International Health Care System Profiles: Selected Health and System Statistics," 2017, https://www.commonwealthfund.org/international-health-policy-center/system-stats.

The chart below summarizes and consolidates the findings:

Measure	Canada	International Ranking (compared to other OECD countries)	The Best Country	The Worst Country
Number of Specialists per 1000		30/32*		
Wait 1 month or more to see a specialist	56%	32/32*[170]	22% (Switzerland)	56% (Canada)
Waited 2 months or more for specialist appointment	30%	11/11 (Last)	4% (France)	30% (Canada)
Waited 4 months or more for elective surgery	18%	11/11 (Last)	0% (Germany)	18% (Canada)
Very/somewhat easy to obtain care after hours	34%	10/11	72% (The Netherlands)	24% (Sweden)

Table 3. Access to Medical Specialists[171]

Do we need more specialists? Absolutely. But the more difficult question is: Where are we going to find them?

Each year, the Royal College of Physicians and Surgeons of Canada releases a survey of newly certified specialists as they complete their training and try to secure employment. Incredibly, in spite of our nation's dire need, 34 percent of new specialists were unable to find a position when surveyed 12 to 17 months after their certification. Looking at data over the years, there is

[170] Based on 2017 data in Steven Globerman et al., "The Supply of Physicians in Canada: Projections and Assessment," The Fraser Institute, 2018.
[171] Ibid.

typically a 60-40 split in employed and unemployed specialists, although employment numbers seem to be on an upward trend.[172]

The majority of respondents to the employment survey (80 percent) and a follow-up survey (93 percent) felt that a major barrier affecting their employment was a shortage of full-time jobs for specialists. Other problems include a lack of transparency in job postings, the consideration of family obligations, and a lack of necessary health-care resources (e.g., the availability of operating room time).

Similarly, the Canadian Orthopaedic Association (COA) reported in 2019 that there have been 478 graduates in orthopedic training over the past six years. Of those, 159 were still seeking full-time jobs and another 74 found full-time work outside of Canada (primarily in the U.S.).

A high number of unemployed specialists does not necessarily mean that they are not needed or there is an oversupply. In fact, in this case, it means the polar opposite. The long wait lists indicate that we desperately need more orthopedic specialists, yet governments cut the number of orthopedic residency posts available in Canada from 81 in 2011 to 52 in 2018.[173]

Where are Canada's health-care planners in all of this?

Given that taxpayers already have heavily subsidized at least a decade of education for these doctors, one would think that Canada would make it a priority to plan for, provide for, and retain, these young specialists in a way that addresses their personal situations and aligns with society's health-care needs.

In conclusion, it seems that Canada's health-care system is just as unhelpful to young doctors seeking employment as it is to the patients who desperately need their care.

---

[172] Royal College of Physicians and Surgeons of Canada, "Employment Patterns of Canada's Newly Certified Medical Specialists," 2019.

[173] Kelly Grant, "Nearly One in Five New Specialist Doctors Can't Find a Job after Certification, Survey Shows," *Globe and Mail,* May 1, 2019.

> "I grew up during the implementation of Medicare in Canada and was proud of that system, thinking it was the best in the world. I now know it was all a hoax. Many countries do this so much better than Canada does. Europe and Australia provide great models to follow, yet we never consider following their example. We have a blind spot about our medical system because we only compare it to the U.S. Our healthcare system is broken beyond repair and needs to be remade from scratch."[174]
>
> Keith, Sechelt, B.C.

Justin, whom we met in a previous chapter, was diagnosed with a rare condition that rendered him completely disabled at the young age of 29. But it took years of visits to doctors and specialists to get a diagnosis that fit the symptoms he was experiencing and he was forced to endure one- to two-year waits to see doctors even as the disease was actively progressing in his body.[175] He writes, "I was healthy, young, university-educated and successful. I know that life isn't always fair, but our medical system is in absolute shambles if you become sick with anything other than a mainstream type illness. We lack doctors, specialists and nurses and yet we live in the most expensive place to live in the world—Vancouver, BC. We pay such high taxes, yet the government and health authorities cannot even look after their citizens. It's truly sad."[176]

Access to Technology

How important is technology to our health care? Most people have no idea until they need it for their own care.

PET (positron emission tomography) imaging is a relatively new technology (to many Canadians) but it can greatly improve the diagnosis, management, and treatment of cancer patients. It is the clinical standard for proper cancer care in almost every country but Canada, where PET scanners are only minimally available. The story of PET use in Canada can be summed up in the stories of two extraordinary men: hockey player Saku Koivu and Sudbury businessman Sam Bruno.

---

174 Keith, "Two Years Ago I was Referred to a Specialist," Charter Health, March 3, 2015, www.charterhealth.ca.

175 Justin, "After Coming Down with a Rare Condition that Completely Disabled Me," Charter Health, February 16, 2016, www.charterhealth.ca.

176 Ibid.

Saku Koivu. On December 4, 2019, the Montreal Canadiens, one of Canada's most storied professional teams, celebrated the 110th anniversary of its founding. A pre-game ceremony to mark the event included the presentation of 11 former captains and an honourable mention to the 12th, Henri Richard, who was unable to attend due to health issues. Together, these 12 men led the Canadiens to a total of 46 Stanley Cups.

The cheers for this group were appropriately legendary. So, it speaks volumes to say that the loudest and longest cheer of the evening was not for that distinguished group of captains and their collective achievements. It was reserved for Saku Koivu, the Finnish hockey player who led the Canadiens for a decade (1999–2009), yet was the only captain in the group who had never experienced the thrill of winning the treasured Cup.

The affection and respect that Montreal natives have for this man goes far beyond his hockey prowess and leadership skills. In the fall of 2001, just as the hockey season was about to get underway, Koivu began to feel ill. Tests were quickly conducted and within days the 26-year-old was diagnosed with cancer (intra-abdominal non-Hodgkin's lymphoma). Koivu began aggressive chemotherapy treatments that were accompanied by devastating side effects that would overwhelm most young men. The drugs were delivered in a four-week cycle that was to be repeated six times.

Would he play hockey again? Definitely not that season. In fact, one oncologist who spoke to the *Globe and Mail* anonymously said the odds of Koivu surviving the next year were "about 50-50."[177]

Fast forward a few months to 2002, when doctors wanted to confirm that the drugs were working. A decision was made to send Koivu to the University of Sherbrooke, which had recently begun using a new diagnostic device called a PET scanner in its nuclear medicine research program. PET scanners have the unique ability to detect the biological activity of cancer cells, while CT and MRI scans can only recognize cells once they have gathered into a mass or tumour. As a result, a PET scan can detect cancer at a much earlier stage.

Since Koivu's cancer was scattered throughout his abdomen and not isolated to a tumour, it seemed that a PET scan would be the perfect technology to determine if the chemotherapy drugs were working. If they were not, the doctors had the option of changing Koivu's therapy and trying another approach.

---

[177] Andre Picard, "Koivu Begins Cancer Treatment," *The Globe and Mail*, September 13, 2001.

The scan proved to be life-changing for Koivu: Almost miraculously, the cancer was gone. Completely! He had not yet finished his six cycles of chemotherapy, but the decision was made to stop treatment in an effort to minimize its detrimental impact on Koivu's physiological resources and give him a greater opportunity to recover and play hockey. Almost unbelievably, Koivu recovered in time to join the Canadiens in their 80th game of the season and just as the playoffs were about to begin.

Fans at the Bell Centre have long been known to be some of the most passionate and intense hockey fans in the NHL, yet what happened the night that Koivu rejoined his team is now considered to be one of the most emotional moments in team history. The fans began to chant "Saku! Saku! Saku!" as soon as he hit the ice and an eight-minute standing ovation continued through the singing of O Canada. The outpouring only ceased when Koivu asked the referee to start the game.

Years later, Koivu is remembered and admired for more than beating cancer. He was so grateful for the PET scan that changed the trajectory of his treatment to his recovery that he wanted every other cancer patient to have the same opportunity. So, he spearheaded a fundraising campaign to raise $8 million for a PET scanner at the Montreal General Hospital.

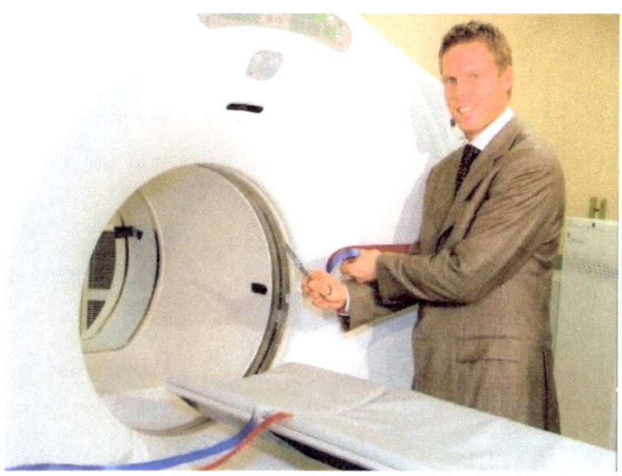

Saku Koivu, former captain of the Montreal Canadiens, cuts the ribbon to open Montreal's first PET/CT facility in September 2005.[178]

[178] Photo credit: McGill University Health Centre Press Release, "Former Habs captain helped raise funds for the MGH's first PET/CT scanner, February 5, 2014, muhc.ca/ways-to-give/article/video-tells-saku-koivu's-montreal-story.

It is difficult to describe the full impact that Koivu had on creating a cultural awareness of PET technology in cancer care in Quebec. His story was followed a year later by a film from another cultural icon, Quebec director Denys Arcand. Incredibly, his movie, "The Barbarian Invasion," has a storyline about a man with a brain tumour, the sorry state of socialized medicine in Canada, and his six-month wait for a PET scan.

These two high-profile events served to educate Quebecers and supercharged the efforts of doctors and patients to ensure that they had access to this critical technology. As a result, Quebec created a network of PET scanners across the province and it has become Canada's leader in the utilization of PET technology in cancer care.

Koivu did far more than beat cancer or achieve hero status as a hockey player. As Arpon Basu wrote for the NHL, "he created as rich a legacy as any NHL player in recent history, especially in Montreal."[179] Cancer care in Quebec was raised to the world standard because of the public outcry, support generated by Koivu's experience, and Arcand's film. It shows us all that sometimes people just need a good story (based on real experience) to energize them to bring about change.

Sam Bruno. While Quebec worked quickly to establish PET as the standard of care for cancer patients, the province of Ontario has done all that it can to limit access to PET technology and deny cancer patients access to its benefits.

There is a host of reasons behind Ontario's stingy use of the technology, mostly revolving around personalities, personal agendas, and costs. Again, the full scope of this issue goes beyond the parameters of this book. Dr. J. L. Urbain, a nuclear medicine physician and past-president of the Canadian Association of Nuclear Medicine (CANM) who left Ontario because of its restrictive PET policies, sums up the province's resistance by saying "Ontario practices financial-based medicine over evidence-based medicine."[180]

In spite of the politics and infighting in that province, one name has become synonymous with the need for PET in cancer care: Sam Bruno. Sam was an award-winning salesman in Sudbury who had an indomitable spirit and dedicated the last years of his life to changing PET funding policies and obtaining a PET scanner for that city.

---

[179] Arpon Basu, "Captain Koivu Created a Lasting Legacy in Montreal," National Hockey League, September 10, 2014, www.nhl.com.

[180] Susan Martinuk, "The Use of Positron Emission Tomography (PET) for Cancer Care Across Canada: Time for a National Strategy," A TRIUMF-AAPS Joint Project, 2011.

When he was diagnosed with colon cancer in 2005, he was determined to beat the odds and did all he could to learn about the disease and the various treatments that were available. According to his brother, Frank: "He asked questions. He talked to others. He read. He made phone calls. It was difficult then, compared to now, but he even sought information on the Internet."[181]

That search led him to discover the superior diagnostic abilities of PET technology, but he was frustrated to discover that he could only access a PET scan in Toronto (400 kilometres away) and that the cost of the scan was not covered by OHIP, the province's health insurance plan. In other words, he would have to pay thousands of dollars to cover travel, accommodations, and the scan itself.

Sam paid the money and, as with Koivu, the results of the scan gave Sam a very different picture than what was expected. The news was devastating. The scan showed a second cancer site in his colon, and this would dramatically change the course of his treatment.

While the scans did not give him the positive results that he so desperately wanted, they did give him a cause. According to Frank, Sam was struck by the unfairness of a health-care system that forced patients from northern Ontario to travel a long distance just "to get fair and equitable access to the machine."

Where was the equity of access in this situation? Why were the scans, considered to be so valuable to cancer care everywhere in the world, not even covered by public insurance in Ontario? In fact, at the time, the province's scanners were only being used for limited clinical trials.

Sam began to educate those around him, took his complaint about OHIP's PET scan coverage to the provincial ombudsman, and began what would become a decade-long effort to get a PET scanner to Sudbury. The government initially denied the request, saying there would not be enough scans to justify the funding.

---

[181] Harold Carmichael, "Sudbury's PET Scanner: A Dream 10 Years in the Making," *Sudbury Star*, October 10, 2019.

> "I've never seen in 25 years of care so many advanced cancers because of the lack of access to this type of technology … Ontario is the most underserved province in Canada (with regard to access to PET services) and remains the only part of the OECD that does not have routine access to PET services."[182]
>
> Dr. J.L. Urbain, Past President of the Canadian Association of Nuclear Medicine

As his health declined, Sam pushed harder to accomplish his mission. He collected 20,000 names on a petition and over the next ten years, his family, friends, and the community would raise $4.3 million to help fund the $8.9 million project. Northeastern Ontario was the last region in the province to get its own PET scanner and it was all due to a grassroots effort, not to government efforts to provide equal access to health care.

Sam passed away from colorectal cancer at the age of 55 on July 15, 2010, never having witnessed the completion of his goal. It was not until September 2019 that a PET scanner came into use at Health Sciences North in Sudbury, and as a tribute to Sam's efforts, the newly designated PET clinic was officially named The Sam Bruno PET Scanner Suite.

> "Sam Bruno exemplified the power of one which leads to the power of many."[183]
>
> Brenda Tessaro, Member, The Sam Bruno PET Scanner Committee

Canada's Diagnostic Inventory

Canada lags far behind the United States, Europe, and almost every other country in the Organization for Economic Co-operation and Development (OECD) in its adoption of diagnostic tools like MRI and CT scanners. It is even worse when it comes to PET scanners, which are only minimally available in Canada even though, as described above, they have long been the clinical standard for cancer care in every other country around the world.

---

182 Susan Martinuk, "The Use of Positron Emission Tomography (PET) for Cancer Care Across Canada: Time for a National Strategy," A TRIUMF-AAPS Joint Project, 2011.

183 Harold Carmichael, "Sudbury's PET Scanner: A Dream 10 Years in the Making," *Sudbury Star*, October 10, 2019.

In Canada, the availability of modern diagnostic equipment is directly related to two factors:

Location. Canada has a sparse population spread over large geographic regions. Most scanners are situated in densely populated cities and it can be difficult to justify their cost in smaller centres even if it is in an effort to serve a large geographic area.

Numbers. The Canadian Agency for Drugs and Technologies in Health (CADTH) is the government agency that periodically reports on the numbers and location of various diagnostic devices across Canada. Its most recent report states that Canada is home to 561 CT units, 366 MRI machines, and 51 PET-CT scanners. There are also three PET-MRI units that are primarily used for research purposes.[184] By way of comparison, the United States had 2,500 and Europe had more than 1,000. When compared to the other countries in the OECD, Canada ranks 21st out of 27 for the availability of CT scanners, 21st out of 26 for MRI equipment and 17/22 countries for PET-CT.

Device	2017 CADTH (Number of Units)	Canada (number of units per million)	Top Ranked Country (number of units per million)	Canada's International Ranking
CT	561	15.9	83.3 (Japan)	21/27
MRI	366	10.4	41.2 (Japan)	21/26
PET-CT	51	1.4	7.1 (Denmark)	17/22
PET-MRI	3	N/A	N/A	N/A

Table 4. CADTH – 2017 Medical Imaging Inventory[185,186]

[184] CADTH, "The Canadian Medical Imaging Inventory, 2017," March 2018, https://cadth.ca/canadian-medical-imaging-inventory-2017.
[185] Ibid.
[186] Baccus Barua and Mackenzie Moir. (2019). "Comparing Performance of Universal Health Care Countries, 2019," The Fraser Institute.

PART IV

HOW DID IT COME TO THIS?

15

Medicare: A History of Missed Opportunities

"History has played a huge part – and at times, an unfortunate role – in how Canadian health care is delivered today. Understanding history gives us a chance to more effectively create a new pathway forward."[187]

Dr. Stephen J. Pinney

Our Medicare system has long claimed to be the envy of the rest of the world; but, in practice, that envy is largely the result of deceptive rhetoric that continues to be propagated by governments of every political stripe:

- Medicare claims to be the best in the world; yet we consistently rank at the bottom of the pack in international health-care comparisons.
- Medicare claims to be free; but costs each Canadian taxpayer more than $7,000 per year in taxes and this is in addition to other out-of-pocket health-care costs (prescription drugs, eye care, dentist, specialist fees, diagnostic scans, etc.) that may be incurred.
- Medicare claims to be universal and comprehensive in its coverage; yet government bureaucrats arbitrarily cut services and make determinations about what treatments it will and will not cover (Dentists, no. Acupuncture, no. Diagnostic scans, maybe. Prescription drug coverage, only for a limited few. Mental health treatment programs, desperately needed yet highly restricted. Surgeries that are not considered to be medically necessary, definitely not. The real problem is that the

[187] Stephen Pinney, *How Hockey Can Save Healthcare: A Principle-Based Approach to Reforming the Canadian Healthcare System,* (LuLu Publishing Services, 2016): 117.

term "medically necessary" can have very different meanings to patients, doctors, and governments).

- Political leaders insist that Canada can afford to maintain an excellent health-care system with Medicare. Yet we know that it can only be sustained by limiting costs through the rationing of care and services. (Limiting access to specialists. Limiting the number of surgeries that a doctor can perform. Limiting access to diagnostic technologies. Denying access to private health care. Limiting the number of doctors that graduate, etc.).

No wonder more than one million Canadians were waiting for medically necessary treatment in 2019. And 2018. And 2017.

So how did we get here? How did a health-care system designed to be universal, equal, and free become a system where it is none of these things? And the only guiding principle that governs day-to-day practice is rationing health-care services? Looking back, it is easy to recognize certain junctures where our nation could (and should) have made a better effort to get Medicare right.

The History of Medicare

A Dream of Free Health Care for All. Canada's experience with universal single-payer health care (known as Medicare) seems perennially rooted in, and associated with, the name Tommy Douglas. He was the premier of Saskatchewan from 1944 to 1961 and leader of the federal NDP party from 1961 to 1971. But half a century later, he is still most commonly referred to as the Father of Medicare. In 2004, Canadians voted overwhelmingly to name Douglas "The Greatest Canadian," thereby putting him and the creation of Medicare above the accomplishments of other noted Canadians including Terry Fox, Alexander Graham Bell, and even the Great One himself, Wayne Gretzky.

How does one get to be "The Greatest Canadian?" Ironically, for Douglas, it all started with falling down.

Tommy Douglas

Douglas was born in Scotland in 1904 and, six years later, his family immigrated to Canada and settled in Winnipeg, Manitoba.[188] But fate intervened just before the Douglas family left their homeland when young Tommy fell and cut his knee on a stone. As was not uncommon in the days before antibiotics, the wound failed to heal and he developed a severe bone infection (osteomyelitis) in his leg. He underwent several surgeries in Scotland to stem it, but when the family arrived in Winnipeg, the infection took hold once more and the Canadian doctors were convinced that it could only be controlled by amputating his leg.

However, just like the stories portrayed on television's medical dramas, there was one doctor who was convinced he could cure Douglas. Dr. R. J. Smith was an apparently well-known orthopedic surgeon who recognized that this young lad's situation presented (what was back then) a unique teaching opportunity. He offered to treat Douglas for free if he could use it as a teaching case and have his students observe. With nothing to lose, Tommy's parents agreed, and Smith eventually managed to save their child's leg.

Like many patients mentioned throughout this book, Tommy Douglas's philosophies and beliefs about socialized health care (where money should never be a barrier to care) were strongly shaped by his personal experience. He went on to become a Baptist preacher with a socialist bent, and then a socialist with a political bent. Ultimately, he became a politician who was best known for his focus on social reform.

As a preacher, a politician, and a great orator, Douglas was well aware of the value of a story to persuade and he often used the narrative of his dramatic childhood experience as a means of convincing his audiences that health care should be free. He would famously tell them: "No boy should

---

[188] Depending on which historical record you use, the Douglas family immigrated to Canada in 1910, 1911, or 1919.

have to depend either for his leg or his life upon the ability of his parents to raise enough money to bring a first-class surgeon to his bedside."[189]

Later on, he would add to his life story by drawing from his experiences as a Baptist minister in Weyburn, Saskatchewan. He would tell the crowds: "I remember burying a girl 14 years of age who had died with a ruptured appendix and peritonitis. There isn't any doubt in my mind that it was just an inability to get her to a hospital. I buried … [two] young men in their 30s with young small families, who died because there was no doctor readily available and they hadn't the money to get proper care."[190]

In light of those comments, one must wonder what Douglas would think of our current health-care situation where people are languishing in pain, out of work, getting addicted to painkillers, unable to care for their families, and even dying because our so-called free and universal health-care system has denied them access to medically necessary care for months and even years.

Saskatchewan Makes Medical History. The Depression of the 1930s overwhelmed the Prairies and left Saskatchewan in particular devastated by unemployment and drought. Such circumstances quite naturally led to the broad acceptance and widespread growth of the Cooperative Commonwealth Federation (CCF), a left-wing political party with ideas that were grounded in socialism. At that point, people had no money to pay for doctors and the idea that the government should be providing health care to its people easily took hold. It became even more popular as wounded veterans from the Second World War returned home while still needing medical care.

The CCF Party took up the cause of socialized medicine and used it as their election platform. Douglas became leader of the Saskatchewan CCF in 1942 and the party was elected to govern the province in 1944, thereby establishing the first democratic socialist government in North America.

---

[189] Hamish MacPherson, "Back in the Day: Tommy Douglas - the Scotsman who gave Canada free health care," *The National*, April 16, 2019, https://www.thenational.scot/news/17575769.back-day-tommy-douglas-scotsman-gave-canada-free-healthcare/.

[190] Tabitha Marshall, "Tommy Douglas," The Canadian Encyclopedia, July 30, 2013, https://www.thecanadianencyclopedia.ca/en/article/tommy-douglas.

The July 1962 doctors strike in Regina, Saskatchewan. Doctors from across the province rallied at the Saskatchewan Legislature to protest the implementation of Medicare.[191]

The CCF was determined to act on its promise to implement socialized medicine, but real change takes time and the CCF was forced to introduce its medical reforms slowly and on a smaller scale. In the first year, Douglas's government established a cancer control agency. This was another socialist first and put Saskatchewan on the map for being the first jurisdiction in Canada (and North America) to cover all cancer diagnosis and treatment costs. Three years later, the CCF introduced universal hospital insurance that covered all in-hospital costs and diagnostic tests.

However, no matter how hard they tried, the CCF could not convince the medical doctors to join their plan for a universal, socialized health-care system.[192] The doctors battled the CCF for years; they were driven by a fear that they would essentially become government employees and lose the autonomy necessary for them to direct their patients' care. (This raises a good question for all to ponder: How much autonomy do doctors have today to ensure their patients receive the timely treatments and scans that they need?)

---

191 Photo credit: Edward Odishaw.

192 Lorne Brown and Doug Taylor, "The Birth of Medicare," *Canadian Dimension*, July 3, 2012.

Fifteen years later (1962), the CCF finally introduced universal medical care that covered doctors' fees in addition to costs associated with hospitals, clinics, and diagnostic tests. The doctors were furious when the Medicare legislation came into effect on July 1, 1962, and approximately 90 percent of Saskatchewan's doctors walked off the job. The infamous doctors' strike bitterly divided the province and even led to violent protests by citizens.

However, as babies continued to be born, injuries and accidents still happened, and sickness refused to leave the province, any political differences among the citizenry fell away and the province's population was increasingly united in calling the doctors back to work. After 23 days, the doctors had lost almost all public support and most agreed to take part in the public insurance program. A government compromise that had been brokered during the strike gave the doctors who most vehemently opposed Medicare an option to continue to practice outside of the system.

Although Douglas is known as the Father of Medicare, he was no longer the premier when his dream came to fruition. By 1961, he had taken his fight for universal health care to the national stage as leader of the just-created federal New Democratic Party. That left his successor, Woodrow Lloyd, to launch the first fully universal Medicare program in 1962.

The Road to National Healthcare: Opportunities Missed Along the Way

A Lost Opportunity to Control Costs. Radical transitions rarely go smoothly or without problems (and compromises) and that was the situation when former prime minister Lester B. Pearson decided that his governing Liberal party would essentially take the Saskatchewan Medicare plan and make it a national one. But as their plans to nationalize Medicare went forward, the CCF government in Saskatchewan lost its first election since taking power in 1944 and a new Liberal government under premier Ross Thatcher was installed in May 1964. In a rare move, he appointed himself as the province's finance minister and he declared that the first order of business for his government was to figure out how to fund the Medicare monster that had been created by the CCF.

As a fresh group of accountants and civil servants began to pore over the financial books left by the CCF, they came to realize that none of the Medicare numbers made sense. According to the numbers in the CCF books, there was no way the province could afford universal Medicare, either now or in the future. Both Thatcher and the Saskatchewan taxpayers were angry at the CCF's deception and Thatcher responded by promptly firing several long-term bureaucrats who had been involved in creating the Medicare system.

It did not take long for the fired bureaucrats to land on their feet. The federal Liberals were struggling to develop a Medicare system that would work on a national scale, and they quickly hired the just-fired policymakers from Saskatchewan and put them to work fine-tuning the federal Medicare program. In other words, the bureaucrats who had just been fired for financial incompetence in creating the Saskatchewan Medicare program were now in charge of creating Canada's national Medicare program.

Pearson had a minority government at that time and he was convinced that a national Medicare program would be the election policy that would push his party to a majority of seats in Parliament. One of Pearson's top advisors, Tom Kent, later wrote in his memoirs that he viewed Medicare as "the jewel in the record of achievement on which the government might go to the people in the following election."[193] Since nobody knew when an election might be called, there was constant pressure on the bureaucrats in the health ministry to finalize the details of Medicare and have it ready to present to the federal electorate.

In the spring of 1966, Thatcher's young executive assistant, a lawyer named Edward Odishaw, was heading to Ottawa for a series of meetings. Before he left, Thatcher gave him one added task: Talk to Mitchell Sharpe, the federal Finance minister, and fill him in on the financial chaos that provincial accountants had uncovered in the CCF documents related to funding Medicare.

Today, Odishaw says, "Thatcher was genuinely concerned about the feds jumping into a massive national program based on wrong financial data. The architects of the Saskatchewan plan were now running the show in Ottawa and they had no idea about how to control the costs." In other words, if the federal government used the Saskatchewan numbers as a basis for a national Medicare system, it would be disastrous. The warning was delivered and when Sharpe spoke to Pearson about the financial chaos in the CCF books, he discovered that those working on the national Medicare project (led by the fired Saskatchewan bureaucrats) were having problems working out realistic costs for the program.

That is, until one of those same bureaucrats came up with what Kent thought was a brilliant way to deal with the problem. In his book, Kent writes: "The government did not need to work out or legislate the details of a shared-cost program—*"it only needed to define, clearly, the principles of*

[193] Tom Kent, *A Public Purpose: An Experience of Liberal Opposition and Canadian Government*, (Kingston-Montreal: McGill-Queen's University Press, 1988): 365.

what it meant by Medicare. Then it would contribute to the costs of any provincial program that satisfied those principles."[194]

That is how the foundation for universal health care in Canada was established -- by sweeping costs and realistic financial details under the carpet to focus solely on the idealistic principles of Medicare. Apparently, they believed that the money would figure itself out later, but here we are, 60 years later, still not sure of how to pay for health care and still focused on ideology instead of establishing the necessary financial underpinnings.

The promise of national Medicare did not provide Pearson with a majority government but he was determined to push the legislation through the House of Commons and Sharpe's concerns about the "fiscal probity" of the Medicare budget were not enough to change his agenda. Ultimately, a compromise was reached whereby the Medicare bill would be passed, but they would hold off implementing it so they could continue to work on budgeting issues.

The *National Medical Care Insurance Act* was passed in the House of Commons on December 8, 1966. Eighteen months later, on July 1, 1968, a free, universal, and national Medicare system finally became reality in Canada.

A Lost Opportunity to Keep Medicare Viable. When the federal architects of Medicare became frustrated in their efforts to establish cost-sharing plans with the provinces, they decided to ignore the budget problems and focus on creating principles that would provide the framework for national Medicare and health-care payments to the provinces. As is the case for each of us in our own lives, the attempt to ignore finances may have worked for a time, but it did not take long before the federal government was forced to confront the massive costs of Medicare.

By the late 1970s and early 1980s, government-insured patient visits to doctors were increasing. Payments to physicians began to spiral out of control and an escalating three-way battle broke out among doctors, the provinces, and the federal government: Provincial medical associations had established physician fees that were beyond what the provinces were willing to pay; the provinces claimed they were not getting enough money from the federal government to pay for the doctors' fees; and the federal government accused the provinces of using their health transfer payments for purposes other than health care.[195]

---

[194] Ibid., p. 366.

[195] Stephen Pinney, *How Hockey Can Save Healthcare: A Principle-Based Approach to Reforming the Canadian Healthcare System*, (LuLu Publishing Services, 2016): 106-107.

A federal investigation was initiated and former justice Emmett Hall, leader of the 1964 Royal Commission on Health Services that had recommended the implementation of a national Medicare program, was called upon once again to determine what was happening in the Medicare system. The second Hall report refuted the federal government's claim that the provinces were misusing transfer payments but declared that user fees and extra billing (two practices that were now commonly occurring) undermined the principles of Medicare and had to stop. Hall's report subsequently became the foundation of the 1984 *Canada Health Act* that now governs our health-care system.

The Canada Health Act

The preamble to the 1984 *Canada Health Act* supposedly outlines the primary objective of the health-care system as:

> "To protect, promote and restore the physical and mental well-being of residents of Canada and to facilitate reasonable access to health services without financial or other barriers."

Obviously, the evidence presented in this book suggests that the system is not even coming close to meeting these objectives, particularly with respect to facilitating "reasonable access" to health services. Once again, instead of establishing health-care objectives and a sustainable financial framework, this 1984 Medicare reboot created five ideological principles that each province must meet to receive federal transfer payments for Medicare.

The five golden principles of the 1984 *Canada Health Act* include:[196]

1. *Public Administration:* The health-care system must be run, directly or indirectly, by provincial governments on a non-profit basis. Note that this prevents governments from making profits on health-care delivery, but it does not prevent provincial governments from delegating the care, delivery, and/or management of some aspects of health care to entities that do make a profit. So, despite this grand principle, there are (and always have been) private individuals and organizations making legitimate profits from health care.

---

196 Ibid., p.109–110.

2. *Comprehensive:* The act states that "all insured health services provided by hospitals, medical practitioners or dentists [in hospital settings]" must be covered by the public health plan. Provinces can extend coverage to other services outside of hospitals (e.g., chiropractors and physiotherapists) but it differs significantly between provinces and providing extended services is increasingly restricted because of budgets.

3. *Universality:* This means that all insured persons are eligible for all health services. The exemptions to this rule include individuals working in the armed forces, inmates at federal penitentiaries, and individuals covered by federal government insurance as discussed under the myth of equal access in Chapter 13.

4. *Portability:* This means that citizens can travel from province to province with the understanding that they can still access medical care. Again, this works well in theory only. Standard procedures are covered, but each provincial government has made its own choices about what care is "medically necessary" and what drugs or types of care it will cover.

5. *Accessibility:* This principle was not present in the original Medicare policy crafted by the federal Liberals in the 1960s and made its first appearance in the 1984 *Canada Health Act.* It calls for "reasonable access" to care and "reasonable compensation" to health-care providers.

How These Principles have Failed Health Care. It seems incredible that the five principles that guide Canadian health care have nothing to do with the practical realities of successfully providing health care to 35 million people. The principles do not:

- Establish objectives to determine if the system is protecting, promoting, or restoring the health of Canadians;
- Provide a means of determining physical and mental status or well-being;
- Ensure that the system is meeting the health-care needs of Canadians;

- Make any mention of measuring progress or determining if any health-care or medical objectives are being met;
- Provide a pathway to encourage innovation;
- Allow for updating and modernizing the system's funding and its delivery methods;
- Offer incentives to produce positive outcomes that relate to the health and well-being of Canadians.

Other problems with the *Canada Health Act* include:

1. *Reasonable Access:* The term "reasonable access" is/has been/and always will be problematic as doctors, patients, and governments continue to debate what, exactly, is "reasonable." The government may believe that waiting one year for knee surgery is "reasonable," but as you have seen in the stories herein, each person has unique and complicating variables that come into play, including their level of pain, ability to carry out work and earn an income, ability to care for a family, and the potential for deterioration of their physical and mental abilities.

2. *Extra Billing:* The compensation for health-care providers essentially bans the practice of extra billing although we all know that theoretical bans are very different from the everyday practice of medicine. Many doctors (primarily specialists) continue to charge patients an extra fee for their services.

3. *Outdated Principles:* There are also growing concerns as to whether the five principles, which essentially lay out the criteria for funding, are realistic given the changing nature of medicine in Canada.

The intention of Medicare was to ensure basic medical care was available to all, but today even the most basic care can be complex and expensive. Doctors' bills, hospital stays, and acute care situations used to be the main line items for expenditures; now even the most rudimentary care can include huge costs for diagnostics (technology and laboratory testing), treatments, and medicines. It also must cover repeat visits and treatments for those suffering from chronic illnesses.

For these reasons, it can easily be argued that, at the ripe old age of 36, the *Canada Health Act* is an outdated piece of legislation that can no longer fully accommodate the demands of even the most basic medical care for all Canadians.

What is Missing?

We give Tommy Douglas credit for initiating universal health care, yet few Canadians realize that politicians and policymakers subsequently stripped three important tenets from his original Medicare plan. Unfortunately, these three missing principles are the very ones that are necessary to maintain and sustain a universal health-care system.

What Happened to Effective, Efficient, and Responsible? Douglas initially called for a sustainable system governed by eight tenets; five of which are largely covered by the principles of the *Canada Health Act,* and three additional tenets that would enable the system to operate effectively, efficiently, and responsibly. In retrospect, these three 'missing' principles would have been germane to sustaining the system. They would have ensured that health-care policies would not (indeed, could not) have been adopted by the government if they were not first properly funded and sustainable. In addition, these terms suggest an openness to innovation and positive change (by striving to be increasingly effective, efficient, and responsible) that is not present in the current system.

More than 50 years since the beginning of national Medicare, and almost 40 years since the *Canada Health Act* was established, funding remains focused primarily on doctors and hospitals. These are still an important part of health-care budgets, but major expenses now include computer technology, laboratory and diagnostic technology (various types of scanners and analyzers), drugs, and highly specialized procedures.

At a minimum, the missing three principles would have forced the system to respond to the rapid changes in medicine, technology, and economics through innovation and updates.

A Long-Term Plan to Save Costs. Governments have also failed to protect the longevity of Medicare by neglecting to invest in its second stage as Douglas envisioned. In a 1979 speech at a conference called S.O.S. Medicare, he reminded Canadians that his vision was to be implemented in two stages: The first was to remove funding as a barrier to access (done) and the second was to change the way health care was delivered in order to "reduce costs and put an emphasis on preventative medicine."

The second stage of Medicare, as Douglas imagined it, was a plan to keep the system sustainable by preventing or controlling these chronic problems that are a huge cost to the system. Douglas had planned for the implementation of regional clinics that were home to a host of integrated clinical and diagnostic services, physicians, home care, public health, and pediatric dentists (the same kind of integrated and coordinated services that people are still talking about today). Doctors would work together in a coordinated practice to offer innovative and efficient medical care that would also promote prevention, health, and well-being among Canadians. Most notably, his plan did not include waiting for medical treatment or being denied medical care.

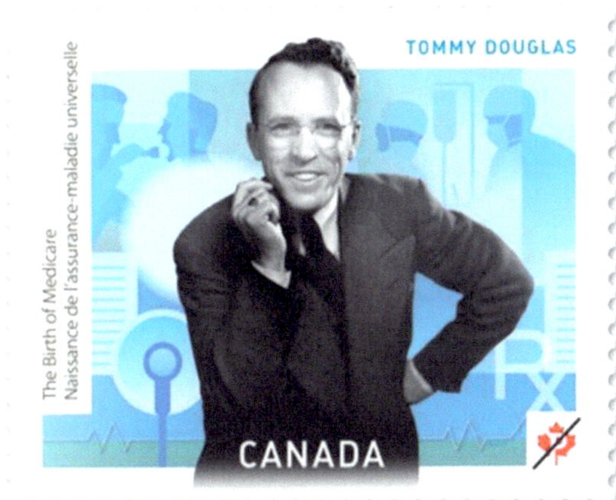

Canada Post honours Tommy Douglas on 50th Anniversary of the Birth of Medicare.

As we look back 50 years later, it seems clear that a few changes back then could have made a vast difference both in the health of Canadians and in the financial health of Medicare.

16

What Happens When Health Care is Based on Ideology?

"The most basic form of human stupidity is forgetting what we are trying to accomplish."[197]

Friedrich Nietzsche

Canada's health-care system is founded on socialism, an ideology that supposedly supports the common good of a society by creating equal outcomes for all. In the matter of health care, it suggests that the primary goal is to provide a social service free of charge and to ensure that every Canadian has an equal and universal access to medical care. In theory, it is a noble goal and one that many Canadians enthusiastically support.

In practice, however, it simply does not work. Our own health-care system (underfunded, bursting at its seams, and unable to provide medical care to more than one million patients each year) is the very proof that socialist-based health care, on its own and as it currently exists in Canada, is not sustainable and cannot provide the medical care that Canadians need.

Ironically, this ideological system cannot even accomplish its own ideological goals, let alone any of the most basic expectations of medical care.

How Socialism Failed Health Care

1. ***Failed to Achieve its Ideological Goal of Equality.*** As described in earlier chapters, as well as in the pages ahead, inequities are rife within the system as to who gets care and when. Although some continue to spread fears that any changes to our current Medicare system will produce a separate, private system to serve only those who can afford to pay, the truth is that this so-called abomination to

---

[197] Goodreads, Friedrich Nietzsche, Quotable Quotes, https://www.goodreads.com/quotes/7517225-the-most-basic-form-of-human-stupidity-is-forgetting-what.

socialism already exists; it is alive, well, and daily thumbing its nose at our socialist dreams.

2. ***Failed to Achieve its Ideological Goal of Universality.*** There may be a public perception that Medicare provides universal coverage for all medical treatments, but it is false. It does not provide comprehensive coverage of prescription drugs, dental care, psychological services, specialist fees, the latest prescription drugs in some categories, and a host of other treatments and services. In addition, each province has independently determined which medical procedures and medicines it will fund, as well as a long list that it will not.

3. ***Failed in its Ideological Goal of Being 'Free'.*** In 2019, each Canadian paid about $7,000 for Medicare through our taxes and, on top of that, we pay for any costs incurred for prescriptions, dental work, and health care that is not covered. Total taxpayer dollars spent on health care that year? More than $264 billion.

4. ***Failed to Provide "Reasonable Access."*** We have the longest waitlists in the world and with the exception of leaving the country for care, there are few, if any, options available to those languishing on a waitlist for two or three years. Five million Canadians do not have a family doctor and Canada has the longest waits in the world for specialist appointments and care.

5. ***Failed by Most Objective Measures of Success.*** By most objective measures, reports show that Canada has the longest waitlists and the second most expensive health-care system in the world. This does not mean that our doctors and personnel are sub-par; it means that the health-care system prevents them from achieving the objective goals that every other wealthy country has for its medical system.

The facts and numbers very quickly make a mockery of Medicare's glorious promise of cradle-to-grave, free, and universal medical care. Provincial and federal governments know it, health-care personnel know it, and it is time for Canadians to accept it and demand something far better for their money.

All of the above may explain why Sir Winston Churchill referred to socialism as "a philosophy of failure" whose "inherent virtue is the equal sharing of misery,"[198] while health-care analyst (and former Canadian) Sally Pipes called the government-run, single-payer health care such as we have in Canada, "a catastrophe for the people forced to live under it."[199]

In his book, *This May Hurt a Bit*, Canadian health-care analyst Stephen Skyvington writes that the problem with ideology is really quite simple: "No one—I repeat, *no one*—is putting patients first in 2019, despite what name they might give to a particular piece of legislation. Unless we, as Canadians and as users of our healthcare system, start demanding better from those in charge—demanding specifically that they stop trying to impose all this crazy ideology on us and start putting patients first—then I'm afraid we're doomed to see Medicare swirl down the drain of mediocrity for some time to come."[200]

Health Care Based on Ideology is NOT Focused on Patient Care

How did a medical system that began with such good intentions become so callous and uncaring to those who need medical care? By losing sight of its purpose and what it was meant to accomplish.

The primary purpose of any health-care system should be to provide medical care and meet patients' needs. There should be health-related goals or incentives and a focus on producing healthy outcomes. Everything should revolve around patient care. But, as evidenced in many stories throughout this book, Medicare has never had this focus. Maybe that was Tommy Douglas's original intention, but after the politicians and bureaucrats had finished shaping his ideas into a health-care system, that primary focus was on the cutting room floor. Instead, we designed a system where the overriding principle is to provide equality to Canadians -- not medical care.

In daily medical affairs, this gift of equality is noteworthy only in that it provides every Canadian with an equal chance to get his/her name on a waiting list. It may be okay to use socialist ideology as the underpinning principle for some systems, but it is clearly not appropriate for health care. Once equality goals trump health-care goals (as is now the case with Medicare), we have surely provided the raw materials for one of Friedrich Nietzsche's most intriguing quotes: "The most basic form of human stupidity

---

198 Churchhill, Winston. Speech, House of Commons in UK, October 22, 1945.

199 Sally C. Pipes, *False Premise, False Promise: The Disastrous Reality of Medicare for All*, (New York: Encounter Books, 2020): 3.

200 Stephen Skyvington, *This May Hurt a Bit: Reinventing Canada's Healthcare System*, (Toronto: Dundurn Press, 2019): 158.

is forgetting what we are trying to accomplish."[201] Perhaps we all need a reminder that our health-care system is there to provide medical care.

Kyle, who lives in Calgary, was forced to wait 18 to 24 months to have an inguinal hernia repair. He not only had to deal with daily pain for months on end, but he had to carry out his physically demanding job while doing so. He is a self-employed labourer who does not have disability insurance and that means his only option to maintain an income is to work, no matter how much pain and suffering he must bear. In his online posting, he asks how such suffering can be acceptable in a system that prides itself on universal access before finally concluding that "universal accessibility means nothing."[202]

There is no equality in how health care is delivered and, as many patients have rightly pointed out, the system has only produced equality in suffering:

> "We are being held hostage by a monopolized system on some false belief that this form of socialized medicine prevents people from becoming marginalized because of lack of access to healthcare. Ironically, our present system can, and does, equally threaten [not help] the health of the poor, the rich, the uneducated, the educated, the young, the old, the healthy and the sick."[203]
>
> Sabrine, Vancouver

Jo and her family in North Vancouver have already experienced this. She clearly sees that our current health-care system functions to first ensure that everyone has access to free health care, as a result, "many Canadians are not getting the health care they need to sustain their lives or be able to provide for themselves because of injuries not getting fixed."

Jo's son had to leave a long sought-after apprenticeship after only three months because he injured his thumb in a rugby game. He could not work or hold anything for several months, yet could not get proper care because the doctor had determined his injury was not serious enough to warrant surgery. Eighteen months later, he is a young man who still has does not have a fully functional hand. Jo concludes her story by saying, "The government is

---

[201] Goodreads, Friedrich Nietzsche, Quotable Quotes, https://www.goodreads.com/quotes/7517225-the-most-basic-form-of-human-stupidity-is-forgetting-what.

[202] Kyle, "Worst Health Care Service in the Developed World," Charter Health, October 24, 2017, www.charterhealth.ca.

[203] Sabrine, Charter Health, n.d., www.charterhealth.ca.

standing behind a 'Fair to All' system that is outdated and no longer works."[204]

Supporters of Medicare tend to pride themselves on caring for all members of society equally. But where is the so-called moral superiority in a health-care system that forces more than one million Canadians to wait months or even years for medical treatment? Where is the compassion? In the end, all Canadians suffer because of our collective (and sadly desperate) need to believe that we are treated equally under universal Medicare.

Health Care Based on Ideology Does NOT Adapt to Technological Change

Canadians have fooled themselves into believing that we are wealthy enough to fund cradle-to-grave, free, and universal health care for all. It may have been manageable at the beginning when health care was almost exclusively delivered by doctors in hospitals and those were the two primary costs (doctors fees and hospital services). From 1975 to 1980, those two expenditures alone accounted for about 60 percent of the federal health-care budget.[205]

> "The primary purpose of a healthcare system should be to provide medical care. Sadly, in Canada, the primary purpose is to provide free healthcare."
>
> Jo, North Vancouver

But health care has changed a great deal since then and costs have exploded. In 1975, national health expenditures were just over $12 billion ($527.10 per person);[206] today they are over $264 billion ($7,068 per person),[207] and it is not a stretch to think that we may soon be spending 50 percent of our federal budget on health care alone. According to some experts, health care will consume as much as 80 percent of provincial budgets by 2030.[208]

The percentage cost of hospital services has dropped from 45 percent to 29 percent since 1975, while physician fees are still responsible for about 15

---

[204] Jo, "My Son Had to Leave His Apprenticeship after Only 3 Months," Charter Health, August 25, 2018, www.charterhealth.ca.

[205] Canadian Institute for Health Information. National Health Expenditure Trends, 1975-2019.

[206] Ibid.

[207] Ibid.

[208] Stephen Skyvington, *This May Hurt a Bit: Reinventing Canada's Healthcare System*, (Toronto: Dundurn Press, 2019):193.

percent of health-care costs. But we now have multiple pills for almost every possible condition and require expensive technology for diagnostics, case histories, treatments, surgeries, and administration. Technology and pharmaceuticals are now major expenditures.

In addition to these costs, many health-care analysts agree that Canada's health-care system and much of its infrastructure, created in the 1960s, has not been modified or adapted to deliver modern care. Today, most modern health care (except for the most acute conditions) occurs outside of hospital settings and often involves specialized personnel who work in home care, communities, and clinics.

In contrast, the funding and organization of our outdated medical system remains concentrated on doctors and hospital services. Not only is this the wrong focus for funding, it also reveals the irony that despite having that same focus for 60 years, we have still not figured out how to deliver or fund medical care in an efficient or effective way.

Modern health care is also characterized by measuring clear health-related outcomes and evidence-based decision-making. Overall, our antiquated system remains focused on trying to achieve equality even though patient experience, studies, and statistics have all repeatedly demonstrated that it cannot provide either equality of care or equality of access. All it has done is to create a system with rationed care and the longest waits in the world.

Dr. Stephen Pinney is a Canadian orthopedic surgeon who trained in Canada and has worked in both the Canadian and American health systems. He writes: "The Canadian healthcare system is a prisoner of its history … it is akin to a large sprawling house built without a solid foundation. The structural organization of the healthcare system was set at the time of its formation. [Our current health-care system] was never designed as a system—it developed piece by piece."[209] That is, Medicare started by funding hospital services, then physicians, and then a hodgepodge of various types of care that vary from province to province. But fragmented funding has led us to the fragmented delivery of care that, according to Pinney, fails to cover the "patient's total episode of care."

Pinney says there is no coordination of care or accountability for a patient's care, communication between doctors and specialists is poor, and the system itself is constrained by outdated administrative systems, physical infrastructure, and service delivery models. This fragmented care and lack of

---

[209] Stephen Pinney, *How Hockey Can Save Healthcare: A Principle-Based Approach to Reforming the Canadian Healthcare System*, (LuLu Publishing Services, 2016): 92.

accountability/communication is exactly what we have observed in the patient stories herein.

In other words, over the past 60 years, many of the foundational elements of our health-care system have not changed. We have failed to develop the kind of coordinated and integrated system that is now required for modern patient care and this is underscored by our woeful results in international surveys.

We are spending more money than almost every other country; Canada ranked second highest in terms of the most money spent (as a percentage of GDP), yet only ranked 26th, 26th, and 26th out of 28 countries, respectively, in numbers of physicians, acute care beds, and psychiatric beds. Rankings were also near the bottom of the list (and far below the OECD average) for diagnostic technology such as MRI, CT, and PET scanners. As you can imagine, our rankings were predictably low in terms of access to physicians, specialists, and elective surgery.[210] When considered collectively, these rankings indicate that we are spending huge amounts of money for health care and getting very little value in return.

Our poor rankings are not so surprising to many who work in health care. Rationing care and services is the only way governments can control a health-care system with finite resources that is faced with ever-increasing demand. But the combination of rationed services and an antiquated system has resulted in a bare bones, no-frills health-care system that you may or may not even be able to access.

Dr. David Gratzer is a Toronto psychiatrist who has written several books describing the problems with Canadian health care and potential solutions. In an article written over a decade ago, he tells readers the so-called "ugly truths" about Canadian health care and how they influenced his thinking about Medicare:[211]

> "My healthcare prejudices crumbled not in the classroom but on the way to one. On a sub-zero Winnipeg morning in 1997, I cut across the hospital emergency room to shave a few minutes off my frigid commute.

---

[210] Bacchus Barua and Mackenzie Moir. (2019). "Comparing Performance of Universal Health Care Countries, 2019," The Fraser Institute.

[211] David Gratzer, "The Ugly Truth about Canadian Health Care," *City Journal*, Summer 2007, https://www.city-journal.org/html/ugly-truth-about-canadian-health-care-13032.html.

> Swinging open the door, I stepped into a nightmare: the ER overflowed with elderly people on stretchers, waiting for admission. Some, it turned out, had waited five days. The air stank with sweat and urine.
>
> Right then, I began to reconsider everything that I thought I knew about Canadian healthcare. I soon discovered that the problems went well beyond overcrowded ERs. Patients had to wait for practically any diagnostic test or procedure, such as the man with persistent pain from a hernia operation whom we referred to a pain clinic—with a three year delay; or the woman needing a sleep study to diagnose what seemed like sleep apnea, who faced a two year delay; or the woman with breast cancer who needed to wait four months for radiation therapy, when the standard of care was four weeks."

Gratzer's description of seeing health care in an entirely new light is powerful and reflects the experiences of many Canadians who were under the impression that health care was okay; perhaps costly and with a few shortages but, on the whole, doing well. These thoughts change very quickly once an individual has an up-close and personal experience in obtaining medical care for oneself or for a loved one.

A System Governed by Ideology Takes Away Autonomy

> "We surrendered our freedom of medical choice many decades ago when, like sleepwalkers, we accepted without much protest a top-down bureaucratic control of government-rationed medicine, and we and our physicians fell under the threat of criminal punishment for attempting to exchange our own money for the treatment of our own bodies, as we had always previously done.
>
> The same citizens who would scream bloody murder if told that from now on they could buy or rent only a government-made home, or had to buy and wear only government made pants, dresses and shoes, or had to buy and eat only government food, suddenly thought it was quite normal to have politicians dictating, regulating, and rationing the quality and amount of healthcare they

would be permitted to have for themselves, their failing parents, or their sick children."[212]

Dr. William Gairdner

A Loss of Collective Autonomy. Many Canadians now living have only ever experienced government overseeing their health care. But in his book, *The Trouble with Canada … Still,* Gairdner makes a point that few of us have ever considered. In giving all our health-care powers to the state, we have also sacrificed our autonomy over our own medical care.

> "We taxpaying Canadians can't get the services we need just to get on with life…
>
> In our universally inaccessible system (unless you are dying), apparently it is appropriate for us all to suffer equally … how very sad is that?"[213]
>
> Annie, Vancouver, B.C.

Few of us realize just how far we have relinquished control over our own health care or how easily we have allowed it to happen. It continues as provincial governments choose the medical services that will be covered under that province's Medicare programs and then determines what geographical areas or hospitals get prime access to technology. The Sam Bruno story in Chapter 14 showed how the residents of northern Ontario had to fight for more than a decade, send petitions, and raise half the money just to get a PET scanner in their area of the province.

The government's over-extended legal powers continue to impinge on our decision-making as it blocks citizens from paying for private medical care in an attempt to maintain its own health-care monopoly.

There is no other country in the world where the government has a monopoly on the provision of health care and also prevents citizens from using their own money to purchase health care when they cannot get timely care in the public system.

As many have stated, the Canadians who defend government-only health care are the same ones who would never allow the government to dictate

---

212 William D. Gairdner, *The Trouble with Canada ... Still!: A Citizen Speaks Out,* (Toronto: Key Porter Books, 2010): 285.

213 Annie, "It's Appropriate for us all to Suffer? How Very Sad is That?," Charter Health, n.d., www.charterhealth.ca.

what sweater or brand of clothing Canadians should wear. What if the federal government made a deal with Nike and ruled that Canadians could only wear clothing and shoes with the distinctive swoosh? Canadians would never tolerate government intrusion on such a personal issue as our choice of clothing. Nor would we accept a law stating that we could only purchase cars made by Ford. So why do we allow governments to dictate our health-care choices?

A decision to put ideology above patient care was recently in the news as Canada (and the rest of the world) struggled with a second wave of the COVID-19 pandemic. As the need for more COVID-19 testing increased, the lines at government-run testing centres became ridiculously long. There were reports of people waiting six hours or more at some centres, while other facilities reached capacity and closed before people could even gain access.

Naturally, many of the private, for-profit clinics that do exist (in spite of the *Canada Health Act*), opened their doors to those who were willing to pay about $250 for a test.[214] That prompted federal Health Minister Patty Hajdu to say that her department would look into the matter because "the law explicitly says that [private clinics] shouldn't exist and we have a number of actions we can take under the *Canada Health Act*." Apparently, any attempts to bypass the long waits at public facilities go "against the essence" of our universal health-care system.

Meanwhile, the media reported that members of Parliament and their families have been able to (and will continue to) use the services of a private clinic in Gatineau, Quebec, to get their COVID tests and, of course, it is all paid for by our tax dollars. Once again, the health-care system has shown that some animals are more equal than others.

Missing in all of this, of course, is any amount of common sense. Consider the following:

1. The lineups at COVID-19 test sites are overwhelming. People can spend their entire day waiting, only to have the facility close because it is over capacity.

2. Some people who can afford to pay for their own tests are choosing to go to private clinics for them.

---

[214] Sarah Turnbull, "Health Canada Looking into Private Clinics Offering COVID-19 Tests," CTV News, October 5, 2020, https://www.ctvnews.ca/politics/health-canada-looking-into-private-clinics-offering-covid-19-tests-1.5133854.

3. This removes them from the lineups at the public centre, thereby allowing more people to be tested there. The government does not have to pay for their tests and our strapped health-care system is thereby spared the cost. Lineups are shorter and costs drop.

4. The government's response is to state that the system's ideology is being violated. It shows no concern that long waits are prohibiting some Canadians from getting tested or that private individuals are reducing the country's health-care costs.

5. In a final show of socialist hypocrisy, MPs and their families are allowed to use private facilities (which, according to Hajdu, should not exist and are illegal) and we, the taxpayers, are paying for their privilege.

That is what happens when the system is focused on sustaining a failed ideology instead of providing patient care.

A Loss of Physician Autonomy. Throughout history, physicians have resisted coming under the Medicare umbrella because of long-standing fears about losing their financial and professional autonomy. Under Medicare, provincial and federal governments both have ample opportunities to enter the once-sacrosanct doctor-patient relationship.

In the extenuating circumstances of the Depression, when no one could pay their medical bills, it was to the medical community's advantage to make an agreement to have the Saskatchewan government pay their fees. That lasted until 1949 when the Canadian Medical Association withdrew its support for this kind of agreement and physicians were free to let the market set their prices. Battles between governments and doctors continued to erupt over billing when Medicare was implemented in the 1960s and when extra-billing became a problem in the 1980s. The struggle continues even today.

A second long-standing fear that physicians have used to oppose Medicare is the potential loss of professional autonomy in directing their patients' care. In 2020, most physicians would admit that government measures to ration care have greatly compromised their autonomy over patient care. A surgeon cannot promise a patient that he can fix his knee within a particular time frame because it all depends on the waitlist. The same holds true for cancer therapies, referrals to specialists, and access to diagnostic technology. When doctors cannot control a patient's access to treatment, provide them with timely treatment, or even prescribe a particular drug for their condition, then we can essentially conclude that the doctor is not in control; the system is.

Chad Curley was a 37-year-old autoworker at the Chrysler assembly plant in Windsor. He was young and strong; when he was diagnosed with brain cancer, he fought hard for five long years. During that time, he endured two operations, and several years of radiation and chemotherapy trials. Eventually, the left side of his body became paralyzed and he was confined to a wheelchair.

After four years, doctors told Chad they had run out of options. His last MRI scan had shown increased tumour activity which suggested that the tumour had become resistant to the chemotherapy drugs. Further surgery would not be beneficial. Instead of giving up, Chad and his wife, Meira, went home and began to search the internet for possible life-saving therapies. They eventually came across a powerful two-drug cocktail (Avastin and CPT11) that had been shown to reduce the size of tumours. Chad went back to the neurologists with his find and three specialists agreed that Chad was a good candidate for this new drug.

The problem, of course, was that the drug was new and not yet on the Ontario government's list of approved drugs. Avastin was on the list, but not for combating brain cancer. They appealed to Ontario's minister of Health but were refused funding for the cocktail even though three specialists had recommended that Chad have access to the cocktail treatment.

The costs of the treatment were substantial, but with the help of friends, they raised enough money to fund the first two treatments. Miraculously, Chad improved and even developed some feeling on the side of his body that was paralyzed. Sadly, it was too little and too late. Chad passed away three months after his second treatment with the cocktail.[215] Under one-size-fits-all Medicare, it seems the doctor no longer knows what is best for his/her own patient; there is no room for innovative treatments or for physician autonomy.

---

[215] Amy Ridenour and Ryan Balis, "Brain Cancer Patient Denied Last-Chance Drug Despite Specialists' Recommendations," Shattered Lives:100 Victims of Government Health Care (Washington, DC: The National Center for Public Policy Research, 2009): 107-109.

A Loss of Patient Autonomy.

Aldo: "If a person has cancer, a heart attack or some life-threatening illness, our system is responsive. But if a person has a quality of life issue, it's different. For three years, I've bounced around from GPs to Orthopods, been fed anti-inflammatory pills and given cortisone shots. To be fair, a few doctors have offered what help they can within the confines of the system—but options are limited. Government-run anything cannot be progressive, that is a historical fact.

For 31 years, I've been paying taxes while taking care of myself and trying not to be a burden on the system. But now that I need help, it is a constant chase. To add insult to injury, I am prohibited from paying for timely medical care. Who gives bureaucrats and politicians the right to control my right to care? I have the right to live pain free. Or do I?"

James: "Canadians have the right to do what is necessary to protect their health and avoid suffering."

Amanda: "For God's sake... let the patient make a choice and pay if they want. It is a win-win as it unclogs the wait times and allows the person to get the surgery faster. If you work and earn money, you should be able to pay for things you want and need. So, make the current health care system less clogged and let those of us who have money, pay. What happened to democracy? If I work and make money, I should be able to have choices. Especially when it comes to my damn health."

Arthur: "Why can I pay for immediate medical treatment for my horse or dog, but not for me? Maybe I prefer to pay for my right to have immediate care rather than having a Starbucks coffee every day!"

Monica: "I just want to say that I am not wealthy and if I choose to mortgage my house, spend my life savings or rack up my line of credit to get faster relief from pain, then it is my right and everyone else's. What is the NDP going to do next? Tell us what type of car we can drive??"

> Vidhu: "I am not sure how our government can decide to take away our choice to use our own money for our own health."
>
> Maureen: "What is wrong with me having healthcare choices? I can choose the quality of where l live, what school my children go to and what food l eat. Why can I not choose the healthcare that I want? I want health care when I decide it is needed. If the taxes that I already pay cannot provide me with access to health care, I should have the right to get medical care where I can."
>
> Al: "I am 68 years old and worked hard to have money in my retirement. I can buy special dental work, I can go on expensive vacations, I can drive an expensive car. Why shouldn't I be able to spend my money on something 'so frivolous' as my health and well-being?"
>
> Fernie: "I pay taxes and yet I have now paid out of my own pocket for something that should be provided - but I can no longer deal with the pain."[216]

Looking at the comments, it is surprising how often personal stories about frustrating health-care experiences eventually turn into questions and/or declarations about "my right," "my choice," or even "my money."The theme repeats over and over.

Patients' frustration is magnified when they discover that the Medicare they have paid for cannot provide them with the medical care that they need, but still denies them the right to use their own money to pay for their own medical care. If the government insists on maintaining its monopoly on health-care services, then it had better be able to provide that care. In any other situation, companies or individuals who cannot deliver the goods they have promised are fired or dismissed. It is only in Canada that we re-elect the politicians and governments who have failed to deliver on health-care promises.

The following comment captures these grievances and rightly places the blame on a system more focused on ideology than helping patients:

---

[216] Online comments at Charter Health, www.charterhealth.ca.

> "I am distressed that in an advanced first world country like Canada, I have found myself in serious discomfort with a significantly reduced quality of life and no option but to wait in interminable queues for specialist appointments and diagnostic tests. Treatment in these situations has been delayed for periods of between six months to a year which, to me, amounts to treatment being effectively withheld.
>
> Ironically, this situation is justified on the basis of socialist thinking although I wholly fail to understand the moral superiority it is supposed to represent. Perhaps it was morally superior when the system could cope with the numbers involved, but when it can't cope, it quickly becomes inhumane. I seriously doubt this is what Tommy Douglas originally intended.
>
> And I certainly do not see it as just or right that politicians should decree that I have no alternative. If I earn money during my lifetime by my own personal efforts and decide to use my personal resources to secure me the help I desperately need, then it is bordering on cruelty and totalitarianism to say you will not have this alternative or receive this help.
>
> In a Western democracy, surely this decision should be mine and not be taken from me by the State?"[217]
>
> Lesley, Sidney, B.C.

What About Autonomy to Choose Positive Outcomes? The ultimate hypocrisy in Canadian health care is that our federal government has recognized the autonomy of the person to make health-care decisions that result in death; yet it denies that same principle of autonomy to those who want to make health-care decisions that will relieve their pain, heal their disease, improve their quality of life, prolong their life, and/or restore their ability to work, provide for their families, and contribute to society. These are all positive outcomes that result in Canadians living better, healthier lives.

In 2016, Parliament passed legislation for what it terms medical assistance in dying (MAID), thereby guaranteeing that Canadians with terminal conditions have the right to request a doctor's assistance in ending one's life. Of course, the list of qualifying conditions continues to expand,

---

[217] Lesley, "I am Distressed," Charter Health, May 8, 2014, www.charterhealth.ca.

and it now includes situations where the prognosis is not terminal. Whether you agree with MAID or not, the point is that Canadian governments are willing to grant autonomy to those who want to die, yet continue to restrict the autonomy of those who want to live by preventing them from accessing the medical care that they need to get on with their lives.

The logic of this once again reminds us that have lost sight of what we are trying to accomplish in our health-care system. We should be striving to do all we can to bring healing and life-enhancing health care to Canadians. If the government cannot do that, then it is truly inhumane to prevent people from pursuing private care and using their own money to pay for that care.

> "Since the 1970s, Canadians have been trapped by their politicians inside an invisible medical jail. There is no other word for it."[218]
>
> William Gairdner

Many years ago, the *Globe and Mail* did a feature on a 48-year-old Montreal poet named Ken Hertz who had been living with a rare, paralyzing form of Parkinson's disease for ten years.[219] As his physical condition deteriorated and his situation became increasingly intolerable, Ken began to ask a friend to bring him right-to-die literature, and then a lethal supply of sleeping pills. His friend did not follow through, but at every meeting, Ken would ask, "Did you get them?"

Then, one day, everything changed. When his friend arrived for a visit, Ken handed him a note that he had painstakingly prepared. It said: "Life is beautiful, and I haven't lost my appetite for life. I have proved the doctors wrong about my capacity to live, despite the disease, for years and years. But if I do not get help, I cannot continue to survive."

Instead of asking his friend to help him die, Ken was now asking his friend to help him live.

For so long, our society has focused on the right to die that it likely has never occurred to many that there are a host of people across this land who want to live, but cannot get the medical care that they need to survive.

Fast forward to July of 2020 when it was reported that a Vancouver woman was prepared to kill herself because she could not get the medical care she needed to get through each day. She has lived with several chronic

---

[218] William D. Gairdner, *The Trouble with Canada ... Still!: A Citizen Speaks Out,* (Toronto: Key Porter Books, 2010): 294.
[219] Listening to a Cry of 'I Want to Live.' *Globe and Mail.* August 24, 1993.

conditions (chemical sensitivities, chronic fatigue, and constant pain) for 25 years, yet can no longer afford the treatments that she needs to help her get through the day.

Her line of credit is almost maxed out and, barring intervention or additional financial assistance from the government, she believes her only option is MAID.

> Question: If we really believe that health care based on socialism is morally superior, why do we not have a moral obligation to provide healing and medical care to those in need?

She says she is not depressed or distressed: But she cannot survive without her daily treatments and supplements. When she runs out of money to pay for them, she says, "There will just be a wall of brutal pain." *She believes that she must kill herself because she cannot afford health care* in our supposedly free and much-admired universal medical system.[220]

At a time when our culture is so overly obsessed with rights and equality, it is difficult to understand why our politicians create laws that offer death, yet refuse to make the legislative and administrative changes that would help people to make medical decisions that would allow them to live a pain-free life.

---

220 Ash Kelly, "Vancouver Woman with Disabilities Living in Pain, Forced into Debt, Seeks Medically Assisted Dying," City News, July 27, 2020, https://www.citynews1130.com/2020/07/27/vancouver-woman-disabilities-medically-assisted-dying/.

PART V

WAITLISTS, THE COURTS, AND COMMON SENSE

17

George

"Access to a waiting list is not access to healthcare."

Chief Justice Beverly McLachlin
Supreme Court of Canada
Chaoulli v. Quebec, June 9, 2005

When governments fail to make difficult decisions, those who want to bring about change in policy and law are often left with just one option—the courts. Since the *Charter of Rights and Freedoms* became a part of Canada's constitution in 1982, our country's highest court has shown a willingness to exert its authority over public policy by declaring long-standing laws unconstitutional and/or by directing Parliament to redraft legislation to fit our modern mores. For that reason, it is hardly surprising that Canadians have turned to the legal system to fix what ails our antiquated medical system.

For the most part, it has not gone well. There have been two significant court challenges where patients and their doctors have had the courage (and made the sacrifice) to challenge the restrictive laws that maintain Medicare's monopoly over the delivery of health care and keep patients waiting months or even years for medical care. In each case, the litigants claimed that forcing patients to wait for months and/or years without treatment was a violation of their rights and freedoms. A brief discussion of each case is integral to understanding why health-care policies remain largely unchanged and fail to put the needs of patients first.

George Zeliotis

You are not likely to find the name George Zeliotis on a list of Canada's great heroes. But perhaps he should be: As a man in his seventies and then again in his eighties, he refused to shrink and fade away when decisions made by health-care bureaucracies made a mockery of common sense.

Just two years ago at the ripe age of 87, he made headlines by challenging Quebec's health-care system on behalf of Alexandra, his wife of almost 60 years. Both of them are fluent in English and Greek, but not French; so, when Alexandra was diagnosed with dementia, George was reluctant to place her in a care home until he was assured that she would have English-speaking caregivers. When he received that assurance, he agreed to put her into the province's care.

Of course, nothing happened as promised and Alexandra was placed in a facility that was predominantly French and her caregivers spoke to her only in French. This language barrier was particularly cruel, given her advanced state of confusion and dementia. The situation became even more upsetting when George would call to check on her condition. The nurses refused to speak to him in English, saying, "Ici au Québec on parle français," meaning "Here in Quebec, we speak French." One nurse even hung up on him.[221]

George Zeliotis - a true health-care hero who fought the system for common sense changes to help his wife and took part in a landmark legal battle over health care in Quebec.[222]

So George took his story to the Montreal media, where he described the lack of compassion offered to Alexandra and to him as he attempted to

[221] Nick Kirmse, "Montreal Man Says Wife with Dementia Denied Care in English," CTV News, August 19, 2018, https://www.ctvnews.ca/canada/montreal-man-says-wife-with-dementia-denied-care-in-english-1.4058770.

[222] CBC photo of George Zeliotis, https://www.cbc.ca/gfx/pix/zeliotis_george050610.jpg.

communicate with her nurses. The publicity immediately moved Quebec's minister of health to declare this "unacceptable" and to promise a swift change in Alexandra's circumstances, saying, "Efforts are being made as we speak to make sure that the patient will be transferred as soon as possible."

Despite public promises, the transfer never happened because there was nowhere for her to go. Alexandra only received a reprieve from the confusion when a case of pneumonia sent her to a local hospital and the media stories caught the compassionate eye of Jennifer Boivin, area manager for St. Elizabeth Health Care, a private, non-profit home-care agency.

The story moved her and she felt that Alexandra deserved to have the comfort and companionship of English-speaking caregivers as long as she needed them in both the public hospital and the nursing home. The leaders at this private agency were able to innovate and act (assess the situation, come up with a solution, and then make the necessary staffing changes) to provide personnel to support a patient who needed help in the public health-care system. In contrast, the public system (whether from a lack of will or an inability to adapt to changing circumstances) was unable to provide some of the most basic needs for patient well-being—human interaction and communication in a language she could understand. George said their response was "like something came from God—a gift."

As you read on, you will realize it is a gift that he and his wife richly deserved, as George's previous efforts in advocating for timely health care inspired positive changes to the medical system in Quebec and spared many people the agony of unduly long waits for medical care.

Fed Up with Waiting

Twenty years earlier, in 1995, George himself struggled to access the medical care that he needed. When the retired chemical salesman had his left hip replaced in 1994, he was left with an unusual complication: His left leg was now 0.5 centimetres shorter than his right. He tried to fix the problem with customized shoes that had a thicker sole on the left shoe, but it was not enough to prevent the agonizing back pain that stemmed from his hip replacement.

George was familiar with the waitlist situation in Quebec because he had waited a year for a cardiac bypass operation that he finally underwent in 1992. He had waited another year for the hip surgery that had left him with searing back pain that was so bad, George says, "There were times when I was in so much pain that I wanted to commit suicide."[223]

The misery of that surgery started George on one more lengthy wait for a second hip operation that would alleviate some of his pain. It was the third time in five years that he had to endure unbearable pain while waiting for Canada's health-care system to find time to care for his medical needs. With his physical resources worn down, he became addicted to painkillers as he waited more than one year again for medical help.

George had no other options to obtain medical care as Quebec laws prohibited patients from purchasing private insurance for treatments and/or services covered by the *Canada Health Act.* Private clinics did exist, but they were too expensive for most people because it was illegal for Quebec citizens to buy private health insurance. As a result, going to the United States for surgery was his only legal option, but the price tag was too high for George in his retirement. If George had been able to purchase private health insurance, surgery in a private clinic would have been very affordable.

At the same, George's physician, Dr. Jacques Chaoulli, was proving to be an innovator in the Quebec health-care system by changing the way medical care is delivered. Rather than meet patients in his office, he attended to them in their own homes. He tried to obtain a licence that, for the purposes of billing, essentially made his services the equivalent of an independent private hospital. However, the province denied his request because of Quebec's laws against private health insurance. That is when Chaoulli and George joined forces to initiate what proved to be a landmark legal challenge to the ban on buying private insurance.

His argument was that patients should not be left to suffer in pain without any options. If the public system cannot provide timely care, then patients should have the right to purchase insurance to cover their own private care. It is a violation of a patient's right to life and personal security to be abandoned on a waitlist without medical care for an unknown period of time.

Their legal journey began with a lawsuit against the province in 1997. In 2000, the Quebec Superior Court stood with the government, reinforcing the notion that the ban on private health insurance protected the rights of all and was therefore more important than private insurance that would protect the rights of a few. In 2002, the Quebec Court of Appeal upheld the ruling.

---

[223] Aaron Derfel, "The Cost of Health Cuts, Part 2: He Made Surgery Wait Times a National Priority," *Montreal Gazette*, October 22, 2014.

But they continued their battle and eventually wound up in the Supreme Court of Canada where they argued that forcing people to wait for medical treatment violated the fundamental protections of Quebec's *Charter of Human Rights and Freedoms* and the *Canadian Charter of Rights and Freedoms.*

George's story captured the media's attention and brought a national focus to the inhumanity of subjecting people to years-long waits for what doctors have deemed to be medically necessary treatment. Their persistence paid off and, in June 2005, after eight years of legal wrangling, the Supreme Court ruled (narrowly) in their favour. The Court struck down the province's prohibition on the purchase of private insurance, by determining that leaving Quebecers like George on a waitlist without medical care is a violation of their right to "life, and to personal security, inviolability and freedom" under Quebec's *Charter of Human Rights and Freedoms.*

Unfortunately, the justices could not decide whether the ban also violated Canada's *Charter of Rights and Freedoms* and so the decision only applies to Quebec. Even so, the ruling is significant in that some Supreme Court justices obviously recognized that waitlists stemming from the government's health-care monopoly have a pernicious impact on Canadians' health and its Chaoulli ruling included these salient statements:[224]

- "Access to a waiting list is not access to health care."
- "The evidence shows that delays in the public health-care system are widespread and patients die as a result of waiting lists for public health care."
- The "prohibition on health insurance results in physical and psychological suffering."

In 2014, a decade after the decision made headlines across the country, the *Montreal Gazette* interviewed George, describing him as the "man who took on Canada's broken health-care system and won." George told the reporter, "It was worth it," while Alexandra proudly proclaimed, "He accomplished something. He wanted the wait times to go down and they did go down."[225]

Years later, the question remains, was it a moral victory only or did it produce concrete changes in Quebec's policies?

---

[224] Chaoulli v. Quebec, The Supreme Court of Canada, 2005.
[225] Aaron Derfel, "The Cost of Health Cuts, Part 2: He Made Surgery Wait Times a National Priority," *Montreal Gazette*, October 22, 2014.

The Aftermath of the Chaoulli Decision

Naturally, the ruling immediately "raised fears that a two-tier health-care system will arise to replace the whole country's universal publicly funded system."[226] Across Canada, throughout government circles, and in the offices of health-care administrators it was said to be the "end of Medicare as we know it," while columnist Jeffrey Simpson of the *Globe and Mail* wrote: "the sacred trust—or sacred cow—of public only medicine is finished."[227]

However, 15 years later, none of these fears have come to fruition. It is safe to say that the Court's decision did not destroy Medicare or create a two-tier health-care system in Quebec or anywhere else. All it did was bring Quebec's laws into line with those of 196 other countries where people can pay to purchase medical care; or to be more accurate, to purchase relief from pain and suffering.

Ten years after the landmark decision, the Montreal Economic Institute reviewed the province's response to the Chaoulli decision and documented three reforms that had taken place:[228]

Duplicate Private Insurance. The Quebec government now allows its citizens to purchase private insurance for the three surgeries with the longest waits (knee and hip replacement, and cataract surgery). Other provinces and territories still prohibit the purchase of private insurance.

Despite all the fears of a madcap frenzy of U.S.-style medical insurance replacing public health insurance, there was no significant uptick in the demand for private insurance and American insurers did not invade the marketplace. Instead, insurers likely considered that the medical insurance market remained quite limited as they could only offer coverage for three procedures.

Specialized Medical Centres. In an effort to retain some amount of credibility, the Quebec government resorted to an old PR trick (change the offending name without changing the issue at the heart of the offence) and "private surgery clinics" were magically transformed into "specialized medical centres." This slight modification kept the clinics up and running, while

---

[226] D. Spurgeon, "Canadian Supreme Court Upholds Right to Take out Private Health Insurance," *British Medical Journal* 330(7505), 2005: 1408. doi: 10.1136/bmj.330.7505.1408.

[227] Ibid.

[228] Y. Labrie, "The Chaoulli Decision and Health Care Reform: A Missed Opportunity?" Montreal Economic Institute. 2015, https://www.iedm.org/sites/default/files/pub_files/lepoint0415_en.pdf.

eliminating opportunities for the public to dwell on the implications of "private" care in our universal health-care system. The centres were allowed to sign contracts with public hospitals to take over a specific number of surgeries and/or treatments.

Better Management of Wait Times. A new database was developed to track wait times for various procedures. While wait times improved and stabilized, about 20 percent of patients still wait more than six months for a hip or knee operation. Like all provinces, wait times continue to increase; although, based on 2019 data, Quebec seems to be in a better position than most provinces. Quebec had the second shortest wait times in Canada (16.3 weeks from date of visiting a GP to receiving treatment), just behind Ontario (16.0 weeks).

18

Dr. Brian Day

"Canada is the only country on Earth in which there are laws that prevent its citizens from accessing private insurance. Last summer, I was invited as an opening speaker at an international conference of health executives being held in Budapest. Delegates from around the world were in attendance. I was invited because of scepticism that a country like Canada could force its citizens to "suffer and die on wait lists" (a phrase from the Supreme Court ruling in Chaoulli). Delegates from China were particularly shocked that governments within Canada could claim sovereignty over the health of its citizens. 'In China, government limits certain freedoms, but would never prevent an individual from caring for their own bodily health,' they said."[229]

Dr. Brian Day
Founder of the Cambie Surgical Centre
Canada's largest private surgical facility

Allow me to introduce you to West Coast health-care innovator Dr. Brian Day, a man who is widely known as:

- The former president of the Canadian Medical Association, an award-winning researcher and a leading orthopedic surgeon;
- A pioneer in bringing arthroscopic (minimally invasive) surgery to Canada;
- A contributor to the development of the world's first surgical robot;
- A world-renowned lecturer who has published more than 200 articles and book chapters;

[229] Brian Day, "A Constitutional Solution for an Ailing Health System?" *B.C. Medical Journal* (62) 5, 12, 2020.

- The founder of one of Canada's first private surgical facilities (the Cambie Surgery Centre); and
- The man who is currently making headlines for challenging British Columbia's laws that prevent patients on long waitlists from using their own money to obtain medical treatment.

Dr. Brian Day[230]

In other words, he is a resourceful and skilled surgeon with impeccable credentials. Perhaps more than that, he is also willing to confront the status quo in the hope of creating a medical system that better serves patients' needs. It is for this reason that, despite his many contributions to the advancement of medicine, Day's most significant contribution to Canadian health care may still lie ahead.

The legal battle began in 2009 when Day asked the courts to overturn B.C. legislation that prevents patients on long waitlists from purchasing private medical insurance and using private health-care options. In 2021, Day's lawsuit was still ongoing and will likely soon head to the Supreme Court of Canada, making it one of the longest cases in legal and Canadian history.

For the past decade, governments and Medicare advocates have vilified him, impugned his reputation, accused him of wanting to profit from the ills of Canadian patients, and wrongly declared that he is out to dismantle our

[230] Photo from www.brianday.ca.

country's health-care system. The hypocritical and petty nature of politics is clearly at play in all of this as the B.C. government spent tens of millions of dollars in an all-out assault to put an end to his lawsuit before it even reached the courts. Of course, it does this even as it continues to utilize his clinic's private services to solve public health-care problems by taking on the province's surgical overloads.

All of this has made for great headlines but, for the most part, the real story behind the media tags is not being told. The truth is that Day does not want to undermine or dismantle Medicare and his lawsuit "is about making Medicare better."[231]

What is his plan? He wants to work alongside—and with—the public health system to enhance Canadians' access to medical care. He wants private care to be an option that alleviates the strain on the public system and gives those who are languishing on waitlists an option to access immediate care. However, that option can only be available to all people if provincial governments legalize the purchase of private medical insurance (as has already happened in Quebec and is described in Chapter 17).

Far from being some kind of angry and selfish villain, Day is soft-spoken, understated, genuine, and earnest in his concern for patients. He is also generous. Over the years, his private clinic has performed more than 600 *pro bono* (or at very minimal cost) surgeries.

In fact, a *Calgary Herald* column by Nigel Hannaford shared Day's generosity and continued commitment to the public health system. Hannaford writes that Day had better equipment than the public hospitals (since the accreditation standards for private hospitals, surgery centres, and their equipment far exceed that which is required for public hospitals) and he would loan Cambie's backup surgical equipment to the public system and even leave it there so it could be used rather than sit unused at Cambie.

Day told Hannaford: "Our anesthesia machinery is brand-new, most of theirs is 15 years old. We lend them our equipment; we keep it there. They're broke; they can't afford their own."[232]

In response, Hannaford wrote: "There's something reassuring about a physician so committed to patient care that he buys surplus machines and keeps them where public system clients get the benefit."

---

[231] Camille Bains, "Debate over Private Health Care in B.C. Heads to Court Next Week," Canadian Press, September 1, 2016.
[232] Nigel Hannaford, "Tireless Agent for Change," *Calgary Herald*, August 25, 2007.

Frankly, Day may well be the best hope that Canadians currently have for restoring Canada's health-care system to its original goal of serving patients' medical needs. Here is his story.

Rationed Health Care Leads to Innovation

As discussed in earlier chapters, Canadian health care began to falter in the 1980s. Doctors continued their Medicare and compensation feuds with provincial and federal governments, and extra-billing (although illegal) became a relatively common practice. Expensive and rapidly changing technology quickly infiltrated the field of medicine, as did costly drugs, complex operations, and pricey diagnostics. The cost of even the most basic medical care grew exponentially as these technological innovations morphed into the common tools of modern medical practice.

Naturally, this growing list of expensive services pushed health-care costs beyond what any public system could afford. As budgets were strained, Canada's health-care system began to reduce costs in the only way it could—by restricting access to operations, diagnostic procedures, and specialists. As the practice of rationing continued, waitlists began and they have been with us ever since.

Day was one of the specialists who was seriously impacted by a decade of cuts. As an example of rationed procedures, Day says his "operating room time was whittled down from 22 hours per week to 17 hours, and then to just five hours per week. I had 450 patients waiting for surgeries, yet I had only five hours of O.R. time and could only do two or three simple surgeries per week."[233]

As the restrictions became commonplace, some surgeons struggled to obtain sufficient operating time to maintain their professional competencies and credentials. Many specialists left for other countries so they could practice medicine without government interference, and this resulted in the brain drain that depleted the ranks of Canada's medical and research communities in the 1980s and 1990s.

Day recalls when he served as chair of the residency academic program in the Department of Orthopedics at the University of British Columbia and says that he saw 16 orthopedic residents graduate over a six-year period, but only five stayed in Canada. What is even worse, according to Day, is, "They didn't want to leave, but we couldn't give them any O.R. time."[234]

---

[233] Michael McCarthy, "Brian Day: CMA's Next President Supports Private Health Care," T*he Lancet*, vol. 368:1321, October 2006, https://doi.org/10.1016/S0140-6736(06)69542-1.

[234] Ibid.

Years later, in 2007, the problem of retaining surgeons was still obvious. Day wrote that 50 percent of graduates in the fields of orthopedic and neurological surgery left Canada within five years of completing their training because they could not get a job.[235]

Day was tempted to leave; that is, until the circumstances prompted him to think outside of the traditional health-care box. He eventually came up with a novel solution—a private surgical clinic and, in 1996, he founded the Cambie Surgery Centre. The for-profit Vancouver clinic created operating rooms for frustrated surgeons who could not get enough O.R. hours in public hospitals. As Day has said, "We had doctors who had patients who needed surgery, but there was no place for them to work."[236]

The surgery centre has grown over the years and today is used by more than 100 surgeons who work as many hours each week as they can in the public system and then use their talents to serve others through the Cambie Clinic. In other words, the clinic was not created to enrich surgeons—it was established out of necessity by surgeons who needed a place to work. Can you imagine functioning as a surgeon if you only have five hours per week in the operating room and 450 patients on a waitlist?

The NDP government at that time (under premiers Mike Harcourt and Glen Clark) did nothing to prevent the creation of the Cambie clinic, and stood by as it grew from a design on paper to bricks and mortar. In fact, at one point, then-NDP premier Ujjal Dosanjh said: "It would do us no good to shut down Day's clinic if we can't provide those services elsewhere."[237]

One would think that logic would still hold true today as waitlists are much longer than they were at that time. But, as will become clear in the next couple of chapters, never underestimate a government's ability to defend, rationalize, and fund that which involves the least amount of common sense.

The Twisted Legalities of Private Health Care

There are hundreds of private health-care and diagnostic clinics across Canada: Fertility clinics (gynecology) offering IVF and other services, plastic surgery centres, and ophthalmology clinics (cataract removal and other surgeries). Dermatologists, vein clinics, foot clinics; the list goes on. They can all be easily accessed at your convenience and with peace of mind (since

---

[235] Brian Day, "Divided We Stand, Divided We Fall," *British Columbia Medical Association Journal*, April 01, 2007.

[236] Sally C. Pipes, *False Premise, False Promise: The Disastrous Reality of Medicare for All*, (New York: Encounter Books, 2020): 45.

[237] Ian Mulgrew, "Private Clinics are the Necessary but Unwanted Foster Child of Health Care," *Vancouver Sun*, April 8, 2018.

private facilities have higher accreditation standards than hospitals and government-run clinics, they tend to have better equipment and facilities).

Provincial and the federal governments do not have an issue with these private clinics because they primarily offer elective procedures. Because each province rather arbitrarily selects which procedures it will cover, the kinds of services available in each province may differ.

The controversy with private clinics emerges when they offer medically necessary surgeries and procedures that are covered by Medicare (such as knee replacements, hip surgeries, etc.). *The government refuses to allow citizens to choose to pay for these procedures and that is why the waitlists grow and patients have no option but to leave the country for rapid treatment.* So you can pay for plastic surgery to enhance your appearance, but it is illegal for you to pay for surgery that will replace a knee or remove a gallstone. That, apparently, is something only the government can do.

This places the legality of surgical clinics (like Dr. Day's Cambie Clinic) into jeopardy under the *Canada Health Act*; it also encourages some federal health ministers (depending on their political stripe) to threaten to withhold health-care transfer payments from provinces that allow such clinics to persist.

The B.C. government was content to ignore the laws surrounding private clinics until Day decided that it was time to banish the laws that were being deliberately ignored anyway. Defending laws that are not being enforced is counterproductive, to say the least. But matters enter into the realm of the absurd when the unbending rules of the *Canada Health Act* obligate the B.C. government to spend tens of millions of dollars to defend those laws in the courts.

That is why Day has spent the past decade in a legal battle with the British Columbia government. He believes that patients on a waiting list should have an option to obtain medical care. *As he often says, the government cannot create a monopoly to deliver health care, not deliver it as promised, and then make it illegal for patients to obtain care elsewhere.* After all, the federal government monitors and even forces the breakup of corporate monopolies that create an unfair market for consumers, so why should it be allowed to continue a monopoly that is so unfair to Canadian patients?

He argues that the restriction on private medical insurance violates patients' constitutional rights by preventing them from accessing timely care and forcing them to sit on a waiting list that is almost certainly measured in months, if not years. A result, this legal case is similar to the Chaoulli case where the Supreme Court ruled that bans on private insurance violated Quebec's provincial *Charter of Rights and Human Freedoms*.

What difference would it make if private health insurance could be legally purchased?

It would make private health care accessible to all Canadians, not simply to the rich or those who have special privileges as outlined below. If people could purchase private medical insurance, private care would become affordable, readily accessible, and a viable health-care option for most people.

Private medical clinics are not going anywhere and allowing the purchase of private health insurance is the only way that private and public health care can be fairly and equally available to all.

Who Enjoys the Privilege of Private Health Care?

Most citizens would be surprised at the kinds of individuals and groups who are allowed to bypass the very laws that restrict most of us from using private health care. Indeed, the list of all who have special access privileges strongly reinforces the notion that Canadians do not share equal access to health care, despite the myth that many believe. So, what kind of people use a private surgical facility? You will be very surprised.

1. ***Those with Money Represent Just 10 percent of the Clientele at Day's Clinic.*** The first inclination of many is to point fingers at "the rich" and "entitled" but that perception is entirely wrong. Those who pay out of pocket for services covered under Medicare comprise just 10 percent of Cambie clinic patients.[238]

   Remember that wealthy people have always had an opportunity to bypass Canadian waitlists by travelling to the United States or some other country for medical care when they find themselves waiting. By using private clinics in Canada, these people are, at the very least, keeping their names off of public waitlists so others can advance and keeping their monetary investment in Canada where it provides economic benefits for the entire health-care system. This includes, but is not limited to, an extended list of health-care personnel (including doctors, nurses, medical assistants, contract labourers, and

[238] Tom Blackwell, "Inside the Nearly Eight-year Long Fight of Brian Day, the Doctor who Would Free Canadians from Medicare," *National Post*, September 1, 2016.

housekeepers, etc.), as well as those who make and sell O.R. supplies and medical equipment, etc.

Further, while the rich may have the added option of seeking private care, many of them continue to make huge donations that help to sustain the public health-care system. Every time you see a name on a building or on a wall plaque, it represents someone who may have a greater opportunity to use private care but has still graciously offered their support to our government's strapped health-care system.

So who are the other 90 percent using private health care?

2. ***Unionized Workers Covered by the Worker's Compensation Board (WCB).*** Unionized workers (through WCB) comprise the "most common single demographic" of a patient coming to the Cambie Clinic.[239] WCB is essentially a private insurance company (owned by employers) and it is cheaper for them to pay for immediate treatment than to make payments to employees who are off work for long periods of time while they wait for medical care in the public system.

   Only workers who have WCB coverage can get prioritized and fully paid surgeries in the private sector. Other workers (of any kind) have to wait (sometimes years) for their medical care, as do WCB workers who happen to injure themselves at home instead of at work.

   One of the witnesses in Day's trial was a welder who had injured the ligaments in his knee while on the job. With his WCB protection, he immediately had his injury fixed at the Cambie Clinic. A few years later, the same worker suffered from a similar injury to his other knee, but it occurred while he was playing sports. The injury affected his ability to work and earn an income just as much as his first knee injury, yet because he was not injured on the job, WCB did not cover the costs of his second injury or provide him with prioritized medical care.

---

[239] Douglas Quan, "'Monopolies are Very Poor for the End Consumer,' Says BC Doctor behind Long Push for Private Care," *National Post*, November 25, 2019.

3. ***Unions, Crown Corporations, and Those with Connections.*** Day testified in the lawsuit against the B.C. government that "health authorities and provincial Crown corporations such as BC Hydro paid for private surgeries for their employees, as have Canada Post and unions including those for nurses, plumbers, postal workers, and boiler workers. He has also provided private surgeries and services for judges and senators."[240]

   The hypocrisy is clear, leading Day to comment, "Strangely, patients treated at our private clinics include leaders from the very groups that are going to court to make sure others can't receive the same benefits that they have enjoyed. Hypocrisy reigns supreme."[241]

   Day later provided more details about the hypocrisy and inequities of those who can access private care in an article he wrote for the *B.C. Medical Journal*: "Those who are injured at work, federal employees, non-residents and federal prisoners all have access to private care. Even at the trial, there was uncontested and unchallenged evidence to show that the representatives of all groups that opposed us in court, including the office of the defendant (the Atty. Gen. of BC), the leadership of the Canadian doctors for Medicare, and the employees opposing trade unions all used private clinics in BC*."*[242]

4. ***Anyone Who is Covered by Federal Health Insurance.*** This group includes federal employees, judges, senators, members of Parliament, members of the RCMP, the military, and even federal prisoners (in fact, it is illegal to put prisoners on a waitlist for medical care). All of these Canadians are entitled to jump the queue to attend private health facilities and to have that care paid for by our tax dollars.

   In other words, the same politicians who have created and upheld the laws that restrict Canadian patients from pursuing medical options outside of the public system are entitled to jump the queue and use the private system at the taxpayers' expense (see text box at end of

---

[240] Ian Mulgrew, "Final Arguments, Finally, in Big Brother Medicare Case," *Vancouver Sun*, November 17, 2019.
[241] Stephen Skyvington, "Tommy Douglas 'Would Not Be Happy' with our System," *Financial Post*, September 8, 2016.
[242] Brian Day, "A Constitutional Solution for an Ailing Health System?" *BC Medical Journal* (62) 5, 12, 2020.

chapter). Members of the RCMP and Canada's military can access private care through their federal health insurance. Professional athletes in all sports have access to private care.

Self-employed people and those who do not have insurance payments to cover them while they are unable to work often turn to private care -- the financial costs of paying for private care can be less than not being able to work over a long period of time while waiting for care in the public system. This was a common theme in many online stories. These people often have no choice but to use retirement money or to mortgage their homes to have surgery immediately so they could get back to work and continue to provide for their families and employees.

5. ***The B.C. government.*** It contracts with the Cambie clinic to take on surgical patients to clear backlogs and this has been common practice for the past two decades. But the incongruities continue and the BC government remains caught in the middle of having to publicly reject private care in order to enforce the *Canada Health Act* and keep federal health transfer payments flowing its way, while making deals with private clinics to take on patients when the public health-care system is overwhelmed. That forces politicians into a corner where contradictory statements are just another part of the job. In 2015, B.C.'s health minister said, "The use of private surgical clinics within the publicly paid and publicly administered health-care system has always been an important part of the system," at the same time as:

   - He declared that B.C. remains fully against a two-tier health system;
   - The Vancouver Island Health Authority was actively seeking private surgical clinics to conduct 55,000 day surgeries over five years;[243] and
   - The B.C. government was spending millions of dollars in legal bills in an attempt to shut down private surgical clinics.

---

243 Rob Shaw and Matthew Robinson, "BC Calls on Private Surgery Centres to Help Clear up Wait Lists," *Vancouver Sun*, June 1, 2015.

- In May 2020, it was also announced that private clinics would again play a key role in helping to clear up the huge waitlists caused by the COVID-19 pandemic.[244]

Confused? You should be. This is blatant hypocrisy. All citizens should understand the clear double standard that exists between the health care for government members (both federal and provincial) and other elites; and the public health care that the rest of the population uses.

Health Care for the Rest of Us

It is one thing for there to be a double standard as to who gets first access to treatment in our overwhelmed medical system. It is quite another for those who enjoy special access to medical care to be the very ones who defend the status quo thinking that keeps the rest of us from accessing the same level of care. Further, it is almost more than Canadians should have to bear when a provincial government spends tens of millions of dollars that could have been used for health care to challenge the legality of providing private care. Perhaps that is why angry patients often take to online forums to express their frustrations.

Two years ago, a Burnaby, B.C., cancer patient named Lynne was furious that the government would "go after private health care providers." She writes that the only reason she had a timely cancer diagnosis is that she "privately paid for two CT scans and a biopsy" and "my actions saved my life!"[245] Lynne reasoned that because she paid for private care, the public health system was more available to help others. Further, if she has the means to pay, why would the government insist she remain on a waitlist and a burden to the public system?

She continues: "Yet the government continues to go after doctors practising privately and their associated facilities."

Apparently, Lynne and her husband used to live in the U.K. where, as she states, "Public and private work alongside one another. Why can't B.C. do this? It truly feels like this province is in the dark ages."

David, another resident of Burnaby, realized how broken the health-care system was after suffering years of debilitating knee pain while waiting for treatment. When he finally had the surgery, it was not successful and left him

---

244 Moira Wyton, "Here's how BC Plans to Clear Surgical Backlog Caused by COVID-19," *The Tyee,* May 7, 2020, https://thetyee.ca/News/2020/05/07/BC-Surgical-Backlog/.

245 Lynne, "I am Upset," Charter Health, September 22, 2018, www.charterhealth.ca.

"barely able to walk due to the pain." His surgeon was not particularly concerned about fixing the problem, so David sought an MRI to "prove" that the operation did not work and an opinion from another surgeon. But both of those would take months or even a year just to get an appointment.[246]

That is when David did the one thing that he could: "I opened my wallet and went private." In less than three weeks, he had undergone an MRI that proved the original surgery had "gone sideways" and had the surgery that fixed the problem. Three weeks for a fix in the private system versus years of waiting in the public system: How can Canadians not cry out for change? This problem surfaced over and over in online stories, and it raises the question of how long Canadians should have to sacrifice their quality of life and their access to medical treatment, just so Canada can maintain a failed health-care system based on ideology?

David vows that should British Columbians lose access to private care, he will take his wallet to Seattle and provide an economic boost to America. His final comments are worthy of note by patients, Canadians, and those in government:

"The very notion that people with financial means to purchase healthcare services should be forced to remain ill instead in the name of 'equal access' is as abhorrent as it is naive. Nothing can stop me from going to Seattle, and I would rather be broke and healthy than suffer debilitating pain for the rest of my life while my money sits in the bank. Every service I buy in the private system is one that the public system doesn't have to pay for, freeing up its limited resources for the people who don't have money and improving their health care as well. Making private health care illegal is just a lose, lose, lose proposition. The poor lose, the rich lose, the economy loses. The only beneficiary is the medical services community in Seattle."

John feels the same way. Several years ago, he ran into a five-year waitlist for sinus surgery at St. Paul's Hospital in Vancouver. He quickly opted for private care and "while it did cost me a significant amount, I was happy to pay for the surgery to get cured. The way I looked at it was that it was the cost of a holiday that I would not be taking."[247]

Today, he is still paying for private health services such as massage, physiotherapy, and drugs to help his sinuses and his back (which was also operated on in a private centre). His conclusion? Why not allow patients to choose the best way to take care of their own pain?

---

[246] David, "I Suffered Debilitating Pain for Several YEARS in the Public System," Charter Health, September 12, 2016, www.charterhealth.ca.

[247] John, "Wait Time for Surgery at St. Paul's was about 5 Years!" Charter Health, September 29, 2018, www.charterhealth.ca.

He writes: "I was retired at the time so had to make choices to spend money on these surgeries. In both cases, I did not hesitate. As my dear mother used to say, 'without your health, you have nothing.'"

Over and over, the same online story with different names repeats itself. Peter, of Nanoose, B.C., was referred to an orthopedic surgeon in Victoria only to find out that his waitlist was so long that the clinic was not even booking appointments.[248]

William from Edmonton wonders: "Why should I risk everything under the current healthcare system waiting for surgery when I also have the option to receive my treatment via private means?"[249]

Tammy, also from Edmonton, says her husband is in severe pain as he waits to see a surgeon. She says: "If I had a dog and it was in this much pain, the veterinarian would treat the animal or put it down. This is freaking ridiculous and we should all call the government to complain. This is inhumane treatment and needs to stop."[250]

Patricia and her family moved to Canada from Australia and she was shocked when she "injured a tendon in my rotator cuff" and had to wait four months, in pain, just to get an ultrasound scan. She says she asked her doctor if he could expedite it, but he simply shook his head and told her, "You'll get used to it." She ended up going to a private clinic, but still feels badly for those who cannot afford to do so.

Patricia says, "In Australia there is the option to go private whereas here in Canada everyone has to wait, and wait, and wait, sometimes in debilitating pain. It's enough to drive us back to Australia. In my opinion, Canada, and especially B.C., gives more attention to the whales, salmon and bears than they do to human beings."[251]

Stanley is a 75-year-old man in Campbell River, B.C., who had a long-time back injury that eventually kept him from sleeping or walking.[252] A trip to the local emergency room put him on a waitlist for an MRI in six months. Then his family doctor reviewed the scan and said he needed to see a surgeon. The wait was a minimum of 18 months just to see the specialist and surgery would be another wait after that. His doctor urged him to try private

---

[248] Peter, Charter Health, n.d., www.charterhealth.ca.

[249] William, "Injured on the Job," Charter Health, October 16, 2016, www.charterhealth.ca.

[250] Tammy, Charter Health, n.d., www.charterhealth.ca.

[251] Patricia, " I Injured a Tendon," Charter Health, December 25, 2018, www.charterhealth.ca.

[252] Stanley, "Had a very Serious Back Issue for 15 Years," Charter Health, September 9, 2018, www.charterhealth.ca.

surgical care in Vancouver, so he did. Within a couple of weeks, he had met the surgeon, had the surgery, and "was amazed when I woke up my back pain was gone." Since then, he writes, "my quality of life has improved substantially."

Why should a seventy-five-year-old have to wait at least three years to get his pain treated? As Stanley says, "When you're 75, three years is a long time."

19

The Blame Game

In the Dr. Brian Day trial, government lawyers described patients seeking to mitigate their pain and suffering as 'parasitic.'[253]

In 2009, Dr. Brian Day launched a lawsuit against the B.C. government claiming that the current laws against private medical insurance prevent patients from accessing timely medical care and force them to endure lengthy wait times that often exacerbate their health problems.

He was joined in the lawsuit by others who are collectively known as the *plaintiffs*. They include Day, the Cambie Surgery Centre, the Specialist Referral Clinic, and six patients who suffered harm as a result of being on an unreasonably long waitlist. Two patient plaintiffs died before the trial began in 2016; two more were children at the time. The other plaintiffs are Walid, whose story is told in Chapter 1, and Sharon, whose story will follow. The stories and names of the two children and Sharon are found in public court documents; however, this book will not dwell on the minors' stories, and "Sharon" is a pseudonym for the plaintiff as she did not wish to be involved in the preparation of this book.

The government's response to the patients in this legal action has been revealing. According to the lawyers, any additional harm from waiting is the fault of the patient because they are either too pro-active (Sharon) or not pro-active enough (Walid) for the public health-care system. The doctors in each case could have taken action, but never did and the lawyers presented this as an indication that the doctors did not believe that the medical problem was urgent. Apparently, problems related to delayed medical treatment are never a function of waitlists.

As *Vancouver Sun* reporter Ian Mulgrew later wrote: "Listening to federal and provincial government lawyers, you'd think people would be

---

[253] Brian Day, "A Constitutional Solution for an Ailing Health System?" *BC Medical Journal* (62) 5, 12, 2020.

grateful for the chance to suffer in surgical and diagnostic queues under the guise of receiving health care."[254]

Sharon

At 35, Sharon was enjoying that stage in life when every cup that you have seems full, and it is hard to imagine things being any other way. She was happily married and the mother of two young children; in addition to these roles, she also worked part-time in a vocation that was very meaningful to her. In short, hers was a world filled with family, friends, and community.

Then, something changed. Sharon experienced abdominal pain, followed by the appearance of blood and mucous in her stool. She was fully aware that these were not indications of anything good and went to see her family doctor. He immediately referred her to a specialist for a colonoscopy and consultation.[255] The process seemed routine enough -- except that her appointment with the specialist was scheduled for November and this was just the second day of May. Sharon faced a seven-month wait to see the specialist and, as the doctor told her, that appointment would be for a consultation only. If the specialist thought it was necessary, a diagnostic colonoscopy would be scheduled some time after that.

For the next month, Sharon waited. She was frustrated about the long wait and as the days went on, pain began to grow in her back and side. At the end of May, Sharon attended a walk-in clinic which accomplished little, as the physician simply told her to go to the emergency department if the pain continued to get worse. Sure enough, it did and by the next day she was in the emergency department of her local hospital. While there, she had blood tests that led her doctor to conclude that she was obviously a "healthy 35-year-old woman."

The news may have been comforting on some level, but a discussion of her symptoms with the doctor was not exactly reassuring. Sharon mentioned that she was waiting for a colonoscopy and asked if there was any way that she could see a specialist right away. But the ER doctor refused, saying that a specialist would "not be very impressed" if he made such a request for a healthy, young woman. Court documents captured his explanation as "a specialist would laugh at him if he made that request."

Sharon's fears deepened as she realized that he did not seem to be taking her complaints seriously. He arranged for an outpatient ultrasound to explore

[254] Ian Mulgrew, "Governments Downplay Public Health Care Failings," *Vancouver Sun*, November 30, 2019.

[255] Defendant's Closing Submissions to the Day court case, para 965.

the pain in her back and side, but beyond that, he did not seem willing to undertake any additional investigations. When she left the hospital, Sharon called the specialist's office to see if her November appointment could be expedited and asked to go on a cancellation list. But, as Walid, Ross, and a host of other patients have experienced, the receptionist was not overly helpful. She told Sharon that "everyone goes on the cancellation list" and it was unlikely that her consult could be expedited.

It was after this phone call that Sharon began to consider getting a diagnostic colonoscopy at a private clinic. Three days later, she had the ultrasound examination. Five days after that, on June 6, she saw her family doctor and her worst fears were realized: She had three masses on her liver.

In spite of these concerning results, her doctor still did not think "it was anything to worry about." He ordered a CT scan to get more information and, before she left the office that day, Sharon asked him what he thought about consulting a specialist at a private clinic to, at the very least, expedite a diagnosis. He agreed that it was reasonable for her to do so given her pain and the masses on her liver, yet still seemed unwilling to take action to expedite her appointment in the public system.

Based on her symptoms, the information gained from the ultrasound and her experience with doctors, Sharon concluded that she had no other option. She had mucous and blood in her stool, pain in her side, and three masses on her liver. Yet, in our broken health-care system that emphasizes equal access above medical necessity, all of that was still not enough to get an expedited appointment to see a gastroenterologist and have a colonoscopy. So, Sharon took action to get the answers she needed through the private health-care system.

By June 21, less than two weeks later, she had undergone both a consult and a colonoscopy at the Cambie Surgery Centre; she was diagnosed with an advanced stage of colon cancer that had metastasized to her liver. Once she had a diagnosis, Sharon was able to book an emergency appointment with a surgeon and met with him about one week later.

She had a successful surgery (in terms of removing cancer cells from her colon) on June 28 and, after a period of recovery, underwent three rounds of chemotherapy (two weeks for each round). On October 11, Sharon was admitted to hospital to undergo a second surgery to remove the cancerous masses on her liver. By November, doctors felt that she was cancer free and this was confirmed by a PET scan. As a preventative measure, Sharon underwent further radiation and chemotherapy over the next three months.

As we consider the trajectory of Sharon's journey, it is important to realize that Sharon completed:

- a consult with a specialist;
- a diagnostic colonoscopy;
- six weeks of chemotherapy;
- colon resection surgery; and
- a second surgery to remove the masses on her liver

before the November appointment date that the public health-care system had assigned her for a first consult with a specialist. By September 25, 2012, Sharon was informed that her disease was officially in remission.

Given her experience, Sharon signed onto Day's lawsuit as a patient plaintiff and submitted an affidavit that described her experience in public and then private health care. She knows the frustration of waiting for medical care and now understands that there are times when patients need to have an option outside of the public system. In her affidavit, she states: "Following my diagnosis, surgeries, and treatment, I am once again able to engage in my life as a wife, mother, daughter, sister, aunt and friend. I just returned to work part-time. I am enjoying life. I am so thankful that I was given the chance to fight the disease that was spreading through my body. It is important to me that I do whatever it takes to stay healthy for my family, particularly my two daughters. I am so thankful I was able to obtain an early diagnosis through SRC (Specialist Referral Clinic) and CSC (Cambie Surgery Centre), which allowed me to access the urgent treatment I required."[256]

Government Lawyers Blame Sharon. Most of us would agree that Sharon very likely saved her own life by being proactive in identifying and treating the problem. After all, the cancer was already in an advanced state and had metastasized to her liver by the time she had her first diagnostic ultrasound at the end of May. In fact, the specialists who diagnosed and treated Sharon told her that if she had "waited until November 2011 for the diagnostic colonoscopy in the public system, the likelihood of a successful outcome of the treatment would have been dramatically reduced." Yet, in the trial, government lawyers somehow managed to twist Sharon's story into an example of how well the public health-care system was working.

In their closing arguments, they wrote: "The plaintiffs allege that [Sharon's] ability to obtain a private colonoscopy allowed her to have more timely access to diagnosis, treatment and surgery than would have been

---

[256] Sharon's story has been adapted from her legal affidavit in the Day case.

possible in the public system. However, the evidence shows quite the contrary and that the public system could have, in fact, expedited [her] services."[257]

While common sense would dictate that a seven-month wait with three masses on one's liver is unacceptable, they argued that Sharon's family doctor had done the right thing in scheduling her for a non-urgent colonoscopy, and claimed that Sharon's seven-month wait for a consult was an "example of appropriate triaging" by a medical professional "who used their best judgement at the time in light of the symptoms indicated."[258] *They claimed that the waitlist did not keep Sharon from accessing treatment at an appropriate time; the real problem is that she chose to pursue care in the private sector and never gave the public system a chance to respond to her circumstances.*

The government lawyers argued that once all the diagnostic information was known, her doctor could have "pursued [an] expedited appointment" and "it likely would have materialized."[259]

Really? The lawyers came up with this determination based on what? The concern and motivation shown by the doctors whom she did see? The length of the waitlists for diagnostic procedures? Or consults with specialists? Even her family doctor, who informed her about the three masses on her liver, admitted he made no attempt to call the specialist and expedite her appointment.

We have already seen in the stories of Walid and Ross that a doctor's promise to expedite a diagnosis or an appointment is no guarantee that anything will happen. Even though Sharon had an advanced stage of cancer, her doctor tried to downplay the significance of the masses on her liver, saying, "he did not think [she] had anything to worry about."

Frankly, even with the off-chance that the liver masses might not be cancer, the mucous and blood in the stool, along with the abdominal pain and the masses, surely indicated that Sharon had a significant medical problem. Yet, the government lawyers argued there was no evidence that Sharon would have been harmed by waiting in the public system and indications of harm were "speculative only."[260] One has to wonder if these lawyers would feel the same way if Sharon had been their wife, daughter, or sister.

Government Lawyers Undermine Cancer Advocacy and Public Education. A second concerning twist is the ease with which the

---

[257] Defendant's Closing Submission, para 988.
[258] Ibid., para 976.
[259] Ibid., para 987.
[260] Ibid., para 980.

government lawyers could simply claim that, in Sharon's case, the plaintiff's lawyers were making a "broad generalization that diagnosing cancer at an earlier stage means it is more treatable."[261] In fact, in their final arguments, they claimed there is no evidence that:

- "An earlier diagnosis of cancer leads to a better prognosis"; or
- Turning to immediate care in the private system "may well have saved her life."

First, it is true that we do not know what would have happened to Sharon if she had waited. There is no way to know for certain that she would have done any better or any worse. Of course, lawyers will always be able to claim that any harm which stems from waiting for medical treatment is speculative: Conditions worsen, chances of a positive outcome decline, and people die on waitlists for medically necessary treatment. Yet, in legal-speak, there is no way to definitively correlate waiting for care to deteriorating health (or death) because the same thing could have happened if the patient had undergone treatment or attended a first an appointment. Even if the patient dies, it is all a game of speculation in a court of law.

However, if it is only speculative that Sharon's early treatment led to her defeating cancer, then surely it can be claimed to be equally speculative that she would have had the same level of care and outcome had she remained in the public system. If doctors are expected to act based on 'speculation,' then surely that 'speculation' should involve action that is in the best interests of helping the patient survive.

Second, it is utterly irresponsible and abhorrent for government lawyers to make claims that oppose all that modern medicine tells us about cancer and early detection. Medical evidence indicates that an early diagnosis offers a better chance at surviving cancer. In addition, Sharon's doctors (the specialists) gave their authoritative opinion that the "likelihood of a successful outcome would have been reduced" if Sharon had waited. Unfortunately, once again, we can never know for sure so that comment (no matter how true) is reduced to mere speculation in a court of law.

Putting all factors unique to Sharon's case aside, the American Cancer Society gives a 90 percent five-year survival rate for colon cancer that is found and treated when it is still localized. But if there are metastases to a distant

---

[261] Ibid., para 985.

organ such as the liver, as in Sharon's case, the survival rate drops to 14 percent.[262]

Debbie and Walid

Debbie and Walid's story is fully described in Chapter 1. Walid spent 30 months on a waitlist for surgery, which is ten times longer than the clinical guidelines suggest. Every day that passed meant Walid had a greater chance of permanent injury and a reduced chance for a good surgical outcome. When he finally had his surgery (in the United States), complications left him permanently paralyzed from the waist down. During periods of extended waits, Walid's mother, Debbie, did everything she possibly could to try to expedite Walid's appointments, obtain diagnostic scans, and get a date for his surgery. But she faced a bureaucratic wall, communications barriers, and received no help or guidance in finding options even when it was apparent that BC Children's Hospital could not help Walid in a timely manner.

Government Lawyers Continue to Play the Blame Game. If, as government lawyers claimed, Sharon's circumstances resulted from "failing to give the public health system a chance," then surely Walid's ridiculous 30-month wait was a result of Debbie putting too much faith in the public system. She is a nurse; she knew how the system worked and she did all she could to expedite appointments and procedures at every juncture, yet nothing happened. The surgeon and the health-care system failed Debbie and Walid in every way:

- The surgeon had said he had a treatment plan for Walid—he did not;
- The surgeon said he would follow Walid closely—he never did;
- The surgeon said he could expedite Walid's surgery if it became necessary—he did not (even when Walid's situation was critical);
- The surgeon said he had booked Walid for surgery—he never did;
- The surgeon said Walid needed MRI and CT scans—but he never made any arrangements for them;

262 The American Cancer Society, "Survival Rates for Colon Cancer," June 29, 2020, https://www.cancer.org/cancer/colon-rectal-cancer/detection-diagnosis-staging/survival-rates.html.

- Debbie offered to take Walid to a private centre and pay for scans, but the surgeon said they could only be properly done at BC Children's Hospital;
- Debbie asked the surgeon if the surgery could be done anywhere else (she was willing to mortgage her house if necessary), but the surgeon said no one else could do it; and
- Debbie asked the pediatrician to call the surgeon and expedite the surgery, but he never did.

At the trial, the surgeon told the court that his experience with Walid occurred at a "fairly desperate" time for BC Children's Hospital. His department was "overwhelmed" by the waitlists and needed more surgeons and operating room technicians.[263]

It is also worth noting that Walid's case triggered an investigation, a damning report by the Patient Care Quality Review Board, and ultimately, an apology from the provincial health minister. The report criticized the surgeon, the hospital, and the Provincial Health Services Authority for not meeting national and provincial surgery access targets, not following provincial and hospital policies to flag cases that had waited too long, not properly communicating with the family, and for its poor scheduling methods.[264] The board also found that Walid did not receive quality care and that treatment delays allowed his condition to unnecessarily deteriorate, increasing the risk to his health.[265]

Despite the Board's findings, the evidence of systemic problems, waitlist issues, clerical errors, and broken promises, government lawyers chose to put the blame on the doctors rather than acknowledge the two-year waitlist as a factor that denied timely care to Walid. They blamed the pediatrician who oversaw Walid's care in Kelowna and first made the "urgent" referral to the spinal surgeon at BC Children's Hospital. When questioned, the pediatrician acknowledged that he had the option of calling the surgeon to expedite matters, yet never did. He also failed to "look into alternative services" for Walid even though he had promised Debbie he would do so. His defence

---

263 Keith Fraser, "Surgeon Defends His Care of Teenage Boy on Lengthy Wait List Calling it a "Fairly Desperate Time,"Postmedia.com., October 7, 2016.

264 Pamela Fayerman, "Mother of Boy Paralyzed After Surgery Delays Throws Support Behind Private Clinic Owner's Lawsuit," *Vancouver Sun*, November 15, 2012.

265 Pamela Fayerman, "A Public Health System that Failed a Canadian Boy: The Saga of Walid Khalfallah," *Vancouver Sun*, November 18, 2012.

seemed to be that he felt the pediatric surgeon "could manage [Walid's] care appropriately."[266]

Then they blamed the pediatric surgeon and his office staff. In February 2011, the surgeon placed a handwritten note in his file to "book OR for this summer, not June." That same day, he wrote a letter to the pediatrician stating that he had already booked Walid for surgery. As it was obvious that the surgeon had not done what he promised, the defence's closing submissions stated: "There were evidently problems with [the surgeon's] booking and communication, which resulted in missed opportunities" and "[The surgeon's] office did a poor job of communicating with [Debbie] and ensuring that the scheduling stayed on track." It was also acknowledged that the surgeon and his office never explored out-of-province options for surgery.[267]

How Much Responsibility Does the Patient Bear?

Both of the above situations raise questions about how much responsibility belongs to the patient in ensuring that they receive timely medical care. Evidence was presented to show that the public system waits put their health in jeopardy, yet government lawyer Jonathan Penner told the judge: "They have not experienced any deprivation. Alternatively, (if they did) that could have been avoided within the existing public health-care system."[268]

Sharon's circumstances appeared critical and she did not wait long before accessing private care to get a diagnosis; yet, at trial, she was accused of "not giving the public system a chance."

For two years, Debbie watched her son's condition deteriorate rapidly and did all she could to try to obtain proper care for Walid in the public system; yet, at trial, she was accused of not exploring other options, being too emotional, acting too slowly to get care for Walid since she knew his situation was urgent, and finally, acting too quickly in taking Walid to the U.S. for surgery.

If the government claims that it is up to the patient to ensure they have timely access to care and to explore the public system for other options when the government monopoly on health care cannot provide timely access to care, then it is truly inhumane to not allow them to pursue private alternatives.

---

[266] Defendant's Closing Submissions, paras 1009, 1010, and 1011.

[267] Ibid., paras 1013, 1016, 1018, and 1019.

[268] Ian Mulgrew, "Private Clinics Haven't Proven Case, Says Government," *Vancouver Sun*, May 13, 2019.

20

The B.C. Government v. Common Sense

"[The government] cannot have it both ways. You cannot promise health care, then not deliver it in a timely way, then outlaw the patient's ability to access it independently."

Dr. Brian Day

This book was not written for the purpose of delving into legal arguments and court documents; it was written to provide a better understanding of how health-care waitlists directly (and negatively) impact patient care.

The B.C. government spent an estimated $70 million (or more) of taxpayers' money to pay lawyers to oppose patients who had already suffered enough by not receiving timely, or even adequate, health care. It did not have to do this; the government could have used Dr. Brian Day's lawsuit as a stepping-stone to serious conversations about what is wrong with public health care and how we can improve it so it better serves Canadian patients. Alternatively, the government that claims it has no cash for health-care services could have used the $70 million to fix the problems and provide more health care to the people of B.C. Instead, the government locked taxpayers into funding a decade-long David vs. Goliath court case which, so far, has only offered evidence that both our health-care and legal systems have lost touch with common sense.

The Day trial in the B.C. Supreme Court was enlightening in that government lawyers were forced to defend waitlists and the health-care system in a court of law. Since there was no credible defence, government lawyers were reduced to using tactics such as legal gamesmanship, blaming the victims, blindly tossing out misleading statements, and over-using taxpayers' money in an effort to vastly outspend and, hopefully, bankrupt the plaintiffs before the trial could even begin.

We do not need to know in-depth legal details, but it is in every Canadian's interest to know about the legal and political games that the B.C. and federal governments played, and to see for themselves the dismissive attitudes their lawyers displayed towards patients, doctors, and health-care waitlists. Any legal details will be shared with as much brevity as possible.

Pre-Trial Games with Taxpayers' Money

Day filed the lawsuit in 2009. Due to a series of delays, the case did not make it to trial until 2016. That means government lawyers were spending a lot of billable hours filing pre-trial motions in an attempt to overwhelm the plaintiffs with paperwork and legal bills.

Game #1: Spend Money. Governments have an unending source of money and they made ample use of the provincial treasury by assigning a team of 20 or more lawyers to create legal issues that would delay the trial and keep Day tied up in pre-trial proceedings for years, in the hope that overwhelming legal costs would force him to drop his lawsuit before even getting to court.

The legal battle is far from over and, to date, Day's costs have been approximately $7 million, funded by donations, a remortgage on the Cambie Surgery Centre, and by Day himself. Even as the government has dragged the case out for years, angry patients and concerned citizens are still making contributions. In sharp contrast, it has also been reported that the B.C. government spent $20 million in just the first six months of the proceedings.[269] The case has now been ongoing for a decade and the best guess is that the government is outspending Day by a factor of ten, suggesting costs of $70 million or more.

The government then sent even more lawyers to the B.C. Supreme Court and the Court of Appeal to prevent the public release of financial information related to its trial expenses. The Canadian Constitution Foundation (CCF), which has provided Day with legal support, requested that the government disclose its trial expenses in 2017. After three years of legal battles at two levels of court, it was ruled that the numbers were subject to solicitor-client privilege and taxpayers will never know how much money was spent to oppose improvements to our health-care system.

Since then, the CCF has ceased its legal battle but commented in a press release that no matter how many millions of dollars are involved, even "a single dollar spent violating the constitutional rights of patients is a dollar too many."[270]

---

[269] Personal communication.

[270] Canadian Constitution Foundation Press Release, CCF disappointed that BC government will continue to hide the taxpayer costs of fighting against patient rights, August 24, 2020.

Game #2: Paperwork. Just weeks before the trial was scheduled to begin, the government suddenly discovered an additional 300,000 documents that it had neglected to disclose as required by law. This resulted in another six-month delay of trial so Day's lawyers could read through them. When that time period was up, the government forced another six-month delay by announcing that it needed more time to have another look at these same papers.[271]

$70 million could have provided B.C. patients with: [272]

- 9,500 days in intensive care
- 93,000 CT or MRI scans
- 45,000 patient-days in a hospital ward
- about 65,000 days of nursing services (based on $45/hour, a mid-range figure for B.C.)
- 300 family medicine doctors at $225,000 per year
- 156 orthopedic surgeons at $450,000 per year
- 215 psychiatrists at $325,000 per year
- 6,400 hip replacements at $11,000/surgery

As an example of government lawyers with too much time on their hands, a single affidavit by one health-care administrator was about 5,000 pages long. Can you imagine how many billable hours went into creating such a tome? It is almost impossible to imagine how many lawyers and billable hours were required to garner that single statement.[273]

---

271 Stephen Skyvington, "Tommy Douglas 'Would Not be Happy' with our System: Dr. Brian Day on his Fight for Medicare Freedom," *Financial Post*, September 8, 2016.

272 Hospital and MRI Rates, Canadian Hospital Rates, http://www.david-cummings.com/documents/canadian_hospital_rates.htm); mid-range nurses' salary taken from BC Nurses' Union Collective Agreement 2019-2022, https://www.bcnu.org/Contracts-Bargaining/Documents/NBA_Wage_Grid.pdf; physician salaries estimated based on CIHI, "Physicians in Canada, 2017…". https://secure.cihi.ca/free_products/Physicians_in_Canada_2017.pdf; hip replacement costs, *Hip and Knee Replacements in Canada: CJRR Annual Report 2018-2019*, CIHI, (https://www.cihi.ca/en/hip-and-knee-replacements-in-canada-cjrr-annual-report.

273 Ian Mulgrew, "Ottawa's Response to Medicare Challenge is, be Afraid," *Vancouver Sun*, April 18, 2019.

Vancouver Sun reporter Ian Mulgrew writes that the length of this trial and many aspects of it demonstrated that we not only have a broken health system, but also a broken legal system. He described the trial as "a stinging indictment of the legal system" and "a living testament to the screaming need for reform—high-priced judges and lawyers operating on essentially a 4 ½ hour working day."[274]

He continues by saying, "This litigation isn't even tilling new ground" since the Chaoulli case in Quebec had already been to the Supreme Court with similar arguments. As a result, much of the case could have been dealt with using "written arguments based on admitted facts about waiting times provided by BC's Medical Services Plan."[275] As Day commented in an interview with health-care analyst Stephen Skyvington, waitlists for access to care are very similar to waits for justice in that they are both "unacceptably long."[276]

What Happened at Trial

The government's arrogance was on full display when one of its lawyers told the media that Day's court case would amount to little more than "political theatre."[277] While he was right in predicting a theatrical production, he was very wrong about who would be putting on the show. During the trial, it was the plaintiffs who produced solid evidence, while government lawyers offered the court little but weary decades-old rhetoric.

A Defence without Evidence. There is no doubt that the lawyers representing the governments of B.C. and Canada were placed in an indefensible and highly unpopular position. How do you defend a health-care system that has one million Canadians waiting for treatment? How do you tell a courtroom that waitlists do no harm as they hear about a young man who was paralyzed by surgery after he waited ten times the recommended benchmark for treatment?

---

[274] Ian Mulgrew, "Court Cases Sail a Sea of Molasses, *Vancouver Sun*, January 11, 2020.

[275] Ibid.

[276] Stephen Skyvington, "Tommy Douglas 'Would Not be Happy' with our System: Dr. Brian Day on his Fight for Medicare Freedom," *Financial Post*, September 8, 2016.

[277] Camille Bains, "MD in Court to Claim Too-long Waits Give Patients Right to Pay for Private Health Care," Canadian Press/CBC, November 17, 2019, https://www.cbc.ca/news/canada/british-columbia/cambie-surgery-centre-trial-1.5363013BC.

The lawyers basically had to prove that the health-care system works and that any harm suffered by patients on a waitlist is justifiable. As a result, it had little to offer in terms of evidence, as shown below:

- The government did not call a single patient or a surgeon to support its arguments;[278]
- The government provided no factual or legal rebuttal to the plaintiff's complaints;[279]
- "How threadbare is the government's defence? It boils down to little more than don't blame us—it's those greedy doctors who don't act appropriately, exaggerate their waiting times and fail to hire good office staff or those patients who don't follow good self help advice."[280]
- "The senior government official offered little evidence to support the view that historically long surgical waiting lists serve the greater good."[281]

A Call to Ignore the Waitlist Data. "The trial has featured incessant government attempts to declare information and the opinion of those who work in the health-care system, including ministers, as irrelevant or to keep it out of evidence."[282]

The only hard evidence that the government had was detailed waitlist data that failed to support its case that the health-care system is working well. Consequently, the government did its best to keep the data out of the trial and asked that it be ignored for legal reasons.[283]

With no useful data in hand, federal government lawyer B.J. Wray tried to claim that waitlist data was not relevant to the case, saying, "The legal question in this case does not require your lordship to conduct a forensic

---

[278] Brian Day, Zoom meeting hosted by the Canadian Constitution Foundation. July 14, 2020.

[279] Ian Mulgrew, "BC Medicare Challenge More Blackeye than Broadway," *Vancouver Sun*, November 19, 2019.

[280] Ian Mulgrew, "Government in Denial over Medicare Crisis," *Vancouver Sun*, November 21, 2019.

[281] Ian Mulgrew, "Ottawa's Response to Medicare Challenge is, Be Afraid," *Vancouver Sun*, April 18, 2019.

[282] Ian Mulgrew, 'Private Clinics are the Necessary but Unwanted Foster Child of Health Care," *Vancouver Sun*, April 8, 2019.

[283] Ian Mulgrew, "Governments Downplay Public Health Care Failings," *Vancouver Sun*, December 2, 2019.

account of wait times, or to consider when waiting is reasonable or not or consider what the benchmark for a particular surgery should be. Those are questions that the government may wish to inquire through a public inquiry or some other form."[284] Frankly, if the judge is being asked to consider the harm that comes from waiting lists, both logic and common sense would suggest that he needs to hear the data.

That forced the plaintiffs' lawyers to call a 'hostile witness' to present the waitlist data to the court. As you can imagine, the testimony was devastating to the government's case. Of course, once the data were admitted into evidence, the government lawyers then insisted that the numbers (prepared by B.C.'s Ministry of Health) could not be trusted.

Day's lawyer managed to elicit the following information from government witnesses when they were queried about the waitlist data from the provincial health ministry:[285]

- 30,000 patients waited longer than the maximum medically accepted wait time.
- "Only 30 to 40% of patients with invasive cancers of the cervix, bladder, and prostate are treated within the maximum acceptable time, and these cancers are at risk of spreading while they wait."
- Government employees manipulated waitlist data. One witness admitted that a large health authority provided incorrect dates on booking sheets to the Government Surgical Patient Registry in an effort to make children's waitlists appear to be shorter than what they are.
- Doctors were forced to falsify waitlist data. A surgeon testified that he had been instructed by hospital authorities to change the number of consultations that he sees in order to make the waitlists for surgical procedures appear shorter than they were. Further, his department also received instructions to re-categorize Priority 4 patients ("moderate to severe pain and functional deficit") to Priority 5 ("mild pain, tolerable functional deficit") in order to make the waitlist seem more acceptable.

---

[284] Camille Bains, "Corporate Profits by BC Doctors Key in Private-Care Trial: Federal Lawyer," The Canadian Press, November 25, 2019.

[285] Brian Day, "A Constitution Solution for an Ailing Health System," *BC Medical Journal* (62) 5, 12, 2020.

In contrast, evidence to show that the system is not working was "damning" and confirmed the following: [286, 287]

- None of the health authorities even came close to meeting the target of providing colonoscopies to 85 percent of patients within the maximal acceptable wait time, thereby compromising their chances of a complete recovery.
- B.C. has never come close to meeting the federal benchmarks for knee or hip replacement surgeries or the maximal acceptable waiting times for more urgent patients.
- Patients (both adults and children) waited well beyond the maximal accepted time for spinal surgeries, with continuing pain, disability, and the substantial risk of permanent damage.
- B.C. wait times for diagnostic imaging (such as MRI and CT scans) are among the longest in Canada and much longer than other OECD countries. Only 46 percent of patients received their MRIs within the maximum acceptable waiting times.
- The capacity to perform additional surgeries exists, but the government will not (or cannot) pay for them.

> "Any denial of health care, by government or otherwise, is, in my opinion, a crime against humanity and is so particularly when it is done by government."[288]
>
> Jennifer, Vancouver BC
> www.charterhealth.ca

Government Witnesses who Lacked Credibility. The B.C. government presented the following 'expert' witnesses:[289]

---

[286] Ian Mulgrew, "Government in Denial over Medicare Crisis," *Vancouver Sun*, November 21, 2019.
[287] Ian Mulgrew, "Final Arguments, Finally, in Big Brother Medicare Case," *Vancouver Sun*, November 17, 2019.
[288] Jennifer, "Denial of Care is a Crime Against Humanity," Charter Health, n.d., www.charterhealth.ca.
[289] Brian Day, "A Constitutional Solution for an Ailing Health System?" *BC Medical Journal* (62) 5, 12, 2020.

- "Expert" witnesses who have been previously admonished by judges in other provinces for providing inappropriate and inaccurate evidence in court;
- A government expert on ethics who gave evidence suggesting that wealthier, productive individuals who pay more taxes should be prioritized ahead of others, including children and the elderly, for surgery.
- An expert witness (who swore under oath to be a non-advocate) who acknowledged that his affidavit evidence was researched and edited by the chair for the Canadian Doctors for Medicare, a participating respondent and an intervenor in the case.
- A government "desk expert" who opined on the New Zealand health system. The plaintiffs responded with a New Zealand "field expert," causing the government to withdraw both the report and its expert from the case.

Other Evidence that Confirmed Waitlist Problems. According to Dr. Roland Orfaly of the BC Anesthesiologists' Society, "the undisputed evidence in this trial demonstrates that patients are not achieving reasonable access to the medical care of anesthesiologists. Evidence of this lack of reasonable access has included facts about closed operating rooms, cancelled surgeries, excessive weight times and growing waitlists." Orfaly testified to the following:[290]

- Operating rooms sit empty while surgeons wait for surgery time;
- "[Patients] are experiencing pain and suffering, irreparable harm. Instead of access to care based on need, access is simply determined by the government's willingness and ability to deliver a certain volume and mixture of priority and non-priority health-care services."
- *The evidence at trial "demonstrates that hundreds or possibly even thousands of patients are dying annually on the waitlist for surgery."* Orfaly stated: "In 2015—16 in Fraser Health alone, there were 308 patient deaths amongst those waitlisted

[290] Ian Mulgrew, "BC Medicare Wait-Lists Leave Hundreds to Die, Court Told," *Vancouver Sun*, November 28, 2019.

for scheduled surgery." [NOTE: When extrapolated nationally, that equates to 6,500 patients a year or about 18 patients a day dying while waiting for surgery].

The Government's Defence of Medicare was Rhetoric, Blame, and Hypocrisy

All of the above presents a frightening picture of the inner workings of B.C.'s health-care system and its claim that waitlists are neither harmful nor justifiable. Highly questionable ethics, manipulated data, and hypocritical arguments about equal access were shown by some who have the best and most exclusive access via federal government employee health insurance. So how did the government lawyers defend the status quo in health care?

Claiming that Change is about Financial Gain. Repeated name calling and groundless speculation appeared to be a major focus of the attack on Day and his fellow plaintiffs. Government lawyers referred to him as "Dr. Profit" at every possible occasion both in court and in the media. Federal lawyer Wray told the court that profit for doctors is at the heart of the trial and that it threatens to undermine Canada's universal health-care system and its principles of equity and fairness. He told the court that the only conclusion to be drawn from this case is that "the corporate plaintiffs want the impugned provisions gone so they can implement their preferred business model and increase their bottom line."[291]

How many people can invest ten years in a legal trial and still make financial gains? Day is now 73 and the court case is nowhere near being over, but the government has told the court and the press that he is doing all this just to get rich. Day has paid dearly for the lawsuit; through legal fees, negative press, sacrifices of time, work, and wages to deal with the legal battle, and the remortgage and sale of the Cambie Clinic. As added proof that Day is not exactly enriching himself with his private clinic, a government audit (called as another delay tactic) showed that the clinic makes a profit of $65 on each $5,000 charged.[292] Do the math on that.

Fear Mongering. One of the intervenors in the case claimed: "This is such a profound threat to the health of everybody in Canada." He then went on to say that a legal win for Day would lead to a U.S.-style medical system, creating

---

[291] Camille Bains, "Corporate Profits by BC Doctors Key in Private Care Trial: Federal Lawyer," Canadian Press, November 26, 2019.

[292] Personal communication.

longer waits for average Canadians and skyrocketing costs as doctors charge patients directly."[293]

This is an interesting statement because there is no explanation as to how allowing patients to pay for private care (thereby removing themselves from the public waitlists) would lead to longer waits.

Skyrocketing costs? It never happened in Quebec or in any other country that has both public and private health-care systems.

As for a U.S.-style medical system, I think it is fair to say that no one in Canada wants that. In international comparisons, the United States is the only OECD country that may show health-care results that are worse than Canada, so anyone familiar with health-care administration and politics knows that we will never turn to the U.S. as a model for health care.[294] It is only used as a scare tactic because we share a border with the U.S. and frequently hear the news of their health-care failures.

There was no evidence presented to support these claims. In fact, to quote the plaintiff's lawyer, Peter Gall: "All we have is hypothetical fears not based on anything that has happened in the last 20 years. None of these concerns have arisen over the last 20 years. There is no evidence to date of any detriment or harm to the public system from private operators that would justify the prohibitions on access to private health care."[295]

Rhetoric. Claims such as those below are routinely made in defence of Medicare and this trial was no exception.

- "Medicare is being put on trial."[296]
- "If their constitutional challenge is successful, the door will swing wide open in British Columbia and across Canada for insurers to sell what will amount to private queue-jumping

---

[293] Camille Bains, "Debate over Private Healthcare in BC Heads to Court Next Week," Canadian Press, September 1, 2016.

[294] Commonwealth Fund, "International Health Policy Survey of Adults in 11 Countries," 2016, https://www.commonwealthfund.org/publications/surveys/2016/nov/2016-commonwealth-fund-international-health-policy-survey-adults.

[295] Ian Mulgrew, "B.C. Medicare Challenge More Black Eye than Broadway," *Vancouver Sun*, November 19, 2019.

[296] Camille Bains, "Debate Over Private Healthcare in B.C. Heads to Court Next Week," Canadian Press, September 1, 2016.

insurance for those who can afford it, potentially harming the rest of us."[297]

- "It's not an exaggeration to say that this case is about the future of Medicare in Canada."[298]

The Blame Game. In closing arguments, the government lawyers tried to claim that the blame for any problems with Medicare lay at the feet of lazy doctors, clingy patients, and justices at the Supreme Court of Canada who are not credible.[299]

- They described the doctor who took time off during the terminal illness of his late wife as cutting back on surgery in order to "to smell the roses."
- They made a similar claim about a doctor who underwent a quadruple heart bypass.
- They described patients seeking to mitigate their pain and suffering as "parasitic."
- They even claimed that the Supreme Court of Canada judges who made the Chaoulli decision to allow private medical insurance in Quebec had been "discredited." The evidence for this claim was opinion editorials written by the judges disagreeing with the decision.

Hypocrisy. B.C. government lawyer Jonathan Penner tossed out the following statements in his final defence:[300]

- "In my submission, what truly is shocking is this complete and utter disregard for the situation of anyone who is not in a position to come up with the funds to pay them to provide rapid surgical services."

---

[297] Ibid.

[298] Ian Mulgrew, "Governments Downplay Public Health Care Failings," *Vancouver Sun*, December 2, 2019.

[299] Brian Day, "A Constitutional Solution to an Ailing Health System?", *BC Medical Journal* (62) 5, 12, 2020.

[300] Camille Bains, "Private Clinics Would Harm Ordinary People Using Public System in BC: Lawyer," Canadian Press, February 25, 2020.

- "They seek the privileged, those few privileged British Columbians who require scheduled surgery and have the resources to pay for private care."
- Therefore, the legal challenge by the owner of a private clinic providing scheduled surgery for "affluent" patients should be denied.

B. J. Wray, lawyer for the federal government, laid out the same concerns, stating: "Canada's position is that if the plaintiffs are successful, the health-care system in British Columbia will be radically altered in favour of the privileged few and the lucky who can afford private care or who can qualify for private insurance."

This is a fascinating remark coming from a lawyer who is employed by the federal government and most likely enjoys special access to private clinics paid for by taxpayers. As mentioned throughout this book, those individuals who have federal government insurance can not only utilize private medical centres to access rapid care, but have the taxpayers cover the tab! These lucky members of society include federal employees, heads of Crown corporations, the RCMP, the military, and most significantly in this case, judges, lawyers on government payrolls, and members of Parliament. Beyond the galling hypocrisy of these statements, they directly contradict the facts that were given at trial and provided earlier in this book: [301]

- The most common profile of a patient at the private Cambie clinic is that of a unionized worker with WCB coverage;
- Only 10 percent of Cambie patients pay with their own funds.

Day said later in an interview "that representatives of all groups that opposed us in court, including the office of the defendant (the Attorney General of B.C.), the leadership of the Canadian Doctors for Medicare, and the employees opposing trade unions had used private clinics in B.C."

In April 2019, the federal government finally presented its argument that Canada's health-care system must be "protected, even as it offered little

---

[301] Tom Blackwell, "Inside the Nearly Eight-Year Long Fight of Brian Day, the Doctor who Would Free Canadians from Medicare," *National Post*, September 2, 2016.

evidence to support the view that historically long surgical waiting lists serve the greater good."[302]

At the same time, the B.C. government justified its existing policy with outrageous claims about the significance of "equity." This deceitfully ignores federally funded, CIHI data showing that low-income groups have the worst access and worst outcomes in Canadian health care. [303] The claim also ignores the many exemptions that are permitted, including their own personal use of private health care.

The Court Rules

In September 2020, Justice John Steeves of the B.C. Supreme Court ruled *that it was lawful for the government to prevent people from buying medical insurance and paying for their own medical care when the public health system is unable to provide that care in a reasonable time frame.* The judge made the determination that even if the waitlists harm some patients, the Medicare system remains an overall good to society and must be protected.

As you can imagine, based on the information presented in this (and other) chapters, it was a controversial ending to a controversial trial.

The case will go forward, as this is just the beginning of a long legal journey. It will first be presented to the B.C. Court of Appeal and then, ultimately, to the Supreme Court of Canada where it will be argued that preventing patients from paying to access private medical care violates a patient's right to life and security of the person, as outlined in the *Charter of Rights and Freedoms.*

In conclusion, the ruling means very little except that the B.C. government paid a minimum of $70 million to keep its citizens on health-care waiting lists. It will likely be several years before the Supreme Court rules on it and that is a very long time to go without any positive changes to the health-care system. While we wait, this government should at least consider the comments by Justice Marie Deschamps in the Court's 2005 Chaoulli ruling:

> "For many years, the government has failed to act; the situation continues to deteriorate … While the government has the power to decide what measures to adopt, it cannot choose to do nothing.

---

[302] Ian Mulgrew, "Ottawa's Response to Medicare Challenge is, Be Afraid," *Vancouver Sun*, April 18, 2019.

[303] Brian Day, "A Constitutional Solution for an Ailing Health System?" *BC Medical Journal* (62) 5, 12, 2020.

The government has not given reasons for its failure to act. Inertia cannot be used as an argument to justify deference."[304]

Hypocrisy Reigns Supreme

"Strangely, patients treated at our private clinics include leaders from the very groups that are going to court to make sure others can't receive the same benefits that they have enjoyed. Hypocrisy reigns supreme."[305]

Dr. Brian Day

---

[304] D. Martin Low, Lydia Wakulowsky and Geoff Moysa. "Failing on the Fundamentals: The Chaoulli Decision," June, 2005, Longwoods.com, https://www.longwoods.com/content/17188.

[305] Stephen Skyvington, "Tommy Douglas 'Would not be Happy' with Our System: Dr. Brian Day on his Fight for Medicare Freedom," *Financial Post*, September 8, 2016.

PART VI

A NEW KIND OF HEALTH CARE

21

The Health-care Tipping Point(s)

A tipping point is essentially the point of no return.

It is the moment when an accumulation of small, seemingly insignificant changes create sufficient momentum to suddenly tip the scales of balance and bring about a sea change of … something. The term began as an explanation for the point in an epidemic when a specific event (such as Canada and the rest of the world recently experienced with Christmas 2020 and COVID-19) turns into a super-spreader frenzy that rapidly and exponentially increases infection rates.

In the early 2000s, author Malcolm Gladwell used the tipping-point theory to describe how modern information is disseminated in a similar fashion through our modern social networks. But when it comes to Canada's health-care system, there are a number of tipping points on the immediate horizon that could effectively cause its outright collapse. They include any, several, or all of those discussed below.

Will the Tipping Point be Money?

Money (as in a dearth of health-care dollars) could well be the beast that brings the Medicare house down. Should our status quo continue, health-care analyst Stephen Skyvington is convinced that Medicare will collapse under its own weight sometime during the next decade. In fact, he estimates that 80 percent of provincial budgets will be dedicated to health care by 2030.[306]

Health care is currently overwhelmed by COVID-19 and the Conference Board of Canada has estimated that the pandemic resulted in additional health-care expenditures of more than $11.5 billion in just the first

---

[306] Stephen Skyvington, *This May Hurt a Bit: Reinventing Canada's Health Care System*, (Dundurn Press: Toronto, 2019): 193.

few months.[307] Taxpayers already pay almost $300 billion per year to cover health care costs and our combined federal and provincial debt now exceeds one and a half trillion dollars.[308]

But it is not enough. Our most basic health-care needs are still not met: We do not have sufficient numbers of doctors, adequate infrastructure to serve a rapidly aging population, or access to the high-tech diagnostic tools that every other wealthy developed country utilizes to ensure a rapid diagnosis (and therefore treatment) for patients. We deny medically necessary care to more than one million Canadians each year because of insufficient funding. We do not have enough surgeons, highly-trained surgical personnel, or operating rooms to cover the health-care needs of Canadians.

The lists of what we cannot do or provide through universal health care could go on and on, as could the list of debts that increasingly preclude the ability of governments to fund and control a universal health-care system.

But counting the full cost of health care goes far beyond calculating the sums of direct expenditures and government transfers. We tend to forget that every tax dollar dedicated to health care depletes the amounts available to cover every other government-run program and service that we rely on. Old age pensions, national defence, education, research and development, unemployment, aid for small businesses, and maintaining necessary infrastructure (roads, bridges, and building) are just a handful of the other government expenses that would suffer or even disappear once health care costs consume 50 or 60 percent of all our tax dollars.

There is little doubt that our health-care system is teetering on the precipice of financial ruin and, without immediate and critical changes, it cannot be sustained.

Will the Tipping Point be Waitlists?

What will happen when we have two million Canadians on waitlists? Will that be enough of an inconvenience for Canadians to shout for change?

This entire book has been filled with stories that describe the consequences of waiting for medical care. Almost every person on a waitlist experiences limitations that impact their families, jobs, income, and ability to live a full and active life. This ultimately impacts all of society as medical conditions go untreated and prevent people from working and contributing to

[307] The Conference Board of Canada, "Health Care Cost Drivers in Canada: Pre-and Post-COVID-19," Impact Paper, September, 2020.

[308] Jake Fuss and Steve Lafleur. (2021). "The Growing Debt Burden for Canadians: 2021 Edition," The Fraser Institute, https://www.fraserinstitute.org/studies/growing-debt-burden-for-canadians-2021.

our economy. As time goes on, mental health issues can arise, as can family problems. If an individual's health problems are exacerbated and require greater care while waiting, so too are the costs and amount of time that the system must invest in caring for that individual both before and after the supposed fix (as an example of this, consider Walid's case in Chapter 1).

In other words, when medical conditions go unchecked, there is a potential impact on our society and health-care costs are magnified unnecessarily.

Will the Tipping Point be our Aging Population?

What happens when we can no longer afford to care for Canadians over the age of 80? And then 70? Given our projected demographics and the rapidly rising costs of health care, we will soon find out.

A recent report reveals that Canada's seniors are far less healthy than those in other wealthy OECD countries. It also suggests that Canadian health care does not do particularly well in treating those with chronic conditions or in treating those who are most likely to have chronic conditions -- our senior citizens.[309]

According to the 2017 Commonwealth Fund international report on the health of seniors:[310]

- one third of Canadian seniors have at least three chronic conditions. This rather sad state of senior health ranks Canada 10th out of the 11 OECD nations compared; in fact, the only country that has more seniors suffering from chronic conditions is the United States.
- Seniors with three or more chronic conditions saw more doctors, had more hospital visits, attended hospital emergency departments on more occasions and had worse emotional health.
- 32 percent of our seniors take five or more regular medications and 14 percent have experienced a mental health problem such as depression or anxiety. Although 14 percent may not seem to be particularly significant, the study showed that almost all seniors (94 percent) who had mental health problems also had other chronic medical conditions.

---

[309] Canadian Institute for Health Information. "How Canada Compares: Results from The Commonwealth Fund's 2017 International Health Policy Survey of Seniors—Accessible Report," 2018.

[310] Ibid.

- Canada's seniors have below average access to primary health care with 59 percent of seniors unable to get a same- or next-day appointment. Close to two-thirds (62 percent) of those had difficulty getting medical care after hours and almost a third (31 percent) reported that the last time they went to the emergency department was for a condition that their regular doctor could have treated.

All of the above bullet points should be of concern to Canadians, particularly when considered alongside demographic studies that show almost one in four Canadians will be a senior citizen within the next decade.[311]

When Medicare was first implemented, Canada was a relatively young country and medical care typically involved acute problems that could either be fixed (with surgery, bandaids, or basic hospital care) or they resulted in an early death. Either way, patients did not have the kind of chronic conditions that are so common today and now require costly prescription drugs, diagnostic procedures, specialist care, and constant medical oversight. This all comes at a high cost and, as a result, over 60 percent of our health costs today stem from the treatment of chronic diseases.[312]

Will the Tipping Point be COVID-19?

Will we one day look back and see that this unprecedented event in our modern world is what forced Canadians to realistically evaluate the limits of relying on a government monopoly to provide our health care? Maybe.

It is difficult to assess the pandemic's full impact on health care as it is still ongoing. However, when the pandemic began, hospitals across the country put all but the most urgent medical procedures on hold and then emptied their beds to deal with an expected influx of coronavirus patients. Whether or not that massive influx happened, the directive shut down basic health care for many who needed it and tens of thousands of surgeries, diagnostic tests, and medical procedures were delayed for months. Waitlists that were deemed unacceptable before the pandemic have continued to grow

---

311 Brian Fitzpatrick, "Canada Today: There are More of Us and We're Getting Older, Statistics Show," *National Post*, September 30, 2019, .https://nationalpost.com/news/canada-today-there-are-more-of-us-and-weregetting-older-statistics-show.

312 Canadian Institute for Health Information. "How Canada Compares: Results from The Commonwealth Fund's 2017 International Health Policy Survey of Seniors—Accessible Report," 2018.

almost unabated and, by some estimates, waitlists that were months and years long before the pandemic could now be as much as seven times longer.[313]

On a more positive note, COVID-19 has also pushed health care out of its comfort zone and forced it to innovate and adapt to new technology. The rapid adoption of virtual care by many office-bound GPs and specialists (whereby office visits are replaced by video or telephone calls) and the swift changes to billing codes (by provincial governments) allowed virtual care to become a viable alternative for many patient consults. These changes are likely to become permanent fixtures that could revolutionize health care in both urban clinics and remote locations.

In addition, cleaning regulations have been changed for hospitals, safe distancing protocols are in place, and there are now clearly defined, multiple supply chains for mandatory items like personal protective equipment and hand sanitizer. Just as COVID-19 forced many Canadian industrial businesses to innovate to provide the products that are now considered to be necessities, our health-care system has had to innovate to provide care under the new rules of social distancing. These systemic changes may be directed towards specific challenges related to the pandemic but, in the most hopeful light, they may also be the first steps forward in creating an adept and efficient health-care system that will continue to effectively evolve to meet the changing health needs of Canadians.

Will the Tipping Point be Politics?

> "It's a dream of mine that one day a politician will emerge from the shadows who has the courage to tell us the truth about our healthcare system. They will not only be honest about the fact we can't go on like this much longer; they'll also stand up and say that in addition to doing all the things I've already mentioned, Canada must grow up and become an adult and embrace the hybrid solution."
>
> Stephen Skyvington[314]

The fact that governments fund and control Canadian health care means that we must rely on our politicians to initiate change and provide adequate

---

313 H. Johal and M. Bhandari, "A Surgical Deep-Freeze: Backlogs, Burden and New Beginnings," *OE Insights*, June 1, 2020.

314 Stephen Skyvington. *This May Hurt a Bit: Reinventing Canada's Health Care System*, (Dundurn Press: Toronto, 2019): 192.

funding to maintain the system. At some point, Canadians will realize the futility of continuing to ask for money and hope for change. But, until that recognition happens, health care will remain in an ideological box and in an inert, stagnant, and unchanging state:

- Conversations about health care will remain vague, highly politicized, and laced with language that is geared more to gaining favour with voters than bringing about positive change.
- Our political leaders will continue to use our tax dollars to fund a highly-flawed system; yet we remain powerless to effect innovative change, even as objective measures show universal health care to be a product characterized by rapidly increasing costs and (just as rapidly) diminishing returns.
- 'Two-tier' health care will remain in place. Politicians and their families (along with those who have federal government health insurance or private medical insurance through unions or workplaces) will continue to receive preferential treatment and have special access to medical care, even as they refuse to change the laws that would allow the general public to purchase medical insurance that would allow them access to the same level of medical care.
- Canada will remain as *the only country in the world* to have a government monopoly on health care. Our governments are quick to investigate and shut down monopolies in any other business sector because they are not in the best interests of the public, yet those same concerns are set aside when it comes to a system that is responsible for the health of Canadians. Governments are willing to interfere if we are paying too much for our cell phones or the Internet, but as was made abundantly clear in the Brian Day trial (as discussed in Chapters 18 to 20), they are content to ignore the obvious damage that their own health-care monopoly has inflicted upon millions of Canadians.

In short, politicians have neglected their collective responsibility to altruistically serve and provide effective leadership in the area of health care. This raises one important question for readers: *How much longer will we allow politics and political groups to control our health care?*

22

How to Make Health Care Better

> "First we have to admit there actually is a problem. Since Medicare was introduced in Canada back in 1968, everyone seems to have been playing some sort of weird game called Let's Pretend. The reality is our country no longer has the best healthcare system in the world—not even close. Nor is there enough money to keep Medicare from collapsing under its own weight. To put it plainly: our healthcare credit card is way over its limit and the payment is due."[315]
>
> Stephen Skyvington

It is time for Canadians to reimagine a health-care system that meets the needs of patients and is sustainable in the 21st Century. Achieving this will require innovation, ideas, an openness to change, and a long-term commitment by governments to put patients ahead of ideology. That said, progressive change has eluded health care for decades because proponents of Medicare, as is, quickly twist any calls for change into calls for an end to universal health care, thereby thwarting any meaningful conversations before they even begin.

That is why the most difficult part of bringing about change is getting the public, provincial and federal governments, politicians, the media, health-care personnel, and all other critical stakeholders to first agree on the following:

Canada's Health-Care System is Not Sustainable

Canadian health care currently hovers on the verge of collapse and to believe otherwise is to ignore the facts, statistics, and the day-to-day realities that patients experience. When first conceived and implemented, Medicare covered the basics that any patient needed -- doctor visits, surgeries, and

---

315 Stephen Skyvington. *This May Hurt a Bit: Reinventing Canada's Health Care System,* (Dundurn Press: Toronto, 2019): 150.

hospital stays. As decades have passed, all aspects of medical care have become increasingly reliant on costly technology and prescription drugs.

In 2019, Canadians spent about $265 billion on health care[316] and that was before the coronavirus pandemic emerged to consume all of our health-care resources and essentially empty the national treasury.

According to a recent study by the Conference Board of Canada, COVID-19 will increase health-care costs by $20 to $27 billion in 2020-2021. Over the next decade, it is expected that the pandemic alone will increase health-care expenditures by $80 to $161 billion.[317]

In 2021, Canada's debt is measured in trillions of dollars and there is no money to spare. We are still fighting this pandemic, five million Canadians do not have a family doctor and over one million patients still cannot access medically necessary care for health problems not related to COVID.

Many analysts believe that politicians at the federal and provincial levels have largely adopted a hands-off approach to health care's systemic problems because they believe that the system is about to collapse under its own weight. If they intervene before that happens, they will be entering a political minefield where Canadians are still clamouring for them to fund a broken model of care. However, once that broken model fails, politicians will have the support of Canadians in designing a new model for health care.

Can we all agree that health care is at the breaking point? Something has to give.

Change is not an Either/Or Proposition

The idea that changing health care is an either/or proposition is a false dichotomy that is presented to Canadians as a means of instilling fear and uncertainty about making changes to Medicare. It is typically the calling card of those who want to keep health care as it is (not for the sake of patients, but because of an association with Medicare, a personal or political agenda, or ties to the unions).

Changing health care is not a choice between two options (maintaining universal health care as it is or creating a 'two-tier' system that offers private health care only to the rich). There are a host of health-care options that have been shown to work well in countries around the world (particularly in

---

[316] Canadian Institute for Health Information. National Health Expenditure Trends, 2020.Ottawa, ON: CIHI; 2021, https://www.cihi.ca/en/national-health-expenditure-trends.

[317] The Conference Board of Canada, "Health Care Costs are on the Rise in Canada and COVID-19 is a New Cost Driver," Ottawa, October 30, 2020.

Europe) yet Canada has made little effort to understand how similar systems could work in Canada because of our unfounded 'either/or' fears.

As mentioned in multiple chapters (and clearly outlined in Chapter 13), we already have a two-tier system whereby those who have health insurance through the federal government (judges, lawyers, MPs, the military, RCMP, prisoners), unions, private insurers (like Workmen's Compensations), professional athletes and Canada's wealthy citizens all have access to private care.

Can we all agree health-care changes are not an 'either/or' choice?

Change Does Not Mean Adopting 'American-Style' Health Care

Changing health care is not a choice between Canadian Medicare or what we vaguely refer to as 'American-style' health care. This particular 'either/or' position is more rooted in anti-American sentiment than any kind of reality, yet it remains one of the highest barriers to introducing positive changes to Canadian health care. As shown throughout this book, most international health-care reports rank Canada at, or near, the bottom of the list for developed countries. The smallest bit of encouragement that Canadians can glean from these reports is that they tend to give similar marks to American health care. In other words, any movement to mimic U.S. health care is ridiculous and would truly be a race to the bottom.

Colleen Flood is a well-known professor in the field of health law and an ardent defender of Canada's public system. She obviously has very different views about Canadian health care than those presented herein, yet she still recognizes the futility in looking to the U.S. for health-care solutions. In a 2014 essay, she commented on the latest Commonwealth Fund study, noting "We had the dubious distinction of beating out only the Americans."[318] It was a dismal comment on Canadian health care then and, seven years later, we are making the same comments. Nothing has changed.

One small fact that Canadians often fail to recall while comparing Canadian and American health care is that we do not provide 100 percent coverage for all procedures and not all Americans rely on private insurers for their medical care. In the U.S., there is typically a 50/50 split between public and private health care, whereas Canada has a 70/30 split. So even if

---

[318] Colleen Flood, "Why Canada Shouldn't Compete with the U.S. for the Worst Performing Health System in the Developed World," July, 2014, www.evidencenetwork.ca, https://evidencenetwork.ca/why-canada-shouldnt-compete-with-the-u-s-for-the-worst-performing-health-system-in-the-developed-world/.

Canadians somehow chose to adopt 'American-style' care (which will not happen), the very worst case scenario is that our public system coverage would fall only from 70 to 50 percent. In other words, even the worst case scenario would not deliver a death blow to universal health care in our country.

Since Canada and the United States each have some of the worst health care in developed countries, surely we can all agree that we do not want 'American-style' health care.

Rhetoric and Fear Mongering Will Keep Positive Change at Bay

As is often the case, those who shout the loudest have the least to say. When the topic relates to Canadian health care, the noisy masses are most likely to gain the media's attention by magically transforming any reasoned or legitimate call for change into calls for an American system (as above) or, perhaps even worse to some, an all out assault on the (obviously failed) ideology that underlies Canada's (obviously failed) health-care system.

This book has covered numerous examples of how baseless rhetoric has undermined opportunities for progressive conversations and positive health care changes. In particular, the Brian Day trial provided numerous examples of statements by Medicare proponents that are, at once, deliberately vague, devoid of facts, and misleading; such language essentially constitutes what is known as 'purple prose.'

Our country fought --and won -- a similar battle against baseless rhetoric during the 1990s when Quebec's political leaders decided that it was in the province's best interests to become a sovereign nation. Frankly, the move was not in anyone's best interests, but sovereigntist leaders relied on rhetoric and verbiage to foster bitterness and a sense of cultural isolation without getting into the finer points of how, exactly, a friendly secession from Canada could be accomplished.

The prime minister at the time was Jean Chretien who, without bothering to contemplate the severity of the situation, decided to stay out of the fray until the end of the campaign, claiming he wanted Quebeckers to make their own choice. As a result, Canadian unity was very nearly fractured by the 1995 referendum as the "Yes" side (those who wanted to leave Canada) was very narrowly defeated by the "No" side (50.58 to 49.42 percent). That put the secession train into slow motion for a time, but it also showed the rest of Canada how close we were to losing the province.

When the vote was over, Chretien finally recognized that Canada had a crisis on its hands. Not long after, he appointed Stephane Dion, a brilliant academic who was not yet an elected Member of Parliament, to his Cabinet as Minister of Intergovernmental Affairs.

In this capacity, Dion was charged with publicly challenging the rhetoric and unsubstantiated claims coming from pro-sovereignty leaders. When the sovereigntists made baseless and unrealistic claims, he immediately responded with arguments rooted in reality. While the sovereigntists offered ambiguous statements about the need to foster a unique culture, Dion talked about the legal and economic specifics of secession. The more Dion provided clarity to the issues, the more the sovereigntist message appeared incoherent and confused.

In short, Dion's work held Quebec's leaders to account for their claims and provided Quebeckers with the substantive information that they needed to make a decision about seeking a formal separation from Canada.

So too, it is time for Canadians to understand the realities that lie under all the verbiage about health care. We could all use a little clarity and holding all groups accountable for the words they speak and the messages they send may be exactly what Canada needs if it is to break free from its stagnant 1960s mentality and move towards the progressive high-tech medicine of the 21st Century.

Can we all agree that any changes to our health-care system need to be grounded in facts? Not rhetoric. Not ideology. For the sake of those who need medical care, it is time to push the hysteria aside and focus on the facts.

The Primary Purpose of Health Care

> "The most basic form of human stupidity is forgetting what we are trying to accomplish."
>
> Friedrich Nietzsche

Nietzsche's quote was highlighted several chapters ago, but it bears repeating now because it is such an apt characterization of Canadian health care today - a fragmented, overly-bureaucratic 'system' where patient care is often subject to the constraints of an intangible ideology that has nothing to do with healing the sick, keeping people well, or providing equal access. Tommy Douglas never wanted health care to be grounded in feckless ideology - his primary motivation was to give people access to proper medical care. So why, decades later, are we so hung up on using ideology to define Canadian health care?

Without the benefits of large sums of money, focus groups, PR specialists, and political influence, I would contend that the primary, most basic, purpose of health care is to help, heal, and restore those who need medical care.

Canadians who use the system regularly are most likely prepared to support the idea of making health-care changes that put the focus on getting care to patients and leaving ideology on the cutting room floor. As would the million-plus patients on waitlists and the five million Canadians who cannot find a family doctor. I venture to suggest that those who have considered suicide because they cannot get treatment or cannot afford the treatment that they need would also support changes to create patient-first health care.

We may not agree on what those changes should be, but once the rhetoric is pushed out of the discussion, it is likely that a majority of Canadians are ready to agree that the system no longer works for patients and changes must be made to put patients first.

How Can We Make Health Care Better?

This book has highlighted a number of patient stories that illustrate some (but certainly not all) of the deficits that are present in our current system. These gaps in care do not just impact a patient's physical health - they create a sense of frustration, anger, and ultimately, a loss of trust that persists and covers every interaction thereafter. It is time to restore patients' faith in the Canadian health-care system.

There are many ways to bring about improvements and positive change, some of which would not even require a huge investment of funds. However, since much of the content of this book relates to patient experience, the list below emphasizes innovations that would greatly improve patient care and access.

Patient Advocates. The stories presented herein make it clear that patients often need help in navigating Canada's fragmented health-care system and communicating effectively with those working within it. Those who are ill, old, alone, weary from disease and treatments, too depressed to function, or simply overwhelmed by the enormity of the decisions that must be made all need someone to come alongside and help them. That person is a patient advocate.

A patient advocate can be a family member, a hospital volunteer, a friend, a hospital employee, or even a paid advocate. His/her role is to stand alongside the patient, attend appointments, guide them as they make decisions, advise them of other types of care available to them through home care, and generally help them to navigate the complex web of bureaucracy that exists between each appointment or procedure. They can even make phone calls, push for appointments, and help them to access appropriate resources through each step of the health-care journey: sickness, diagnosis, treatments, waiting, surgery, and home care.

In short, advocates can be the "squeaky wheel" that ensures the patient does not fall between the cracks.

Harold was in his late 80s when he collapsed suddenly in a stairwell and was rendered unconscious. He was taken by an ambulance to the same hospital that he had attended on many occasions but, for some unknown reason, the hospital could not locate any of his medical records. Staff who might have known who he was were not present on that day.

A quick assessment suggested he was somewhat dishevelled, underweight, dehydrated, and had some rather odd-looking burns on his back. With Harold still unable to communicate, hospital staff had no context for his symptoms and they began to make assumptions about his medical, psychological, and social issues. It seemed likely that he required some sort of psychiatric care. They ordered a number of expensive diagnostic tests.

It was only after the examination that they looked through his jacket and found a scrap of paper with just one name and phone number on it; he had kept it in his pocket for months just in case he was ever in a situation like this. When they called, they learned that his contact was a friend who had been helping him through a series of appointments and treatments for terminal cancer -- the burns on his back were from past radiation treatments. He was obviously dehydrated and delusional but he did not need to undergo the numerous and expensive diagnostic tests that they were considering; nor did he need psychiatric help. As his health-care advocate, she was able to put his medical condition into proper context so he could get the treatment that he needed.[319]

Advocates can help patients of all ages cope and make choices when they are diagnosed with a critical or terminal illness. It can become difficult to take in all that a doctor is saying in a brief 15-minute appointment; once the bad news has been spoken, any understanding is lost amidst the sudden barrage of emotions and the inevitable medical jargon. Doctors rarely have time to repeat explanations or answer a host of questions, but a knowledgeable advocate can join patients in appointments and then spend time with them, answering questions and guiding them as they select a treatment pathway amidst the myriad options that exist.

---

[319] Personal Interview.

Canadians who have never had health issues that required medical care may be surprised to discover the importance of having an advocate who can counsel them on the need to be proactive in obtaining care. Many people naively believe that the health-care system works and assume that they can obtain timely care when, and if, they need it. They have no idea how difficult it can be to access diagnostic testing and specialist care; as a result, they will passively wait for the phone to ring with an appointment. It can be rather alarming when these people first come to the realization that health care does not run smoothly in Canada and it may take months to access the medical care that they need. It does not take long for this group of patients to understand that there is no virtue in waiting when medical care is required.

Right now, many Canadians cannot even take that important first step to getting help because they cannot access, or find, a family doctor to begin the referral process or perhaps even guide their care as they seek a diagnosis and treatment. They also need an advocate.

Not all family members or friends understand that medical care, in and outside of hospitals, has changed. At one point, entering a hospital meant a transfer of care from the family to the professionals; family was supposed to be "hands off" and only visit for a few hours per day. But things have changed and helpful family members are often welcome to stay through the day and even the night. They can alert nurses if care is needed, help with feeding and medication and, perhaps more than anything, keep the patient feeling calm and secure.

One woman said she was worried about leaving her husband overnight at a hospital because the nurses were so busy. Once the nurses noted that she was extremely helpful and "did not crumble or fall apart" at the sight of blood, they were quite grateful to have her stay and care for him throughout the night.[320]

Many American hospitals have patient advocates who are with patients from the beginning to the end of their stay. They explain what is happening, discuss medical options, go over test results, and answer any questions. Neil Macdonald (Chapters 4 and 7) has also written about this experience and notes that such advocates are even present at public hospitals and for every category of patient whether they are insured through a private corporation, Medicare, or Medicaid.[321]

---

320 Personal Interview.

321 Neil Macdonald, "Canada's Health Care System is Hopelessly Sclerotic. We Need to Wake Up," CBC News Commentary, June 12, 2019.

In Canada, many hospitals have a patient relations or advocacy department, but they often only come into play after problems have arisen and complaints have been made. Patients need an advocate that offers proactive help; they need someone to tell them what to expect, not someone to justify why something went wrong.

The Canadian health-care system could make a huge step towards patient-centred care by providing patient advocates to those who need or request them. Paid professional advocates who have their own patient loads of people they must stand alongside and guide during their care would be ideal. Most people will have a friend, parent, family member, or even a helpful physician to help them, but there is a huge opportunity here for volunteers, church networks, and advocacy groups for diseases to contribute manpower and make health care just a bit easier for someone.

Patient Education. Patient education has increased exponentially over the past decade, largely due to the efforts of patients themselves. Internet sites and support groups help individual patients to learn more about their conditions, what to expect during treatment, what treatment options they might have, and even where to get the best care.

There is one patient advocacy group in Toronto that invites different specialists (in fields related to that particular cancer) to join monthly meetings with patients. The physician is not there to provide a speech about the latest research or give them encouragement about their chances of beating the disease. The doctors are there only to respond to the unanswered questions of patients and their families. In doing so, these physicians bridge the knowledge gap that has been created by too few specialists and limited time periods for appointments.

Thus far, most of this education has been focused on how to understand and cope with specific diseases; we now need to amplify that education by covering issues related to navigating the health-care system, itself.

Minimize Bureaucracy. Since most calls for improving health care are related to demands for more money and Canada has no more money to give, we need to carefully reconsider how our highly-rationed health-care dollars are spent.

Various studies have declared Germany to have the top-ranked (or almost top-ranked) health-care system and copious amounts of data exist to prove that it deserves this rank. Of course, this raises the question -- what does the best health-care system (Germany) have that one of the worst systems (Canada) does not?

There is one striking difference between the two countries: Canada has ten times as many health-care administrators as Germany, even though Germany has twice the population of Canada.[322]

This is a glimpse at their respective ratios of health-care bureaucrats to populations:

Country	Healthcare Bureaucrat Ratio to population
Canada	1 to 1,415
Germany	1 to 15,545

Table 6. Canada has 10-times the number of health-care bureaucrats as Germany.

Every system needs some sort of administration but this statistic strongly suggests that we may be overburdened by bureaucracy and so-called 'paper pushers.' One realistic prescription for improving the public health system may be to hire fewer administrators and a lot more doctors, specialists, and health-care workers instead.

According to a 2019 comparison of universal health care in OECD countries, Canada spends more on health care than Germany as a percentage of GDP (11.1 and 10.2 percent, respectively) and slightly less than Germany when calculated per capita (US$4,995.60 and 5,324.50, respectively).[323] Based on these figures, we can assume that the amount of money spent on public health care is essentially the same in each country. Yet international studies show that Germany has more physicians, more specialists, and many more acute care and psychiatric beds. It far surpasses Canada in its inventory of diagnostic equipment (CT, MRI, and PET scanners) and just one percent of its population waits more than four weeks to see a specialist, compared to 17 percent in Canada.[324]

---

[322] Matthew Lister, "Canadian Health Care Needs to be Leaner," *National Post*, November 21, 2011,https://nationalpost.com/opinion/matthew-lister-canadian-healthcare-needs-to-be-leaner.

[323] Bacchus Barua and Mackenzie Moir. (2019). "Comparing Performance of Universal Health Care Countries," 2019. The Fraser Institute.

[324] Ibid.

The cost to patients to use this superior public system? Seven percent of Germans claimed that cost was a barrier to care in the past year, compared to 16 percent of Canadians.[325]

In sum, Canada and Germany spend about the same amount of money on universal health care, yet Germany's public system serves about 75 million people and is one of the top ranked systems in the world, while Canada's public system serves half as many people (about 38 million) and is rated as having one of the worst public systems in the world. We do, however, have ten times as many administrators.

Invest in Physicians and Other Health-care Personnel. Based on the above statistics, it should be relatively easy for patients to locate a health-care administrator when one is needed, but family doctors and medical specialists remain relatively scarce and, for many patients, sightings are rare. That is a sure indication that Canada needs to reallocate its health-care resources and invest in the education and training of physicians and specialists.

A plethora of data exists to show that we have extremely low numbers of physicians and specialists compared to other OECD countries[326,327,328] but most Canadians do not need statistics and tables to know we need more doctors. Our waitlists for specialist care (the longest in the developed world) and the high percentage of Canadians who do not have a family doctor provide sufficient evidence of our nation-wide problem.

Unfortunately, the fix for this relies heavily on federal and provincial governments for input, long-term planning, and money (all involve bureaucracies which, when conflated, rarely produce the most practical or efficient outcome).

Enrollments at medical schools have been unevenly matched with public needs since the 1992 Barer-Stoddart Report[329] came to the still-controversial conclusion that Medicare's formidable costs were the result of too many doctors on the payroll. Aside from contributing to the so-called Brain Drain

---

[325] Ibid.

[326] Ibid.

[327] The Commonwealth Fund, "Selected Health and System Statistics," 2017. https://www.commonwealthfund.org/international-health-policy-center/system-stats.

[328] Steven Globerman et al. (2018). "The Supply of Physicians in Canada: Projections and Assessment," The Fraser Institute.

[329] Barer, Morris L., and Greg L. Stoddart (1991). Toward Integrated Medical Resource Policies for Canada. Centre for Health Services and Policy Research, University of British Columbia.

of the 1990s (where a dearth of funding sent physicians and researchers scattering to other areas of the globe), the report called for a 10 percent reduction in both medical school enrollments and residency positions for post-graduate training. In combination, these factors created a decade where the number of doctors plateaued even as Canada's population continued to rise.[330]

Data from CIHI (Canadian Institute for Health Information) claims that the increase in numbers of physicians has exceeded that of the general population for the past 13 years (and even doubled the growth rate of the general population from 2015 to 2019).[331] But this PR claim from a government-funded body does not mean much when our population remains grossly underserved by doctors (as shown by comparisons with other wealthy developed countries) particularly in rural areas.

Incredibly, Canada has never had a 'plan' whereby medical school enrolment numbers are correlated to the numbers of doctors that we need. The lack of long-term planning in medical schools fuels frustrations in finding employment and options for further training once students have graduated. For example, some newly-graduated medical students cannot find positions at Canadian facilities even when they wish to pursue further training[332] and that trend continues as newly-trained specialists cannot find employment.[333]

As discussed in Chapter 14, a report by the Royal College of Physicians and Surgeons suggests there is typically a 60/40 split in the number of employed and unemployed specialists in Canada.[334] This obvious disconnect that exists through medical school enrollments, residency positions, and the number of physicians needed in our medical system clearly points to a lack of planning and insufficient funding for specialty training in specific areas that are most needed by Canadians (e.g. psychiatrists, orthopedists, surgeons).

---

330 Steven Globerman et al. (2018). "The Supply of Physicians in Canada: Projections and Assessment," The Fraser Institute.

331 Canadian Institute for Health Information. Physicians in Canada, 2019. Ottawa, ON: CIHI; 2020, https://secure.cihi.ca/free_products/physicians-in-Canada-report-en.pdf.

332 Jonathan Gravel and Max Deschner, "Medical School Enrolment is an Expensive Mystery," February 17, 2016, www.healthydebate.ca, https://healthydebate.ca/2016/02/topic/medical-school-enrolment-is-an-expensive-mystery/.

333 Royal College of Physicians and Surgeons of Canada, "Employment Patterns of Canada's Newly Certified Medical Specialists," 2019.

334 Ibid.

Currently, Canada seems content to rely on immigration of foreign-trained doctors to fill the gap. It certainly helps, but such an approach can also be associated with issues related to language barriers and quality of training that may not equate to Canadian standards. Beyond those concerns, a reliance on foreign-trained doctors can impinge on the need to plan for the employment needs of Canadian-trained doctors. There is no reasoning behind a policy that promotes the training of new physicians and specialists and then exports them to other countries because of insufficient opportunities for employment or further training.

The undersupply of primary care physicians can be altered by effective planning (as above) and by a more efficient use of other medical personnel. Gone are the days where doctors had one set of skills and nurses another; now we have highly-trained professionals such as physician assistants, nurse practitioners, and pharmacists who have the capabilities to take on some of the physicians' duties. It has been estimated that as much as 40 percent of medical care traditionally carried out by doctors could be accomplished by a less expensive group of professionals.[335]

Creating a system that relies more on other health-care professionals and moves medical services out of the hospital and into a community clinic setting have all proven to be beneficial. Specialized clinics that serve as a one-stop service for orthopedic or dermatology patients are also known to reduce the burden of care on hospital services and specialists. Some clinics utilize specialized health-care workers to complete intake assessments before a patient sees the specialist. This provides the specialist with more information to make a determination about the problem and more time for constructive conversation with the patient.

Invest in Medical Technology. Canada ranks far below OECD averages for the numbers of diagnostic equipment such as CT, MRI, and PET scanners.[336] Coincidentally, we have outrageous waits to access this technology in the public system and, in many provinces, private groups are

---

335 Brian Golden and William Mitchell, "More Doctors won't fix Canada's Health-care Woes," *The Conversation*, October 16, 2019.

336 Bacchus Barua and Mackenzie Moir. (2019). "Comparing Performance of Universal Health Care Countries," 2019. Fraser Institute; Eurostat Statistics, Medical Technology Imaging Equipment 2017, https://ec.europa.eu/eurostat/statisticsexplained/images/c/c4/Availability_of_medical_technology_%E2%80%94_imaging_equipment%2C_2015_or_2017_Health2019.png.

making money by providing this service in a timely way to Canadians, even though such groups are technically illegal.

The answer to this problem is simple: If the government does not have the finances to provide the medical equipment that is required for rapid diagnosis of injuries and diseases, then it should allow the private sector to take over this aspect of health care. In doing so, the health-care system can rid itself of one expensive line item on its budget, which is particularly relevant since the COVID-19 pandemic has escalated medical costs to the point that a massive investment in technology is almost impossible.

Canada also lags in its adoption of other technologies such as telemedicine and electronic records. In February 2020, a task force working under the auspices of the Canadian Medical Association released a report calling for greater use of virtual care technology. Based on surveys, the task force reported "fewer than one in 10 family physicians" allowed patients to book appointments electronically, less than 25 percent of doctors were available to their patients via email, and just four percent provided video visits.[337]

That creates the kind of scenario faced by Jason, a 32-year-old man, who was on several prescription drugs that required physician renewals every three months.[338] He did not have a family doctor to monitor his care, so he attended a local walk-in clinic when needed. As the clinic did not provide specific appointment times, a prescription renewal involved lining up alongside other patients outside the clinic when it first opened at 8:00 am and then being assigned an approximate time (usually two or three hours later) to return for a consultation with a doctor. That is, a simple prescription renewal that involved not much more than a five-minute appointment with the doctor, required Jason to invest several hours of his time every three months when it could just as easily have been resolved by a telephone or video call, text, or even an email. No wonder Canadians are increasingly turning to virtual health groups like Telus (formerly Babylon), Maple, Virtual Clinic+, and a growing list of others.

Depending on the province, a virtual visit with a physician can be covered by the public health system and, as the pandemic gained strength, other provinces moved quickly to create new fee codes that would ensure that patients had virtual access to medical care.

---

337 Lauren Vogel, "Canada has Long Way to go on Virtual Care," CMAJ March 2, 2020, www.cmajnews.com.
338 Personal communication.

Establish a Long-term Health-care Plan and Separate Politics from Health Care. Canadian health care is random and Dr. Stephen Pinney refers to it as a "large, sprawling house built without a solid foundation."[339] Because there has never been a long-term plan, we have multiple, add-on, fragmented systems that do not function well together and, at every step of their journey, patients must rely on an unpredictable and ineffective system of referrals and communications to access care. Continuity of care, patient flow, coordinated efforts, and ease of navigation are all lacking -- and the result is the kind of health care that frustrates Canadians, produces waitlists, requires more bureaucracy, and fails patients like those whose stories are told throughout this book.

To further confuse the situation, Canada essentially has thirteen different health-care systems. The federal government provides funding, but each province and territory is free to use the money in a way that supposedly best meets the needs of each area.

If Canadians and their politicians want to get serious about improving health care, there has to be a commitment at all levels of government to work together without political bias and provide long-term funding.

Health care remains under the control of the federal and provincial governments, and with each change in government there is a shift in philosophies of governing, spending, and how to deal with health care. This is why there is no grand design to our system: Governments do not want to commit big, long-term money to projects if there is a possibility that they may not be around to gain the credit and adulation upon its successful completion; nor do they want to invest heavily in a plan that might be co-opted and altered by another political party should there be a change in governing power.

To effect positive change, political leaders will have to agree that the need for a better health-care system is too critical for political bias to be the maestro that leads the way. If they are not willing to provide non-partisan support for healthcare, the only realistic option is to disconnect health care entirely from politics and create a new health-care system outside of government control. This is not the solution that Canadians want, but it is the only option if governments refuse to come together to rescue the sinking ship of health care.

---

[339] Stephen Pinney, *How Hockey Can Save Healthcare: A Principle-Based Approach to Reforming the Canadian Healthcare System.* (LuLu Publishing Services, 2016): 92.

Before this system collapses under its own weight, Canadians have to decide if they want to keep health care under political control or create a system outside of government; or call for legislative changes that would allow what is called a hybrid or parallel system.

A Hybrid or Parallel Health-care System. Canada is the only country in the world that has government-controlled health care only and this book has clearly demonstrated the results of that philosophy. Every other country that boasts of universal health care also has a parallel, private system and this amalgamation of care is often termed a hybrid system. For example, Germany has universal health-care coverage and every resident must have public health insurance (cost is based on income). Those who wish can purchase additional private health insurance and just 10 percent of the population does so.[340]

Politicians and those who have an investment in perpetuating universal health care tend to express hypocritical and fallacious outrage that a private, parallel system could exist in a nation that prides itself in providing a social safety net for its people. Yet European countries that we would never consider to be bastions of conservative principle (e.g. Sweden, Denmark, Norway, and others) all have private-care systems that run alongside public health-care systems. Even communist Cuba, a nation governed by an ideology that extends further left than socialism, has an option for its citizens to get private medical care.

We need to keep two things in mind as we contemplate legalizing a hybrid health-care system for Canadians:

- We already have a 'two-tier' system that allows some favoured groups to 'jump the queue.' Taking steps to allow all Canadians to buy insurance that would give them access to a private facility would be one step in levelling the playing field.
- Our current system is not by any means fully funded and, at present, only 70 percent of our health-care system is public.[341] The other 30 percent is already covered by Canadians' private insurance or out-of-pocket payments.

---

[340] Yvonne, "Private vs. Public Health Insurance in Germany, Expat Guide," Simple Germany, February 1, 2021, https://www.simplegermany.com/private-vs-publichealth-insurance-germany.

[341] Canadian Institute for Health Information, "Health Spending," n.d., https://www.cihi.ca/en/health-spending.

A parallel system that is accessible through the purchase of private insurance is the only way to provide patients on a waitlist with an affordable option; other than that, they must leave the country to get timely medical care.

Many provinces already rely on private medical clinics to clear outrageous waitlists.[342] There is a stronger media focus on it right now because of the COVID-19 pandemic but this same arrangement has been taking place on a smaller scale for years. The government already contracts private clinics to perform cataract surgeries, back surgeries, and hip replacements, among other procedures. Why not simply acknowledge that it exists, that it helps patients, and then work to establish a dual system that is mutually supportive and works together to ensure patients are treated in a timely fashion?

Those who oppose changes to the status quo typically resort to reckless and unfounded comments to claim that a private system would decimate the public system, but there is no evidence from any country that a parallel private system strips resources from the public system. For example, Ken Manning, lawyer for the government of Canada at the Brian Day trial, claimed that a private system would, "siphon resources from the public system, increasing administration costs, contributing to the escalation of cost of services and reducing efficiency and effectiveness." There is no evidence to back up Manning's claims and his fears have not been documented in any nation with a hybrid system or in the province of Quebec where a dual system has been legal for the past 15 years.

To the contrary, in every other country, public and private systems collaborate and integrate closely for maximal benefit to patients. There is plenty of evidence in international comparative studies by the Fraser Institute, the Commonwealth Fund, and even the Canadian Institute for Health Information to show that countries with public/private systems have superior results, reduced wait times, improved access, and better health.[343]

---

342 Daniel Boily and Davide Gentile, "Quebec Signing More Contracts with Private Clinics to Help Clear Surgery Waitlists," February 5, 2021, CBC News, Sammy Hudes, "Alberta teams with private clinics to clear surgeries delayed by COVID-19," *Edmonton Journal,* March 5, 2021.

343 Canadian Institute for Health Information. How Canada Compares: Results From The Commonwealth Fund's 2017 International Health Policy Survey of Seniors — Accessible Report. Ottawa, ON: CIHI; 2018; Robin Osborn and David Squires, "Commonwealth Fund 2016 International Health Policy Survey of Adults in 11 Countries," The Commonwealth Fund, 2016; Bacchus Barua and Mackenzie Moir. (2019). "Comparing Performance of Universal Health Care Countries 2019," The Fraser Institute.

> "Every other industrialized nation with universal health care, except Canada, has a parallel private-care system ... Private treatment is an essential component of the system because it allows patients to alleviate their suffering and protect their health in the face of lengthy waiting times."[344]
>
> Peter Gall, Lawyer

Let the People who Know the Problems Fix the Problems. We have to know exactly what to fix before we rush in to create massive change. Too many hospital boards and local health authority boards are laden with lawyers, businesspeople, and administrators who may have never even seen the inner workings of a busy hospital ward or clinic. It is time to let those who know the problems do the fixing. That means putting nurses, doctors, and hospital personnel into creative roles where they can identify issues and come up with innovative solutions.

[344] In Ian Mulgrew, "B.C. Medicare Challenge More Black Eye than Broadway," *Vancouver Sun,* November 19, 2019.

23

Where Do We Go from Here?

It is estimated that 18 Canadians die every day as they wait for medical care.[345]

Each one is a son, daughter, brother, sister, mother, father, grandmother, grandfather, and/or friend; and each one leaves behind devastated family members, co-workers, and friends who will always wonder if they could have done more while they waited. Inevitably, the following questions arise:

- What if we had acted sooner or pushed harder to get an appointment or a date for surgery? What if we had mortgaged the house and taken him/her to another country for treatment?

- What if we had known more about the problems in our health-care system *before* our mother started on the long journey of being diagnosed and then treated for cancer? What would or could we have done differently?

- What if we had been more assertive in pushing for care? Would he/she still be alive if we had been more willing to be known as that 'pushy' family who dared to demand faster or better care for their loved one?

No one can ever know the answers to these questions, and this lack of certainty is one more reason why it is so difficult for Canadians to demand change to health care.

Are Canadians Divided on Health Care?
Discussions throughout this book have suggested there is a deep divide between those who want to maintain a universal system based on ideology

---

345 Brian Day, "A Constitutional Solution for an Ailing Health System?" *BC Medical Journal*, 62(1), 2020, Pages 5, 12.

(no matter how badly it has compromised patient care) and those who have personally experienced or witnessed others as they have been denied access to medically necessary care.

Surprisingly, it is in this divide that we can also find some common ground: After all, most of us would agree that there is something very wrong with a health-care system that cannot provide care to those who need it. Sharing the stories of those who suffered because they could not access medical care can create a common sense of compassion and help us to realize that our basic hopes for health care are the same -- we all want a system that provides care to those who need it.

Recall that Tommy Douglas, our first national advocate for health care, took action when he saw that people were dying because they could not access health care. Similarly, Dr. Brian Day has taken part in a decades-long legal battle to change health care because he has seen thousands of patients who were denied the medical care that they needed. In retrospect, Dr. Day's motives are essentially the same as those that inspired Tommy Douglas to lead the charge for health care reform almost a century ago.

What Tommy Douglas and Dr. Brian Day Have in Common

Both men are champions of patient-first health care, and they each reached that determination as they travelled remarkably similar paths.

Tommy Douglas was a fighter at heart who endured many difficult circumstances. He immigrated to Canada with his family and, at the young age of 15, entered the boxing ring as a lightweight fighter. A few years later, he had a broken nose, missing teeth, a severely injured hand, and several local amateur titles to his name. He was small, but scrappy and learned to persevere through any fight.

His vision for what Canadian health care could be was strongly shaped by his own experiences. As a child, he almost lost a leg to an infection; ultimately, it was only saved because one doctor was willing to treat him for free. He lived in Saskatchewan during the Depression and, as a young Baptist preacher, conducted funeral services for several young people who had very treatable illnesses but died because they could not access medical care in a timely way.

Times were tough for everyone, but Douglas believed it was morally wrong for patients to die because they could not access, or pay for, health care. For the next several decades, he worked within the political system to ensure that patients in Saskatchewan and, later, Canada would never again be denied access to medical care.

Seventy-five years later, another man is carrying on this same fight - working within the medical and legal systems to ensure that no Canadian is denied access to medical care.

Like Douglas, Brian Day grew up in the United Kingdom. He lived in a rough and tough working-class neighbourhood in postwar Liverpool. Violence came with the territory and his hand still shows a scar from a knife fight at age ten. His father was murdered by a gang that broke into his pharmacy to steal drugs. Like many in that era and in that city, Day took his fighting spirit into the amateur boxing ring and onto the soccer pitch.

At 18, he left Liverpool to attend university in nearby Manchester and, from then on, his life was filled with academia and medicine. He became a medical doctor and travelled the world to undertake surgical fellowships and research opportunities. He eventually ended up in Vancouver.

In Canada, Day experienced the frustration and the agony of having to say no to patients who needed surgery. Health-care rationing meant his allotted time in the operating room was reduced from 22 to just five hours per week, even as he had 450 patients on a waitlist for his surgical care. Operating rooms were sitting empty while people who needed medical care were forced to wait; the privileged few with money left Canada to get care in another country.

Like Douglas, Day saw patients living for years in unnecessary pain or even dying because they could not access timely care. He took notice when patients like Walid suffered adverse outcomes because of unreasonably long delays in getting treatment. *He could see that the health-care system was overwhelmed yet, because of its rigid structure, the system could only respond to greater numbers of patients by further rationing medical care.*

Like Douglas, Day's vision was shaped by his experiences and as he watched his patients suffer, he concluded that our health-care system made no sense. Like Douglas, Day believed it was morally wrong for patients to die or lose all quality of life because they could not access or pay for care. Like Douglas, Day decided to change health care to ensure that patients would never again be denied treatment when they needed it.

He built a private surgical clinic in 1996. More than 100 surgeons are associated with it because they do not have enough operating room time to perform surgeries in the public system. The clinic primarily serves unionized patients and patients with federal government insurance. On many occasions, the B.C. government has contracted the clinic to take on surgeries in an effort to diminish waitlists in the public system. As Day saw the inequities associated with access to medical care, he *decided he would go to court to ask for changes that would grant every citizen the right to use the very services that the government turns to when waitlists are unmanageable.*

Like Douglas, changing health care to serve patients' needs has become Dr. Brian Day's fight. He too has worked for several decades to better conditions for patients and that fight continues today in Canada's courts.

The Next Champions of Patient-First Health Care

To quote an infamous but fictitious broadcaster named Howard Beale, health care will not change unless Canadians "get up, go to their windows, open them up and shout 'I'm mad as hell and I'm not gonna take it anymore."[346]

In Canada, CBC reporter Neil Macdonald has called for the same. Instead of congratulating ourselves on how wonderful our health care is, he says we should be "screaming" about how bad it is.[347]

The government may have control over health care, but Canadians have the power of the vote. Patients and those who have experienced suffering and/or loss because of waitlists need to make other Canadians aware; they need to share their stories with the mainstream media as often as possible. We need to write letters to newspapers and not be afraid to complain about the system when something goes wrong. We need to get active and we need to get loud. People need to know what is happening and only those who have experienced it are properly positioned to inform others.

So, who are the next champions of patient-first health care in Canada? We are.

In the Meantime, Tip Your Umbrella

Change takes time. While we push for it and, no doubt, argue extensively about it, there is one thing we could all do to make things better for patients and that is to *'tip our umbrellas.'* It is a rather strange directive but most Vancouverites know exactly what it means.

The idea comes from Slack Technologies, a software company that was valued at almost $20 billion just four years after it came into existence. It is led by a young Canadian businessman named Stewart Butterfield and while it is headquartered in San Francisco, there is also a satellite office in Vancouver.[348]

---

[346] "Network" movie (1976).

[347] Neil Macdonald, "Canada's Health-Care System is Hopelessly Sclerotic. We Need to Wake Up," CBC News Commentary, June 12, 2019.

[348] David Ebner, "Sharing Information with Slack CEO Stewart Butterfield," *Globe and Mail*, March 3, 2018.

Butterfield is obviously well accustomed to the rain-soaked winter days in both cities and he has a rainy-day story that he shares with all of his new employees to illustrate the simplicity and importance of thinking about others.

One winter day, Butterfield and an employee were enjoying a short walk down a narrow Yaletown street when the clouds burst, and a typical Vancouver downpour began. The sidewalks were immediately covered with brightly coloured canopies as people opened their umbrellas for shelter. While lovely to look at, such scenes also create problems for pedestrians as they are forced to zigzag around, or duck under, oncoming umbrellas to protect themselves from the sharp metal ends protruding from the rims of every open umbrella.

At this point, Butterfield observed, an individual can extend a small courtesy to oncoming walkers by tipping his/her umbrella, so the metal points face away from them. It is a simple act that takes almost no effort, yet it makes a huge difference in allowing others to safely navigate the streets. Still in spite of it being an effortless task, not everyone extended this courtesy to others.

Upon subsequent reflection, Butterfield decided that empathy made the difference in whether a person took the time to make things easier for another person.

This story is now part of the office culture at Slack Technologies and the term "tipping your umbrella" is commonly used to encourage employees to take a moment and think if there is one small thing that they can do to make things better, simpler, more productive, or even more pleasant for another person in the workplace. Butterfield says the act of "tipping your umbrella" is like a catalyst; it spreads like a chain reaction throughout the office, making it a better day for everyone.

Surprisingly, tipping umbrellas could play a large and valuable role in today's health care. It just takes a moment to think about what we can each do to make things better for a patient who is in pain, or unable to work and provide for a family, or on a long journey that everyone knows will inevitably end in death.

If every doctor, nurse, receptionist, administrator, and staff member tipped his or her umbrella to each other and to patients, the kinds of frustrating situations faced by Ross, Bill, Debbie, Walid, and others might be avoided. It works the same way for patients: take time to tip your umbrella to those who are doing their absolute best to help you while working within the constraints of a broken system.

Until health care undergoes significant change, a little bit of kindness may be the only form of healing that we can offer one another.

Alphabetical Index of Patient Stories

A

B

C

D

E

F

G

H

J

K

L

M

N

P

R

S

Index for the book

A

B

C

I

K

M

N

O

P

R

S

T

About the Author

Photo Credit: Todd Korol

Susan Martinuk is an accomplished, nationally recognized researcher and writer who has consistently challenged the status quo policies that govern Canada's health-care system and limit the scope of care available to Canadians. The former columnist and talk show host has published more than 1,500 commentaries, articles, and reports on themes related to health care and public policy. In 2012, she was awarded the Queen's Diamond Jubilee Medal for her contributions to Canadian society through her writing.

Prior to working in public policy, Susan was a medical researcher; she and her colleagues achieved a world-first medical breakthrough when they were the first to visualize and record human ovulation. More recently, she published a ground-breaking, peer-reviewed report that identified the factors restricting the utilization of PET (positron emission tomography) imaging in cancer care programs across Canada. Susan currently serves as a Research Fellow in Health Care for the Frontier Centre in Public Policy.

Frontier Centre for Public Policy

Founded in 1997, the Frontier Centre for Public Policy is an independent, non-profit research and educational charity more commonly known as a "think tank." Frontier's mission is to explore options for the future by undertaking research and education that supports economic growth and greater opportunities for Canadians with the goal of improving their quality of life for generations to come.

The work at the Centre is supported by generous donations of many friends from across Canada. In order to assure its independence, the Frontier Centre does not accept government funding.

Frontier includes a world-class team of research fellows including academics, retired judges, and former senior policymakers from both the public and private sectors. Over the years, these researchers have partnered with experts from Canada and around the world.

The Centre is dedicated to foundational Canadian values including individual rights, economic freedom, and a strong civil society that maximizes citizens' choices and standard of living within a market-based economy. The Centre is committed to results-based public policy and high-performance governments that better serve the needs of Canadians. The Centre believes that the best government is as close to citizens as possible (subsidiarity) so that it is effective, accountable, flexible, and transparent.

Frontier serves Canadians by improving the level of thinking, research, and policy discussions, and it focuses on many key policy areas, among which are high performance government, education, civil society, healthcare, environment, local government, asset valuation and divestment, equalization reform, and Aboriginal empowerment.

For more information, please visit our website at www.fcpp.org. You're welcome to get involved with Frontier by donating, volunteering, attending events, and subscribing to the newsletter.

FRONTIER CENTRE
FOR PUBLIC POLICY

Manufactured by Amazon.ca
Bolton, ON

24150229R00146